IMAGINARY LANGUAGES

IMAGINARY LANGUAGES

MYTHS, UTOPIAS, FANTASIES, ILLUSIONS, AND LINGUISTIC FICTIONS

Marina Yaguello

translated by Erik Butler

THE MIT PRESS
CAMBRIDGE, MASSACHUSETTS
LONDON, ENGLAND

Originally published as *Les langues imaginaires: Mythes, utopies, fantasmes, chimères et fictions linguistiques* © Editions du Seuil, 2006

This book was set in ITC Stone and Futura Std by New Best-set Typesetters Ltd. Printed and bound in the United States of America.

Library of Congress Cataloging-in-Publication Data

Names: Yaguello, Marina, author. | Butler, Erik, 1971- translator.
Title: Imaginary languages : myths, utopias, fantasies, illusions, and linguistic fictions / Marina Yaguello ; translated by Erik Butler.
Other titles: Langues imaginaires. English
Description: Cambridge : The MIT Press, 2022. | Includes bibliographical references and index.
Identifiers: LCCN 2021030652 | ISBN 9780262046398 (hardcover)
Subjects: LCSH: Imaginary languages. | Languages, Artificial. | Glossolalia. | Language and languages in literature. | Language and languages—Origin.
Classification: LCC P120.I53 Y3313 2021 | DDC 499/.99—dc23
LC record available at https://lccn.loc.gov/2021030652

10 9 8 7 6 5 4 3 2 1

publication supported by a grant from
The Community Foundation for Greater New Haven
as part of the **Urban Haven Project**

CONTENTS

PREFACE

Imaginary Languages is a new, thoroughly revised and expanded version of a book published in 1984, *Les fous du langage: Des langues imaginaires et de leurs inventeurs* (translated in 1991 as *Lunatic Lovers of Language: Imaginary Languages and Their Inventors*). When the original edition went out of print, the title remained unavailable for years. However, the subject—which had received little attention when I started my research—continued to garner interest among scholars and in the broader public. Notable works that subsequently appeared include *La linguistique fantastique* (1985), a collection of essays edited by Sylvain Auroux; Umberto Eco's *La ricerca della lingua perfetta nella cultura europea* (1993), which was based on a seminar at the Collège de France (and translated into English in 1995 as *The Search for the Perfect Language*); Paolo Albani and Buonarroti Berlinghiero's *Aga magèra difùra: Dizionario delle lingue immaginarie* (1994); and *Aux origines des langues et du langage* (2005), a volume edited by Jean-Marie Hombert.

The same period witnessed an unexpected boom in the *practice* of inventing languages across a wide range of cultural spheres. Spiritualism is evidently experiencing a resurgence, and Pentecostalism is on the rise, with the attendant phenomena of speaking in tongues (*glossolalia*) or in languages unknown to speakers beforehand (*xenoglossia*). Largely thanks to the Internet, a great revival of interest has greeted artificial languages meant to facilitate international communication. Nor do enthusiasts and advocates of Esperanto have the last word: inventing languages has become a popular pastime with a market of its own (including specialized software and countless websites) and a dedicated fan base—around forty thousand people in the United States alone. Some of these languages—Lojban, for instance—have been designed to illustrate linguistic theories.

In turn, television and film have offered any number of fictions featuring an invented linguistic component. The cult series *Star Trek* has Klingon; there are rumored to be some quarter of a million speakers who use this language to communicate in secret and separate insiders from outsiders. J. R. R. Tolkien's trilogy *The Lord of the Rings* was adapted for the screen between 2000 and 2003; the films grant a prominent role to "Elvish" tongues. And lest we forget, Anthony Burgess made up the language of cavemen for Jean-Jacques Annaud's *Quest for Fire* (1981).

Finally, on more academic terrain (particularly in Russia and in California), theorists interested in the origin of language have turned back to monogenetic schemes of explanation, rejecting the dogmas and preconceptions of the past and enlisting new insights from the fields of genetics and paleontology. In a word, as a new century and a new millennium dawn, "logophilia"—the love of languages—is alive and well. I was very sorry I'd been unable to explore such developments in the original book, so I took advantage of this new edition to add material and modify its organization. Hence the new title.

—M. Y., September 30, 2005

FOREWORD: THE LOVE OF LANGUAGE

Why write one book and not another at a particular time of life? Without any narcissism, I'd say that a certain number of questions, encounters, coincidences, and circumstances gave rise to the work at hand. At least in part, I *had* to write it.

First came the coincidences—wide readings on a range of topics, which hardly seemed destined to yield a book of my own. They included science fiction novels like Ian Watson's *The Embedding,* which has a plot based on the Chomskyan postulate of a universal structure common to all languages, as well as Romanian author Vladimir Colin's *Babel,* which connects the primal tongue of Bab-ili (or Babylon) and a cosmic language of the future. Other books were J. R. R. Tolkien's *The Lord of the Rings,* featuring languages constructed along the lines of those depicted in seventeenth-century journeys of imagination, and, of course, George Orwell's *1984* and Anthony Burgess's *1985,* in which linguistic engineering controls how people think and standardized language is meant to erase social differences.

The last two titles, in particular, brought to mind the well-known arguments advanced by Edward Sapir and Benjamin Lee Whorf about how language shapes thought. I also couldn't help but think of the theories of Nikolai Marr in this context.

A book by the Russian semiologist Mikhail Bakhtin that I had translated[1] made frequent reference to Marr. Having read a few hundred pages of his writings, I decided to publish a selection of excerpts with a critical introduction. Marr's works were all but unavailable in French,[2] and almost all that anyone knew about him was that his speculations about the origin of language and desire to eradicate "class languages" had prevented Soviet linguistics from evolving until 1950—the year Stalin declared that the emperor had no clothes.

Marr's linguistic madness recalled another memory: Raymond Queneau's *Children of Clay*. The protagonist of the novel sets out to compile an encyclopedia of writers given the epithet of "literary madmen" or "reasoning madmen." Passages from their works are embedded throughout the text. I rushed to the Bibliothèque Nationale and, to my great surprise, discovered that Queneau was referring to actual books. These mad inventors had really lived; a number of them even claimed to have tracked down the primitive origins of human language. Later, I learned from Paul Braffort, Queneau's collaborator in the Oulipo (*Ouvroir de littérature potentielle*, or "Workshop of Potential Literature") that the author had collected the material for a university thesis that he never completed; the only remaining traces are published in this work of fiction.[3]

Strolling one day among the book sellers in the Latin Quarter, I got my hands on *La grammaire logique* and *Les origines humaines* by Jean-Pierre Brisset—two of the finest examples of literary madness to address the origins of language.[4]

The picture was growing clearer and clearer. Back at the Bibliothèque Nationale, I pored through the catalogs in the hope of discovering curiosities of the same magnitude. All of a sudden, one title jumped out at me: *Le langage martien* by Victor Henry. From there, I found my way to Theodore Flournoy's

Des Indes à la planète Mars: Étude sur un cas de somnambulisme avec glossolalie (*From India to the Planet Mars: A Case of Multiple Personality with Imaginary Languages*),[5] a work to be discussed at length in the pages to follow. A new vista opened before my eyes: the unconscious creation of unknown languages.

Although I've never been in the habit of reading the Bible, while reorganizing my books, I found a volume of the New Testament. Providentially, it contained the Epistles to the Corinthians, where Paul treats the matter of religious glossolalia, or "speaking in tongues." I'd made passing mention of the phenomenon in an earlier study, *Language through the Looking Glass*, and a reader had sent me a long letter about his experience of glossolalia as a manifestation of the Holy Spirit.

Scattered threads of memory began to come together. I recalled a recording of Pentecostal services that one of my students had brought back from the United States but I hadn't given much notice at the time. Coincidences continued and connections multiplied. While looking over an American bibliography, a title by John Sherrill, *They Speak with Other Tongues*, caught my eye. I tried to find the book in Paris, to no avail, and considered an expedition to the British Library in London. Then, one fine day, tidying up my own collection, a slim volume found its way into my hands—the very book I'd been looking for. Some ten years earlier, another student had given it to me as a gift. Suspecting her of being somewhat inclined to exalted states, I'd filed it away without looking inside.

Having published several books that discuss sexism in language, I'd also received, from an appreciative reader, a work of science fiction on the subject: Suzette Haden Elgin's *Native Tongue*. The time had finally come to read the novel and discover how a language for expressing women's experiences was invented.

I also remembered Louis Wolfson's wonderful *Le Schizo et les langues*. This book, written by an American in French, develops an idiosyncratic philological method to transform the author's mother tongue into a unique pidgin that evokes the "neo-Babelian" or "vernacular European" of another one of Queneau's novels, *The Blue Flowers*.

Little by little, the theme of my own study started to come into focus. Languages can be invented for serious purposes. Like my colleagues, in the classroom I'd used what linguists call *Kalaba-X*: series of phrases in a made-up code consisting of pieces of real languages; students are asked to decipher these puzzles and explain how they function.

Associations now were running wild: languages invented wholesale, Esperanto, Volapük, hybrid idioms, pidgins, Queneau's Babelian, the tongues of Middle-earth, jargons spoken in the works of Swift and Rabelais, and scientific—but still fantastical—efforts to reconstruct Proto-Indo-European.

From one day to the next, the material piled up, and I found myself more and more enthralled. Whenever I told friends, relatives, or students about my project, they came up with something new: a work of science fiction describing the workings of an alien tongue, a fantastic journey, a bizarre theory, a reference book I hadn't know about, an artificial language created by some obscure autodidact. . . . I learned that Esperanto is only the most well known of the approximately four hundred artificial languages on record; if one counts those lost to history, even more have been created.

My questions about artificial languages and their construction were compounded by phenomena such as *linguae francae* and pidgins, the formation of interlanguages in zones of cultural contact, as well as the process of acquiring one's mother tongue and learning foreign languages. As one thing led to another, the question of linguistic universals came up again and again in different form.

More and more, I recognized that I was working on a magnificent topic—and doing so, yet again, under the aegis of Raymond Queneau (to whom I had dedicated *Language through the Looking Glass*). A veritable fever, a state of constant intellectual excitement, gripped me for three years as I pursued research and reflections, reading and rereading texts as varied as the Old and New Testaments; Arnauld and Lancelot's *Grammaire générale et raisonnée de Port-Royal*; Freud and Lacan's writings on paranoia and hysteria; Leibniz and Descartes on the universal language of philosophy; Fontenelle and Flammarion on the plurality of inhabited worlds; studies on Galileo, Copernicus, and the Age of Discovery; the works of Rabelais and Swift, Thomas More, and John Amos Comenius; biographies of mystics, from Hildegard of Bingen to Therese Neumann; the Book of Mormon; books on spiritualism, occultism, witchcraft, shamanism, language development, cryptophasia, communication among the deaf and mute, aphasia, children's acquisition of language, planned languages (interlinguistics), computer languages, and translation machines. Of course, I read everything I could about linguistic universals—which represent the philosopher's stone, as it were—and countless theories about the origin of language (many of them by "literary madmen"). For comparison and contrast, I added all I could find in the way of utopias, imaginary journeys, and science fiction or fantasy novels about invented languages, a body of work reaching from antiquity to the present day.

What, I wondered, did the elements of this heteroclite assemblage have in common, drawing them to each other like so many magnetic particles? Where do they ultimately converge? What unites chimerical theories born of the myth of Babel, speculations on interplanetary and intergalactic communication, the vigorous fiction animating utopian schemes of a universal language, and instances of possession-by-language which give the elect the ability to speak in the tongue of God, angels, Adam, the Holy Spirit, Martians, or the inhabitants of the Sun or Moon?

The common denominator, the element that comes back time and again like a refrain, might well be the idea of universality: the uniqueness of human language projected into the future, past, and all directions at once—the infinity of space and time—whether in a work of fiction, a scientific study, or a pseudo-scientific project. This idea has been conveyed by myths (that of Babel, for instance); by respectable—and respected—theories (that of the *Grammaire générale et raisonnée de Port-Royal*, generative and transformational grammar); by idiosyncratic speculations like those offered by Jean-Pierre Brisset or Nikolai Marr (to say nothing of others to be found at the Bibliothèque Nationale or, now, on the World Wide Web); by logical schemes that some of the greatest minds developed in their search for a philosophical language from the sixteenth to the eighteenth centuries; by pragmatic and political projects to create the language of the future, which promised to put an end to conflicts between individuals and nations alike; by the coordinated expansion of trade languages that developed based on economic and political criteria. The idea has also flourished through practices such as the cosmic communication proposed by Emanuel Swedenborg or the "gift of tongues" in certain religious communities. There's no counting the works of fiction—which always reflect the contemporary state of learning and prevailing notions about the world—that have spread this vision to all corners of the Earth.

Accordingly, this book draws on three types of document; particularly interesting (or curious) examples are reproduced in the appendix:[6]

1. theories on the origin and nature of language;
2. imaginary languages constructed by design, whether in a fictional framework or with an actual utopian or didactic aim;
3. unconscious productions (glossolalia or xenoglossia) that seem or claim to be true languages.

One might think that the invention of languages (2 and 3) and theories on the origin and nature of language (1) belong to different fields of inquiry, and that spontaneous creations (3) must necessarily be distinct from intentional creations (1 and 2). But in all these cases, isn't a *metalinguistic* activity at work, even if it's unconscious?

At the same time, logical and, as it were, necessary relations unite these three types of production, however dissimilar they might seem at first.

To begin with, theories of origin almost always involve *reconstructions* (which can be more or less elaborate) of the primordial tongue and its subsequent stages of evolution.

Second, the myth of an Adamic language serves to *justify* the creation of future artificial languages and spontaneous linguistic productions of a mystical or spiritualist nature; most commonly, the connections are *explicit*. Historically, claims about the origins of language (which, for the main, have been monogenetic, then, from the nineteenth century on, polygenetic) and projects for universal languages have developed in parallel. Even though they entail constructions that are different in nature, both types of endeavor belong to the same current of thought. Most often, the same party winds up working in both senses at once.[7]

Finally, we can say that all such productions—theorized or not, rational or not, conscious or unconscious—display the same attitude toward language on the part of the creative subject: an ambivalent, love-hate relationship arising from a demiurgical will and a ludic sensibility in equal measure.

The speaking subject stands front and center in this story. Hence the second guiding idea of our inquiry: language "possesses" humankind, and vice versa. This is why the book does not examine only the myth of a universal language; it also explores the relationship between human being (or human beings) and language. The reflexive capacity they share means that taking up the matter of language means taking interest in people's interest in language. No distance between subject and object exists on this terrain. One is always already invested—simultaneously the subject of desire and its object, for the relationship passes through love: love of language and love of self.

Inventors of language are madly in love. They love an object that belongs to them only to the extent that they also share it with a community.[8] And yet, each of them entertains an exclusive and particular relationship with it. Language reaches into a mythical past and casts light on the future while remaining profoundly anchored in human history; it extends to the known and the unknown alike. Language makes human beings human, that is, beings similar and dissimilar at one and the same time.

Although many of the texts I have chosen have a poetic or aesthetic quality, however unintentional it may be (in the case of Brisset's mad elucubrations, for example), I should explain why invented languages in more purely literary texts are not included here. Burgess, Rabelais, Swift, James Joyce, Lewis Carroll, Antonin Artaud, Henri Michaux, and many others have received—and will continue to receive—the attention of academic scholarship. Only cases that meet the following criteria will be examined:

1. Writers must present their *language* as an *autonomous system*, complete unto itself and for communal use. Martian, as it emerged from the unconscious mind of the medium Hélène Smith, meets this requirement just as much as does Esperanto, the language her contemporary, Dr. Ludwik Lejzer Zamenhof, constructed patiently and deliberately.
2. The system must be *imaginary* and set in opposition to *natural languages*,[9] on the one hand, and to *historically attested* languages,[10] on the other.
3. The projects at issue stem from an individual effort—intentional or not, ludic, functional, or utopian—to lay hold of language. Therefore they stand opposed to society (as a social fact, language escapes the individual) and, at the same time, address society (in the form of proselytism, by serving didactic or philosophical purposes, representing a privileged connection to other worlds, and so on).

It is clear that "poetic" inventions do not meet these criteria, even though the procedures employed are often similar—and especially in the case of people "speaking in tongues" or the insane. If the latter prove to be poets in spite of themselves, subjective intent marks the line of division.

In turn, texts taken from novels retain our interest for two reasons. First, they attest to the uninterrupted hold of the myth of an original language on the collective imaginary. Second, they provide the best reflection of the state of knowledge in the general public throughout history. To be sure, expert insight takes a popularized form—one that is necessarily schematic and distorted—as it spreads. However, precisely this feature is why works of fiction provide a guide, coming back like a leitmotif from one chapter to the next. Each author, whether pursuing didactic and philosophical aims, or merely seeking to entertain, transmits positive information, however corrupted, about the ideas and visions circulating in his or her day.[11]

The Creation of Languages: Increasing at an Exponential Rate

SOME STATISTICS

> At some point in the next century the number of invented languages will probably overtake the number of surviving natural languages.
>
> —Cullen Murphy, *Atlantic Monthly*, October 1995

The site operated by Jeffrey Henning, who "holds watch" over the realm of invented languages, provides the following tally for the period from 1100 to 2005:

1100–1499	1	(Hildegard of Bingen's *lingua ignota*; see box on p. 30)
1500–1599	1	(Thomas More's Utopian)
1600–1699	5	
1700–1799	4	
1800–1829	0	
1830–1839	1	
1840–1849	1	
1850–1859	2	
1860–1869	2	
1870–1879	3	(including Martin Schleyer's Volapük; see box on p. 74)
1880–1889	6	(including Ludwik Zamenhof's Esperanto; see box on p. 77)

1890–1899	2	
1900–1909	15	
1910–1919	8	
1920–1929	5	
1930–1939	11	(including C. K. Ogden's Basic English)
1940–1949	7	
1950–1959	13	
1960–1969	15	
1970–1979	24	
1980–1989	33	
1990–1999	204	
2000–2004	298	

From 1960 on, creations have been essentially fictional and "private" languages with a playful or cryptic purpose—no longer intended to serve philosophical or vehicular ends. The language of the Star Trek series, Klingon, is the best known example, and many young fans use it as a code for insiders.

This trend therefore represents a counter-current to the disappearance of minority and nonstatus languages; the phenomenon is an item of concern for linguists who, like Claude Hagège, have sounded the call, "Stop the death of languages!"

Each act of creation draws on the collective imagination. It is advisable, then, to situate where the sources of imaginary languages lie: in connections between myth and utopia, the dreams of sleep and those of waking life. Part I of the book is devoted to this task. And since it's impossible to pass judgment on individual endeavors outside of prevailing notions, part II takes the reader on a quick tour of the history of linguistic thinking—a tour whose landmarks include languages invented in works of fiction from the sixteenth to the twentieth centuries. To illustrate linguistic fantasy in action, I have chosen the exemplary cases of Nikolai Marr and Hélène Smith, who are discussed in the penultimate section of part III. Part IV undertakes the "defense and illustration" (to borrow a phrase from the Renaissance poet Joachim du Bellay) of natural languages.

POSTSCRIPT

While writing this book, I had one deep-seated concern. By pursuing linguistic universals, wasn't I condemning myself to survey more or less the whole of human knowledge—an impossible task? As I found myself on the terrains of psychology, psychoanalysis, philosophy, logic, history, sociology, ethnology, and the history of ideas and ideologies, I realized I was leaving the realm of linguistics, properly speaking. But do the borders of the study of language need to be so clear-cut? Even though linguistics has the right—indeed, the duty—to establish itself as an autonomous field (a process that has been unfolding since the end of the nineteenth century), it still exists on a spectrum that includes other "human sciences": "man" stands at the heart of language, and vice versa. The great linguist Émile Benveniste hoped to construct a fully articulated anthropology: either linguistics would be totalizing or not. In turn, Roman Jakobson declared, "I am a linguist; I consider nothing linguistic foreign to me." For my part, I would gladly replace *linguist* with *speaking subject,* because language belongs to everyone and is everyone's concern. That said, I hope readers who are specialists in the aforementioned disciplines will pardon any omissions or shortcomings they may find.

PART I FROM MYTH TO UTOPIA

When the sleeper awakes, the dream dies.
    But when the dreamer dies, what becomes of the dream?
—Nietzsche

1

FROM AUSTRAL TO ASTRAL VOYAGES: FOUNDATIONAL MYTHS

How myth came to take the place of history . . .

How it came to feed both fiction and utopia . . .

How fiction, in the form of dogma, took the place of science . . .

How science, more and more, could dominate fiction . . .

How history, by eliminating myth, became a science itself—at the price of mortal combat against ideologies (a battle of uncertain outcome, still today) . . .

This history reads like a novel. And doesn't the word *history* evoke—over and above a sequence of events in time—a tale, a fable, an imaginary account?

In Romanian author Vladimir Colin's *Babel* (1978),[1] Ralt Moga, an earthling and a poet, has lost his beloved, Arla. In the company of a woman from Venus and a man from Mars, he betakes himself to the planet that lends the work its title. Like the Earth, Babel belongs to an integrated cosmos of ten planets controlled by a single "Office." But Babel is an artificial place; everything is an illusion. The collective unconscious of galactic humankind takes refuge here; hidden memories and a reservoir of fantastic visions are what Babel *is*. Consequently, our hero can travel both in space and time, and he finds himself in the city of Bab-ili—ancient Babylon, or, by another name, the Babel of myth. Instead of Galactic, the language used in the integrated cosmos (with "regional" accents varying from planet to planet), Babylonian is spoken here. The poet, now named Ra-lit,[2] can communicate right away, without having to learn the language first (an example of xenoglossia). His search leads him to an incarnation of Arla from the past; together, like Orpheus and Eurydice, they will regain the present. The myth of the original universal language, ideal and natural—the tongue of Babel-Babylon, which every human being carries within without even knowing it—is linked with the utopian (or anti-utopian?) theme of a language unified on a global and, indeed, a galactic scale (colonizers setting out from Earth have brought it to other planets). Future and past meet up, space and time merge, and reincarnation effected by thought and language ensures the continuity of human life.

A single novel, then, presents both aspects of the dream. On the one hand, we have the vision encountered in sleep, which can only be put in the past ("I dreamed that . . ."); as an expression of the collective unconscious, it refers back to human origins. On the other, we have the waking vision, which finds expression in the present and refers to the future ("I dream of . . ."); naturally, it is sustained by the first. Both forms of dream exist outside of history—indeed, *against* history—and respond to anxiety in face of the unknown. The acknowledged function of myth is to explain the mystery of origins—the origin of man, the origin of language. The goal of a utopia—a kind of prefabricated myth—is to direct and organize the future.

The border that divides utopia from myth is identical to the one that divides waking dreams from those of sleep. Thus, dreams that arise in the twilight state between unconsciousness and conscious life hold a particular interest.[3]

Languages belong to a space that includes the known world but also, as soon as the imaginary enters the picture, to another world, one that is unknown and invisible. They are inscribed in historical time and in mythical or utopian time (or both).

Etymologically, *utopia* means *u-topos,* or "non-place"—a site that does not exist. In literature, the idea extends to what might be called *u-chronia*: a time that doesn't exist. This duality opens space for *u-glossia,* "language that doesn't exist," to take hold.

U-topia and u-chronia form the two sides of *elsewhere*. Journeys of imagination and works of science fiction are always about hypothetical places (unexplored islands or planets, say, or the center of the Earth) and/or epochs for which no documentation exists, where the goings-on cannot be empirically verified. This is why, whether they raise scientific claims or not, the history of imaginary languages—which unfolds in an imaginary elsewhere—cannot be separated from the exploration of the world (or worlds). Whatever is supposed, or imagined, to exist invites speculation as a matter of course. It is inseparable from the history of ideas and linked, in particular, to the latter's driving force, the history of ideologies.

Great milestones of discovery have fed our linguistic imagination and influenced how we think about language: Marco Polo's voyage to China; the circumnavigation of the globe and conquest of the Americas; the hard-won and belated acceptance of the Galilean-Copernican system; expeditions in the South Seas and the discovery of new lands; the invention of the telescope, which brought the stars closer to Earth; nineteenth-century polar expeditions; the opening of Africa to trade and missionary work, permitting the scholarly description of new languages (in addition to those of Asia and the Americas, which were studied from the seventeenth century on); twentieth-century space travel; the rise of information technology . . .

Speculation precedes each and every new discovery. One only sets out to find what has been imagined beforehand. Often results prove to be quite different than expected. Only then do empirical facts enter the picture, which are manipulated and distorted in order to fit theoretical presuppositions, for ideological reasons. It takes an immense force of rupture for a new theory to emerge from any discovery, however novel it may be.

As the frontiers of the known world recede, speculations shift from one terrain to another. This is why trips to the Moon, the Antipodes, the center of the Earth, and uncharted continents provided literary themes before anyone thought of journeys to Mars or the outer reaches of the galaxy. Human imagination always stakes a claim before objective knowledge is available—hence the projection of questions of communication into an interstellar dimension. By the nineteenth century, when science fiction took the place of the fantastic voyages of old, there was nowhere left on the Earth to locate a utopia.[4]

What we see, then, is imagination soaring forward at full throttle, with science and empirical data following only after the fact. Hereby, fiction becomes confused with science, and it can even take its place. In order to install itself in a position of authority, science must first take care of myth. But myths are tough and not easily dispelled. It's not enough to muster proof based on the direct observation of phenomena; science must also be confirmed—and bolstered—by ideology. When a line of thinking or theory has gained the status of dogma, mere facts are powerless. The history of ideas in general, and of ideas about language in particular, is a series of conflicts between products of the imagination and facts—and ideology is what settles debates. Otherwise, there's no way to explain why the claim that language is divine in origin persisted for so long, or why Nikolai Marr's theories enjoyed the success they did. A further example is learned discussion of "primitive" languages in the nineteenth century; the theory of stages of linguistic and cultural evolution (cf. chapter 5, p. 54) underpinning it represented a way to reconcile colonialist ideology with positive science.

Myths are born, grow, and die; sometimes they are reborn—all in direct parallel to prevailing notions about the world. Often enough, they overlap and cross-pollinate, provided that they're not manifestly opposed to each other (although myths have little problem harboring contradictions). There are myths about language that have shaped Western thought since antiquity, and their traces can be found in scientific, religious, philosophical, and literary works. The best known of them concern *lingua adamica* (or *lingua humana*) and the story of Babel. Because of the authority of the Bible and the religions it has brought forth, these myths have grown intertwined with others, especially myths about the discovery of new worlds: that of *Terra Australis Incognita*, for instance, or stories of life on other planets.

UNKNOWN WORLDS

The idea of inhabited worlds other than our own, which dates back to antiquity and provides a cornerstone of science fiction even now, found its most celebrated expression in *Entretiens sur la pluralité des mondes* (*Conversations on the Plurality of Worlds*, 1686) by Bernard Le Bovier Fontenelle. The notion was heretical in the eyes of the Church, of course, being contrary to the teachings of the Bible. Although the Galilean-Copernican revolution had opened a breach in the dogmatic edifice built on Holy Scripture, the Church clung to the Ptolemaic system. At the end of the seventeenth century, when Fontenelle wrote his work, the theories of Copernicus (who had died in 1543, a century and a half earlier) and of Galileo (d. 1642) counted as subversive. They were gaining ground, however. If the Earth no longer occupied the center of the universe, and if the universe no longer represented God's creation for His creature, "Man," there was the possibility that human beings are not the only form of intelligence possessing the faculty of language. Other worlds would have tongues of their own.

The thesis of many inhabited worlds—an idea that preceded the Christian era but had no scientific patent—could come back into circulation. In the nineteenth century, Camille Flammarion became its vocal proponent and wrote a series of best sellers on the subject. The theme of planets inhabited by speaking beings (starting with the Moon) had flourished during the seventeenth and eighteenth centuries. At the same time, the dogma of the oneness of human language as a divine gift came to be called into question, opening the way for other modes of linguistic reflection.

Similarly, the myth of Terra Australis Incognita had posited the existence of an unknown continent that, sprung from the southern tip of Africa, sealed off the entire Indian Ocean and met up with Southeast Asia to create a kind of second Mediterranean.[5] During the Middle Ages, the torrid zones of the Earth were thought to be impassable; it seemed the truth about this continent might never be known. All the same, the idea of balance between North and South made it probable, if not necessary, for another world at the bottom of the globe to exist. The Church was divided on the issue. Some clerics argued that there could be no such continent: not only would people have to walk upside-down, but worse still, the Apostles would have been unable to cross the fiery Equator to preach the Gospel to them. Hadn't they received the gift of all human tongues for precisely this purpose? Other learned parties insisted on finding out whether there were people "down there" so the Word of God might be spread to all of humankind.

The Portuguese explorer Lopes Gonçalves proved that the Equator could be crossed when he did so in 1471. In 1479, Vasco da Gama sailed around the Horn of Africa to India; in the process, he showed that no adjacent continent existed. Expert opinion shifted the location of Terra Australis Incognita to South America. Magellan's voyage put an end to this theory, too. When New Guinea was discovered in 1526, it was held to be part of the mythical continent—then came the Solomon Islands and the New Hebrides. Each new site on the map had a turn. Around 1642, Dutch navigators explored the western coast of Australia, which they called New Holland. For most of the eighteenth century, the "austral continent" was still hypothetical and believed to extend all the way to the South Pole. Only in 1770 did James Cook finally discover Australia as we know it today.

It's easy to understand why, up to the eighteenth century, the Antipodes and the Australia of myth offered a site for utopian landscapes as favorable as the Moon or the center of the Earth—and for unknown languages, too.[6]

THE ROLE OF MYTH: FROM LINGUA ADAMICA TO BABEL

Where does language come from? How can one explain the diversity of languages spoken all over the globe? The function of myth is to explain the questions that human beings ask concerning where they come from.

In Judeo-Christian cultures (and among Muslims, who, we shouldn't forget, share the same founding myths), the theme of a shared origin and the dispersal that followed it have come to stand as dogma. The Bible provides an account in five stages, divided between the Old and New Testaments. The first four represent foundational events. The fifth enables passage from myth to history.

Myths of Linguistic Origin

The most familiar myths of the origin of language and the diversity of human tongues have come from the Bible, and they are shared by the three great revealed religions. However, other civilizations have sought answers to the same questions by means of their own legends and myths.

Thus, a pharaoh of ancient Egypt, Psammetich, is said to have had a child raised by a mute nurse in order to see what language it would finally speak. One day, the child uttered a sound close to the Phrygian word for bread (*bekos*), and its guardians concluded that this was the native tongue of humankind. Having heard of actual cases of children found in the wild, Frederick II of Prussia conducted the same experiment. Instead of spontaneously commanding "the primitive tongue," such children do not speak any language at all: their linguistic ability has atrophied.

The native inhabitants of Australia tell the tale of Wurruri, a sorceress who traveled the land, constantly sowing strife among families and villages. One day, she died. Since people were cannibals in those days, they decided to eat her body in a great feast, to which they invited all the inhabitants of the Earth. Alas, when the assembly started to sing, people found that different words issued from their mouths, in keeping with the part of the witch they had eaten. Wurruri had taken revenge by causing discord among communities that previously spoke the same tongue.

A Thai legend treats the same theme. Once upon a time, a free-spirited princess was fond of living among the beasts. To keep her at the palace, the king ordered her to count the grains of rice in the kitchen stores. The princess fled into the forest and vanished. Guards sent to pursue her encountered a python and killed it. In fact, the python was the princess. At the very moment their spears struck the royal creature, they changed form and began to speak unknown tongues. They promptly began to fight and scattered abroad, all over the Earth.

First, in the Book of Genesis, God gives language to Adam so that he may apprehend the universe. Adam assigns names to creatures and things as he discovers and takes possession of the world, for everything must have a name to exist. "And out of the ground the LORD God formed every beast of the field, and every fowl of the air; and brought them unto Adam to see what he would call them: and whatsoever Adam called every living creature, that was the name thereof." Such is lingua adamica, the original universal language, an essential component of the dogma of the oneness of God's children. Up to the dawn of the twentieth century, the Church held to the thesis of monogenesis with all its might and refused Darwin's theory of evolution. Indeed, to admit a plural origin of language would mean accepting that Adam was not the ancestor of humanity as a whole.

Of course, lingua adamica was the most vital part of the myth. As dogma, it had to be defended and affirmed, which gave rise to a truly fantastical strain of scholarship (could it have been otherwise?) on the divine origins of language, which didn't end until the nineteenth century. This did not mean, however, that the search for the mother tongue of humankind ceased—far from it; scholars simply no longer assumed that it was a matter of celestial benefaction. In fact, from 1866 on (when the Société de linguistique de Paris was founded), the enterprise continued at the margins of official learning. The torch had passed to "literary madmen." Only at the end of the twentieth century, mainly in the United States and Soviet Union (then Russia), would the project return with an air of general respectability, now in the context of advances in the fields of paleontology and human origins.[7]

The next part of the Biblical account is the Flood. Only Noah and his descendants escape destruction. Where did Noah manage to build his ark? What if, as John Webb surmised in the seventeenth century,[8] he had done so in China? This land was eminently suited to the enterprise. It followed that the language in use before the Flood was Chinese. There was no limit to Webb's esteem for Chinese art and culture. In his eyes, the language of people here had retained its original purity. The Westerners of the day had to come to terms with the antiquity of Chinese civilization, which threatened ideas about European preeminence. What's more, the writing system used throughout Chinese territory erased dialectal differences, which commanded further admiration (see chapter 4). Webb had struck upon a way of "recuperating" China for standing notions without imperiling the Bible or Christian orthodoxy. Simon Berington took up the same line of argument in 1750.[9]

Indeed, what if certain, exceptionally high mountains had escaped the Flood altogether? The search for traces of the Garden of Eden—and thus the Adamic language—shifted to elevated sites, and even to the Moon, since it had escaped the cataclysm, too. Scholastic thinkers held the latter opinion. As late as 1884, the Flood still provided the basis for arguments in favor of a monogenetic origin, language given by God. To counter evidence that the myriad languages in existence could not derive from the same mother tongue, a certain Georges de Dubor[10] got around the problem by claiming that the waters had not reached the black, red, and yellow races; if the Semites, Hamites, and Aryans make up a single racial and linguistic family descended from Noah, other races and languages do not belong to this lineage.

The question of where to situate Paradise—both the earthly one, where Adam and Eve lived, and the heavenly one, where departed souls abide—represents a point of intersection between linguistic and topographical imaginaries. Like the Greeks (Plutarch, for instance), Gaulish druids deemed the Moon to be the heavenly body to which souls ascend upon death. Such belief passed into Christian belief, in various forms. Indeed, it's hardly surprising, since Paradise must be located somewhere hard to reach (if it's not altogether imaginary—like the lost continent of Atlantis); hence the coincidence of paradisiacal and utopian *topoi*. The bowels of the Earth, on the other hand, have traditionally been thought to contain Hell, the *topos* of anti-utopias.

Ariosto's *Orlando Furioso* tells how Astolfo journeys to the kingdom of the Moon, a kind of paradise where everything lost by mortal men and women is now to be found: the sighs and tears of lovers, vanished time, unrealized projects, reason, and common sense. In Dante's *Commedia*, the poet travels down through the circles of Hell, arrives at the heart of the Earth, and comes back out at the Antipodes, where earthly Paradise and Purgatory are located; then he passes upward and onward to each of the seven heavens matching the seven planets (as understood at the time): the Moon, Mercury, Venus, the Sun, Mars, Jupiter, and Saturn. These celestial bodies all house souls. The uppermost spheres of the cosmos belong to fixed stars and the *Primum Mobile*. The Empyrean realm crowns it all; here dwell the saints and angels of Heaven.

The voyage Cyrano de Bergerac describes in *The States and Empires of the Moon* (1656) reveals a paradise lost to the Earth after the Fall. There he meets a young man named Mada, a transparent anagram of *Adam*. First on the Moon—then later on the Sun—the voyager finds ideal languages in use (cf. chapter 4, p. 55). In a very different spirit, Emanuel Swedenborg claimed to have made a similar journey in 1758 and to have discovered the first language of humankind on Jupiter (cf. appendix, p. 271). Finally, in the late nineteenth century, the spiritualist Hélène Smith (see chapter 8) communicated first in Martian, then in Uranian, with disembodied spirits that had ascended to the heavens.

The third foundational event recounted in the Old Testament is also the most familiar: the construction of the Tower of Babel and the confusion of languages that ensued—a kind of second Fall cementing the effects of the first once and for all. *Babel* is the Hebrew word for Babylon, or *Bab-ili*, which means "Gate of God." The text in Genesis (11:9) contains a pun, playing between *bab-el* and *bal-el* ("He confounds, confuses"): "Therefore is the name of it called Babel; because the Lord did there confound the language of all the earth: and from thence did the Lord scatter them abroad upon the face of all the earth."

The myth of Babel represents the necessary counterpart to the myth of the Adamic language, shining light on the mystery of the many tongues spoken by human beings and the lack of concord between them. At the same time, it opens the prospect that order, which once existed, will again prevail. Thus did myth give birth to utopia. From the sixteenth to the twentieth centuries, in parallel to the search for an original language—traces of which were presumed to exist among one remote tribe or another that didn't participate in building the accursed tower—the project of constructing a universal language thrived.

We now turn to the New Testament. If Christ has come to redeem Man, the creature once driven from Paradise, he also—and this fact is not as well known—comes to put an end to the curse of Babel. This happens in two stages.

The first is the miracle of Pentecost, which has been interpreted in different ways. Either it enables the Apostles to speak the foreign languages of those who have come from many lands to hear them (the first case of xenoglossia), or it means that although they speak Aramaic, their listeners can understand them as if they were speaking each man or woman's native tongue (in Chomskyan terms, one might say that communication is occurring at the level of deep structure, guaranteeing the oneness of human language). Alternatively, the Apostles express themselves in a kind of mystical Esperanto—a new language that revives the lost lingua adamica. Note the profound implications of the Pentecost for theology: banishment from Eden and the curse of Babel are the work of a vengeful deity; the Christian God is a God of mercy.

A second manifestation of divine grace in language—which, appearances notwithstanding, is quite different—occurs in Paul's First Epistle to the Corinthians (13 and 14).[11] Here, one reads of a singular practice that has emerged in the Primitive Church: "speaking in tongues." In contrast to what happened at Jerusalem on the day of Pentecost—the miracle of perfect intelligibility without the aid of translation, pellucid communication—at Corinth the faithful speak languages that neither they nor their listeners understand; by this means, the Holy Spirit places them in direct communion with God. Unlike xenoglossia, which occurs in an identifiable language, glossolalia involves a language unknown to speakers and listeners. This is not communication between one human being and another, but between a person (or persons) and the Deity (or spirits from the other world).

Rise up, speak or make a sound—keep making sounds, and the Lord will turn them into a language, urged Joseph Smith, the founder of the Church of Jesus Christ of Latter-day Saints. Yet there will always be confusion between two orders of phenomena. Even though Mormonism and Pentecostalism affirm the miracle of xenoglossia (which involves human languages), they are essentially reliant on glossolalia (supernatural tongues).

Without condemning glossolalia altogether, Saint Paul voiced strong reservations. He set the "gift of tongues"—an emotional (if not infantile) outpouring—in opposition to prophetic speech, which addresses the intellect. In fact, Corinthian glossolalia marks the passage from the realm of myth to History, writ large—the first instance on record of a linguistic practice occupying a defined historical position oriented and justified in terms of myth.

Yet myth precedes science and history, and it perpetuates itself even as history unfolds and science advances. Though assigned a lesser status, it animates human endeavor, representing the most universal form of thought and, in this capacity, shaping worldly events.

After all, doesn't myth—if on another register—say the *same* thing as science? Doesn't it unveil the truth in a different light, fusing the worlds of imagination and of reason?

2

THE DREAMER DREAMING: PROFILES IN LOGOPHILIA

All voyages of madness cross over the horizons of reason.

—Gilles Lapouge, *Le singe de la montre*

How admirable it is to have been born opportunely.

—Charles Nodier, *Bibliographie des fous*

Who, then, possesses the privilege of bearing this utopian and mythical current of thought, which develops on the fringes of science and history yet permeates them?

Michel Pierssens has denominated the parties in question—those who are "crazy" about exploring or creating languages—"logophiles." For his part, Umberto Eco calls them "glossomaniacs."[1] These people are the kind of dreamers who take their visions for reality.

As we've noted, the creation of a universal language most often rests on nostalgia for the primal tongue predating the Tower of Babel, a divine gift shared by all humankind. What inspires its inventors, then, is the quest for a lost paradise—a seamlessly integrated lingua adamica, or lingua humana. Their efforts, when rationalist in conception, are geared toward society. When glossolalia is involved, normal communication is disrupted, and the thrust is antisocial. But either way, logophiles occupy an eccentric position. They seize language and make themselves its master, whether to the benefit or detriment of common understanding. Logophiles want to escape the standing social consensus on which language is based. This is why the idea of universality is not enough to characterize the phenomenon. The struggle pitting the speaking subject at odds with the language-object is just as important as the myths previously discussed.

What inspires such demiurgical will? It would seem that, having received language from God, Nature, or Culture (in keeping with personal motivation or prevailing belief), the logophile wished to take the place of God, Nature, or Culture and shape what has already been given, transforming the past, present, and future of language. Logophiles always emerge defeated from the struggle—but never discouraged. Isn't it the nature of dreams that they never come true? Illusion may condemn the dreamer to failure, but human beings never stop dreaming; it's the only way they can go on living.

"When the dreamer dies, what becomes of the dream?" Nietzsche asked. When one dreams about the perfect language, there is always another dreamer to come along and take it up, so others will continue the search by embracing a vision of the future in which it will ultimately come true.

Although its shape, features, and conditions of emergence are historically determined, the dream still forms an archetype inscribed deep in human being. At heart, the dream of man-as-demiurge is to create perfection and harmony, to achieve progress by returning to one's origins, to attain unity, establish universal communication with God, spirits, extraterrestrials, or, quite simply, with other people and oneself—a dream of fusing with Nature. The burden of lost innocence and vanished wholeness weighs heavy on the unconscious mind of the peoples of the world.

The following concerns the dreams of both nighttime and waking life, visions that can be sober, drunken, or otherwise intoxicated. The scene does not always offer a pleasant illusion or a generous utopia; at times it takes the form of a nightmare or delirium.

Our story unfolds between opposite poles, then:

dreamed/real
utopia/history
myth/science
nature/culture
child/adult
primitive/civilized
emotion/intellect
fantasy/reason
unconscious/conscious
faraway/near
perfect/imperfect
divine/human
innocence/experience
simple/complex
feminine/masculine

We can picture the logophile in a study crammed with books; all around lie vast quantities of information yet to be collated, classified, listed, and indexed on countless tables and cards. A delirium of naming, taxonomical madness, has seized this solitary figure. Everything in the world awaits its true name, but first the overarching categories and concepts must be identified and arranged, so a system of notation, hierarchies, and models spans the whole universe. It may be a fool's errand, yet there's something majestic about it that one can't help but admire: so much energy is mustered for such scant results. It seems no other mirage has ever been pursued with as much ardor—except, perhaps, efforts to find the philosopher's stone or prove the existence of God. No utopian design has ever led so much ink to flow, with the possible exception of socialism.

A man possessed, our inventor sacrifices both his private life and financial resources; more often than not, editors won't touch what he writes and he must bear the costs of publication himself. He recognizes that the enterprise exceeds what a single lifetime will allow. If he's lucky, he has a child, disciple, or friend who will continue work he leaves unfinished. Bishop John Wilkins (1614–1672) went to the grave without managing to conclude his project for a philosophical language, and he bequeathed the task to a group of his associates. Charles Nodier's *Archéologue ou système universel des langues* (1810) had in fact been started by Charles de Brosses (1709–1777); a pupil of Antoine Court de Gébelin (1725–1784) took charge of seeing that someone saw it through. The work of Charles Callet is mainly known thanks to his son's efforts. And so on, and so on.

Let's say our inventor does manage to bring the project to completion. The demon of glossomania will spur him to start another one—and then yet another. Many creators of artificial languages have thought up other systems in succession, or even at the same time. For instance, Petro Stojan, who was born in what is today Ukraine, wandered all over Europe between 1910 and 1960, leaving behind more than a dozen languages. What's more, logophiles are perfectionists; never satisfied, they're constantly making improvements. Adolphe

Nicolas, who was employed as a ship's doctor, reworked his language, Spokoil, thirty-four times between 1889 and 1904.

Now suppose that our inventor's labors meet with some success—as happened with Zamenhof's Esperanto. Any number of people will show up and set about trying to improve the endeavor. Esperanto has provided the basis for a host of derivative languages, so-called Esperantides. One enthusiast—René de Saussure—proposed three new versions between 1919 and 1942.

Even though they labor for the good of humankind and try to "spread the word," logophiles most often remain isolated and alone. Each time one of them emerges from the study to address the public at large, he meets up with rivalries, intrigues, critics, and intellectual tribalism. The scene repeats itself time and again. Marcel Monnerot-Dumaine, an advocate of universal language and a historian of efforts to bring it about, notes the fate of his predecessors: "Almost always unrecognized, they were met with scepticism and obscurantism, sometimes even mockery."[2]

Inventing a language means being a passionate amateur,[3] in both senses of the word: a lover and a dilettante. Often, logophiles know nothing about the scientific study of language and their concerns are aesthetic: they want to produce something complete, a totality, a closed but exhaustive whole that exhibits perfect symmetry, with gears that move smoothly; it should be free from grating ambiguity and harbor no room for waste, doubt, or misunderstanding. This edifice is meant to be pleasing to the eye, ear, and mind—in contrast to all the exceptions, defects, and gray areas one finds so readily in natural languages.

The enterprise requires idealism. In the case of a philosophical language, the goal is to match up the ways people speak and the ways they think. When international communication stands at issue, the aim is to reconcile human beings with one another. A significant number of language inventors have come from Central Europe: disputed territories torn apart by history. Many of them were born in either the Russian or Austro-Hungarian Empire at the turn of the twentieth century. Their ranks included clerics, teachers, and physicians—in other words, the bookish sort. The portrait gallery in Monneret-Dumaine's study—one of two "bibles" in the field of interlinguistics—shows one bearded face after another gazing earnestly through wire-rimmed glasses.[4]

Some logophiles look to the future. Others look to the past. Occasionally, the same individual does both.

Imagine what it's like trying to reconstruct the primitive language at the origin of all others. It means gathering words and roots from all the known tongues spoken throughout the world. Any one person might know two or three—in rare cases, some half-dozen. But if this is so, there's no question of investigating grammatical structures with any perspective. That would be too complicated—and besides, it can be hard to recognize that one's native tongue (or, say, Indo-European languages) isn't the only model out there. So work proceeds at a remove from primary sources, relying on second-hand accounts and descriptions of "exotic" languages written up by travelers. There's neither world enough nor time to conduct fieldwork everywhere. Foreign tongues wind up being learned at home, at a desk.[5] In this setting, there's no chance of studying the relationship between oral and written forms. Surely, the amateur supposes, the letters match up with sounds. Who would think that phonetic rules follow some other system? One might not know about Franz Bopp's comparative grammar or Jacob von Grimm and Karl Verner's laws of consonant change—or maybe it seems best to ignore them. Nikolai Marr was familiar with comparative, Indo-European research, but his Stalinism made him despise "bourgeois" scholars and their science.

Logophiles know what they want to prove, but they still have to convince everybody else. This means:

1. gathering data;
2 classifying it;
3. finding a principle of explanation—say, the imitation of sounds of nature, or the correspondence between words' meaning and the way they're pronounced;
4. organizing information in a family tree, with a mother tongue that has brought forth all the languages of humankind, past and present.

The glossomaniac faces the immense task of laying hold of all languages—the sum total of human communication—in a desperate bid for exhaustiveness; it's vital that nothing be omitted. Then, in a second step, he must progressively reduce this totality to its core elements. Marr, for example, arrived at four fundamental components; he would have been happier still to have found a single, primordial word.

Boiling all languages down to a common denominator demands seeking out points of intersection and resemblance, however remote they may be. From time to time, comparisons hit the mark, but what are they worth without a system? There are all kinds of tricks for transforming the irreducible mass into manageable units; in many cases, features of natural languages show the way. Yet the question persists: what's it worth without a system? Logophiles play in earnest, juggling between registers of meaning by way of metonymy, metaphor, and antiphrasis; by trying to reconcile antonyms; through metathesis, epenthesis, and anything else that might occur to them. One means is as good as the next; so long as words are taken in isolation, similarities abound.

Those inclined to seek the origins of language in imitation will be attentive to onomatopoeia. "The names of things when spoken," Charles Nodier declared in this spirit, "were the imitation of their sounds, and the names of things, when written, the imitation of their form. Onomatopoeia, then, is the very *type* of vocalized language, and the hieroglyph the type of written language. *For Nature names itself:* everything abstract derives from something concrete, and all extended meaning from primitive noises is made by the interplay of figures." To prove as much, Nodier observes that "the speech of children abounds in images . . . , like that of primitive peoples and women [sic]."[6]

Parties who hold that language originates in nature will trace everything back to the grunts, whistles, growls, and bellowing of prehistoric humankind.[7] One might also stress the influence of climate and build on a theory dear to Rousseau. Nodier describes the perspective as follows: "In torrid lands, the vocabulary is loud and flowing. Greek displays a full, majestic resonance, like the sound of the river god Peneus's words. The murmur of cascades and the trembling of olive trees roll in the sonorous syllables of Italian. But the vocabulary of frigid lands is harsh and consonantal. The sound of words, thunderous and jagged, evoke the roar of torrents, firs creaking in storms, and the crash of falling boulders."[8] Another view—one advanced by Jean-Pierre Brisset—is that language emerged in response to sexual urges. Supreme effort devoted to phonetic and semantic shifts (much in the manner of Lacan's famous puns) reveals how words ultimately refer to the bare facts of life (cf. appendix, p. 223).

Still other possibilities exist. It's only logical for the first language to have been less complex than modern ones. Chinese has miraculously preserved this quality and points the way. After all, Chinese must be pretty simple: it's an "isolating language" (one without inflection, that is) consisting of monosyllabic elements.

Good Christians mindful of Scripture know, of course, that the first language can only have been Hebrew. One need only take a handful of familiar Hebrew words and track down obvious matches in other tongues. Indeed, in his *Harmonie étymologique* (1606), Guillaume Postel was so intent on deriving Greek from Hebrew that he read it from right to left! Strangely enough, Celtic has often been enlisted to throw a bridge between the language of the Bible and modern vernaculars. Reverend Paul Pezron (1639–1706), whose works Queneau unearthed, was convinced that Celtic was one of the tongues brought forth by the post-Babelian diaspora. The Celts, he claimed, are descended from Gomer, Japheth's eldest son; as any number of similarities prove, their tongue is related to Hebrew. What's more, inasmuch as they've inhabited the greater part of Europe and Asia, they're the original "Indo-Europeans."[9] Louis Poinsenet de Sivry (1733–1804) advanced the same thesis and found, in hundreds of names for places and peoples, a wealth of supposedly related Indo-European and Semitic roots, all connected with fire.[10] On this basis, he concluded that the Celts had managed to conquer the globe thanks to an enormous conflagration following the Flood (which has also left toponymic traces). His *idée fixe* was finding the word for "fire" and related vocabulary all over the vast expanse of Eurasia, in order to prove how the Celts—the "fire people"—had spread far and wide; all the world's races are descended from "Urian, or incendiary, colonies among the Gauls, where the first blaze was started and from where the name, use, and cult of fire passed on to all the countries of the globe, which the Celts were the first to conquer."

A mystical bent will lead the logophile to spirits from other worlds—like those sought out by Swedenborg—for traces of the first language. To obtain a single explanatory principle accounting for how the universe is organized, keys are provided by esotericism, numerology, and cabalistic or Llullist tradition,[11] to say nothing of astrology. François Drojat, author of *La maîtresse-cléf de la tour de Babel* (1857), discovered Voconte, a language that belongs to all humanity, and invented a phonetic alphabet for bringing together the various tongues in relation to the five senses, colors, and numbers. According to Joseph Bouzeran's *Essai d'unité linguistique raisonnée* (1847), the holy number of the Trinity explains the threefold oneness of language. The author deemed it a matter of course that the world's peoples all have the same alphabet, perceive phenomena along the same lines, and have languages with the same parts of speech. Three categories of sound—gutturals, labials, and dentals (which are semantically equivalent)—structure every human language, just as the Father, Son, and Holy Spirit govern the world. In turn, *La langue basée sur l'idéographie lunaire* (1868) by Rémy-Amand de Vertus declared that observation of the Moon and its cycles led to the analogies at the origin of the first human language. This study is the very epitome of the eureka moment: the heteroclite lexicon detailed page after page culminates in a single flash of insight a posteriori.

Nationalists, or parties moved by chauvinist stirrings, will try to prove that Adam and Eve spoke the language of their native land—Swedish (Anders Kempe), for instance, or Dutch (Gropius Becanus).[12]

Nostalgia for a lost paradise can also lead to Polynesia—where the language of our communal ancestors first was spoken.[13] Unless, of course, the answer lies in America and some mysterious tongue used by the Indians there.[14]

Even if they belong to specific historical moments, the cast of mind and passion that one encounters among logophiles represent something abiding and permanent that stands outside of time—and especially outside the present day (whenever that may be). Here, myth and utopia meet up in a universalist vision transcending ages and epochs. More than anything, I have tried to evoke a particular kind of personality—an archetype—and to treat it without making value judgments. One particularly striking feature of this portrait provides the focus of the next chapter. Before turning the page, the reader might want to venture a guess.

3

THE DREAM OF THE DREAMER'S RIB: FEMALE BODIES, MALE SCIENCE

We have seen our dreamer in the throes of his dream. But is it possible for the dreamer to be a woman? Who are these people who invent languages, whether to philosophical or to practical ends? What kind of person devises theories on the origin and development of speech and communication? Who comes up with imaginary voyages and works of science fiction?

Time and again, it's men who do so. Among the approximately four hundred authors inventoried first by Louis Couturat and Léopold Leau, and then by Monnerot-Dumaine, we find only one woman, the celebrated Hildegard of Bingen; and the language she created is more a matter of glossolalia or cryptophasia than anything else.

But as soon as our attention turns to glossolalia and xenoglossia—cases of all kinds, and at all historical periods—the names of women abound, and men represent the exception. Among mediums and mystics, women play the starring role.[1] However vexing, the fact is undeniable. The challenge, then, is to interpret this state of affairs without appealing to biological arguments. Is this another example of the age-old division of gender roles that perpetuates prejudices about the "nature" of men and women? Men supposedly excel at intellectual tasks, abstract reasoning, philosophical and theoretical thinking, conscious and reflected endeavor; women are said to be emotional and imaginative, and unfettered by intellectualism. Men think with their heads; women act on gut feelings. . . .

The First Known Case of Linguistic Invention

Lingua Ignota per simplicem hominem, by the abbess Hildegard of Bingen (1098–1179)—a language devised to cryptic and/or mystical ends—counts as the first example on record of an actively created language. It dates to the year 1100.

Far from presenting a complete system, Hildegard's invention comprises a glossary of some thousand words written in an alphabet of twenty-three signs. As such, this "language" implies simple lexical substitution within a single tongue (German or Latin); this is also what happens in other, more recent examples of cryptic languages—for instance, Louchébem, Verlan, and other forms of slang. We don't know whether Hildegard's *lingua ignota* was intended for a group of insiders or as something private. The abbess claimed that it originated in a divine vision, and she employed it in the hymns she composed. The following sample follows Latin syntax:

> O orzchis Ecclesia, armis divinis praecincta, et hyacinto ornata, tu es caldemia stigmatum loifolum et urbs scienciarum. O, tu es etiam crizanta in alto sono, et es chorzta gemma.

Significantly, lingua ignota is a woman's creation, whereas the overwhelming majority of imaginary or devised languages that have been attested are the work of men.

It isn't hard to see how these roles are culturally determined. We needn't dwell on how, until recent times, it has fallen to men to be creators, inventors, and theoreticians. Plenty of ink has flowed, and the history of women's exclusion from scientific endeavor has already been written. The same holds for the realm of pseudo-science. It's more interesting to look at the other side of the picture, the place assigned to women. Here, history provides an answer to our questions.

Following the excesses of Montanism in the second century, the Church rejected the practice of speaking in tongues, which grew increasingly marginal over time. During the Middle Ages, however, the activity resurfaced among women who ultimately earned sainthood: Hildegard of Bingen and Elizabeth of Schönau, for instance. (In the twentieth century, the Church denied canonization to their latter-day sister, the Bavarian mystic Therese Neumann.) Moreover, speaking in tongues has persisted, without interruption, in dissident Christian sects (the prophetic movement in seventeenth-century southern France, the 1904–1905 Welsh Revival, North American Pentecostalism, and so on). In this setting, men and women have played active roles.

The official Church has condemned the deviant practice because of its emotional and sensual charge, which adds too much of the body to the spirit; at times, a whiff of sulfur seems to attend the proceedings. These sects are held to be irrational and infantile, suited for women and simple souls. Sociological studies of membership in the United States reveal many more women, people of color, illiterates, and parties of modest means than so-called upper- and middle-class denominations. A real class division exists, then. The model speaker-in-tongues is poor, Black, and a woman. Everyone knows that mediumship has always been the province of "the weaker sex."

We can discern two radically opposed approaches to language, then, two wholly different modes of relation. On the one hand, we find intellect, or rational comprehension, which is analytical, logical, and out to establish order in the world—a utopian and constructive bearing that counts as masculine in essence. On the other hand, we find intuition: an attitude that is instinctive, spontaneous, globalizing, sensual, primitive, infantile, fanciful, and hysterical—in a word, everything that is supposed to define women, children, and the mad.

There you have it. I swear I didn't make it up. But madness, scrupulous readers will observe, occurs across the board.

Madness takes many forms: the criminally insane, people who need to be locked up for their own good, gentle dreamers, harmless nuts, visionaries, village idiots, feeble-minded innocents, as well as complete lunatics endowed with uncanny subtlety. The latter sometimes even pass as reasonable individuals. They're always men.

The "literary madmen" who have the good fortune of having been "born opportunely [*à propos*],"[2] in Nodier's phrase, enjoy the esteem of their contemporaries. What border separated Louis Wolfson's genius from outright schizophrenia? Why did Brisset—who was paranoid but also certain that he would receive the acclaim of future generations—represent a danger to some of his contemporaries while Marr, who proposed a theory just as crazy (and at exactly the same point in time), came to stand at the summit of Soviet linguistics? Nodier flouted the esteemed opinion of Voltaire when he rehabilitated Cyrano de Bergerac. He also wrote a book of his own on the onomatopoeic origins of language; it was well received in his day, but now it seems clumsy and nonsensical.

It's often tough to draw a line between (sound) reason and (mad) reasoning. It's a matter of simple fact that the judgment passed on any given work depends on the state of learning and dominant ideology of the time and place. The Christian dogma of language's oneness and divine origin is what gave rise to efforts to find humankind's primal tongue. Likewise, in a different context, cloaking his theory in Marxism enabled

Marr to pass off his ideas as scientifically valid. Under the right conditions, the search for a philosophical language (in the seventeenth and eighteenth centuries) or schemes to devise a linguistic means for facilitating international relations (in the nineteenth and twentieth centuries) didn't seem silly at all. No one would dismiss Descartes, Comenius, or Leibniz as fools.[3] Nor, for that matter, would anybody subject Zamenhof to such treatment, even now. Although cultural factors are important, the diagnosis of madness is made along lines that are the province of medicine. At any rate, the judgment of one's contemporaries affects career prospects. Brisset and Callet only became more paranoid. Marr qualified as a genius (and his megalomania and paranoia passed unnoticed).

Among projects for universal languages, some are silly or naive. Without the slightest idea how language works, authors just take their mother tongue and come up with some arbitrary code, convinced that all languages follow the same design. The same mistaken beliefs are found among the theorists of linguistic origins.

The true madman is fairly conspicuous: obsessive, exalted, and, in particular, inclined toward defensiveness. "They called me simple, ignorant, deluded, and 'ridiculous.' I was accused of bad faith and of knowingly attributing false meanings to foreign words in order to support my ramblings. That's the treatment meted out to bearers of new ideas. . . . This 'trash talk' doesn't mean a thing.[4] So runs the opening of Charles Callet's *Le mystère du langage*. The psychiatrist Jaroslav Stuchlik cites one patient who came up with no fewer than sixteen fully-fledged languages.[5] As Monnerot-Dumaine observes, "There's no doubt that a large number of paranoiacs are to be found among these authors, and that many of their creations should be considered the product of inflated self-importance."[6]

Megalomania, obsessive thinking, desire for power, and delusions of persecution combine with a predilection for playing with words to shape the dominant traits of language inventors. At what point does the game become pathological?

To make things even more difficult, all such inventions—whether the result of conscious reflection or the outpourings of the unconscious mind—employ the same procedures and exist on a continuum. Often the ludic aspect is plain, even when the inventor is classified as mad. As a rule it's impossible to distinguish between "mentally ill" and "healthy" individuals on the basis of formal criteria such as the level of observation and detail they demonstrate. Some languages created by the insane display a high level of sophistication, and there are nonpathological cases of glossolalia resembling the babble of children; in fact, there's no formal way to tell the difference between aphasic glossolalia and some forms of poetry that are wholly intentional.[7] The languages spoken by Hélène Smith—which, according to Théodore Flournoy (1854–1920), were the product of a second, infantile personality—came out in a somnambulistic trance; they offered many points of resemblance to forms of slang and literary idiolects, as well as the cryptophasic utterances of the insane and the jargon brought forth by aphasics.[8] Wolfson's personal language was based on philological principles that caricatured real ones. Justinus Kerner (1786–1862) described a mystical seer speaking a tongue that was supposed to be the original language of humanity before the Fall;[9] its hybrid nature makes it look like Volapük *avant la lettre*.

Like "dream," the words "fool," "mad," "insane," and so on harbor ambiguity that the discussion here gladly exploits. Madness does not describe only what fails to satisfy the criteria of "normality." Equally, the term is applied to people who love to excess. Seventeenth-century Protestants in southern France were said to be "mad about God," and more recent times have witnessed so-called Jesus freaks; fanaticism can signify insanity in a social sense. People who are "crazy about language" can't help but occupy a marginal position.

While products of the unconscious mind, dreams can also be consciously constructed. In dreams, as in madness, there's no clear line of division—especially where language is concerned. Instead, it's a spectrum. Indeed, even without falling into pathological excess, is there a single linguist—or any poet—who isn't a bit of a logophile, a sorcerer's apprentice when it comes to language and words?[10] Consider the monumental grammar of Jacques Damourette and Edouard Pichon (1911–1940), which is written in a metalanguage invented wholesale, a work so overflowing, excessive, and poetic it makes one's head spin.[11] Likewise, much has been said about the "madness" of Ferdinand de Saussure's research on anagrams. And what, if not collective logophilia, inspired comparative linguists to reconstruct a fantastical "mother tongue"?

Since we've already brought up the stereotypical distinction between the ways that men and women relate to speech and language, there's no avoiding a well-worn cliché. On the one hand, there are the imperious but capricious ways of women: inconstant, unpredictable, illogical, unfaithful, deceitful (inherently ambiguous), fickle, unstable, self-indulgent (full of redundancy), and refractory. On the other, there's masculine straightforwardness, duty-bound to tame the feminine tongue and bring the speaker to heel. Such defects are precisely the faults that inventors of languages—all of them men, lest we forget[12]—have found in natural languages and set out to remedy. To be sure, these inventors declare that they want to put an end to linguistic confusion, but in the process they place a premium on rationality, regularity, and logic. The same principle applies, if for different reasons, to theoretical projects ("mapping" language by means of taxonomies, formulas, and other hierarchies), as well as to poetic or simply ludic endeavors. Men are destined to master language with a firm but loving hand. *Qui aime bien châtie bien*, the French saying goes.[13]

Time and again, the history of imaginary languages records gestures of exclusion. Women are banished from the field of theoretical reflection and creation, however unreasonable the latter may actually be. They are confined to a domain imposed by culture as if it were a matter of natural fact: the realm of affect, emotion, intuition, and practice (as opposed to the philosophically dignified sphere of praxis).

All those excluded from power—and from the power of speech, in particular—wind up in a ghetto: holy women who contradict the official (male) clergy, spiritualists and mediums, and members of marginal sects whose desire for the innocent state of the Primitive Church takes the form of a return to childhood—the childhood of the human race. Speaking in tongues is a second infancy.

PART II IN THE COURSE OF TIME (THE SEVENTEENTH TO THE TWENTIETH CENTURY)

Wherein evolving conceptions and theories of language take literary root in vernacular form.

4

THE UNFINISHED QUEST: THE SEARCH FOR AN IDEAL LANGUAGE IN THE SEVENTEENTH AND EIGHTEENTH CENTURIES

And out of the ground the LORD God formed every beast of the field, and every fowl of the air; and brought them unto Adam to see what he would call them: and whatsoever Adam called every living creature, that was the name thereof.

—Genesis 2:19

Find a language;—Besides, every word being idea, the time of a universal language will come!

—Rimbaud, *Les lettres du voyant*

Until the end of the nineteenth century, fictions of imaginary travel culminated in positive utopias combining utility and pleasure.[1] Although meant for amusement, they often included didactic or edifying aims. Ideal societies would have ideal languages serving the purposes of communication. The age of the anti-utopia began with *The Coming Race*, by Edward Bulwer-Lytton (1871). From this point on, imaginary tongues appeared in literary works with a pessimistic cast. Instead of furthering communication or philosophy, these languages represented instruments of subjugation and manipulation. A dream turned into a nightmare. Much of what would come to be known as science fiction didn't find inspiration in universalist linguistic schemes like Esperanto.

Umberto Eco has written on the history of the quest for the true philosophical language, a form of symbolic communication free from the imperfections tainting languages now in use.[2] The latter are often ambiguous, illogical, irregular, and unsuited for clear reasoning inasmuch as the categories they employ are said to hamper the expression of autonomous thought.

Thomas More's *Utopia* (1516) represents the first—and exemplary—station in this quest. Even though the author describes it only in schematic fashion, the utopian tongue is the standard and model for subsequent inventions. Close to Greek and Persian (the relationship between which was unknown at the time), Utopian enables perfect communication, faithfully translating the essence of things into human terms that are simple, straightforward, and harmonious: "a language both copious in words and also pleasant to the ear, and for the utterance of a man's mind very perfect and sure."[3]

The philosophical project of the perfect language had long been exercising the greatest minds on both sides of the Channel when, finally, the English bishop Francis Godwin (1562–1633) provided a literary treatment in his *Man in the Moone* (published posthumously in 1638).[4] Soon, the work was emulated by Cyrano de Bergerac (1618–1655) in France.[5] Godwin's hero Domingo Gonzales betakes himself to the Moon and finds that, unlike the inhabitants of the Earth, people there all speak the same language. What's more, it's a musical language, and each utterance forms a melody (cf. appendix, p. 231). This form of communication is so natural and easy that the traveler masters it in just two months.[6]

Later in the narrative, Gonzales winds up in China—where the language is also musical and broadly intelligible. Although dialects exist for everyday use, the tongue of the ruling class, Mandarin, is spoken in all provinces of the land. This is the first literary record of China's influence on linguistic thought in Europe. It continued unabated until the end of the nineteenth century.[7] For this duration, the theme of China intersected with that of music, which, like mathematics, counted as a universal code. More still, the Chinese system of writing was held to transcend regional variations, translating concepts instead of mere sounds. For generations of philosophers seeking a universal form of communication, it represented the model par excellence.[8]

The musical language that Godwin invented holds interest mainly as a documentary source for understanding the culture of his day. The good bishop didn't bother to work out a model beyond substituting notes for letters of the alphabet; his scheme represents a kind of cryptography. John Wilkins—another bishop—took up the same idea in two works that likewise addressed questions of communication and life beyond the Earth: *The Discovery of a New World or a Discourse Tending to Prove that it is Probable that There May Be a Habitable World on the Moon* (1640) and *Mercury or the Secret and Swift Messenger* (1641). The former posits a connection between notes and concepts: "But now if these inarticulate sounds be contrived for the expression, not of *words* and *letters*, but of *things* and *notions* . . . , then might there be such a general Language, as should be equally speakable by all People and Nations; and so we might be restored from the general curse, which is yet manifested, not only in the confusion·of *writing*, but also of *speech*."[9] Wilkins was a member of the Royal Society of London for Improving Natural Knowledge, and he devoted his life to studying problems of communication. Even educated Europeans were growing less and less sure about the virtues of Latin over the course of the seventeenth century. Wilkins was one of the chief advocates of a universal tongue that would eliminate room for error or ambiguity and convey the simple truth.

The same idea had been introduced to France by René Descartes and Father Marin Mersenne.[10] Soon, Comenius and Leibniz made contributions of their own. From 1650 on, the prospect and problems of a universal language formed part of the conceptual horizon of civilized Europe as a whole. Significantly, it emerged in tandem with the Galilean view of the cosmos and its corollary, the idea of many inhabited worlds. The idea of a universal language implied a broader view of the Universe itself.

Like Godwin, Cyrano de Bergerac found the model for a philosophical language in a realm beyond the Earth. His novel unfolds as the account of a dream. The first leg of the journey takes its hero to the Moon, where the higher social echelons speak a musical tongue and commoners employ a system of gestural signs. Yet again, the lunar world matches up with European notions about China, with different modes of communication for different classes. At the same time, and also in keeping with convention, the Moon offers a version of earthly Paradise, where the Adamic language has been preserved. Cyrano encounters not only Mada (*Adam*, spelled backward) but also the prophet Elijah.

While more comic and picaresque than didactic in tone, the novel bears the imprint of contemporary philosophical concerns—especially in the second episode, which takes place on the Sun (or, more precisely on "one of those little Earths that wheel about the Sun, which the Mathematicians call Spots"). Here, the voyager finds a small man sitting naked on a stone:

> I cannot call to mind whether I spoke to him first, or if it was he that put the Question to me: But it is as fresh in my Memory, as if I heard him still, that he discoursed to me three long Hours in a Language, which I knew very well I had never heard before, and which hath not the least resemblance with any of the Languages in this World; notwithstanding I comprehended it faster, and more intelligibly than my Mother Tongue. He told me, when I made enquiry about so wonderful a thing, that in Sciences there was a *true*, without which one was always far from the *easie;* that the more an Idiom was distant from this *truth*, the more it came short of the Conception, and was less easie to be understood.[11]

This miraculous language is the mother tongue spoken by the father of all humankind. Its perfection is evident in the fact that "the several Names which he gave to several things, declared their Essence." Cyrano's interlocutor tells him: "When I speak, your Soul finds in every Word of mine, that *Truth* which it gropes after; and though her Reason understand it not, yet she has Nature with her that cannot fail to understand it."

Through language, one lays hold of reality. When God gives the world to Adam, He has him name what he finds—the first step in making it his own. This primal scene repeats itself throughout history. "Languages which have progressively evolved," Leibniz wrote, "have words which have been created as the need arose, on the basis of an analogy between the sound and the emotion which accompanied the perception of reality. I incline readily to believe that Adam did not go about it any differently when he wished to name things."[12] A truly philosophical language would be a matter of nomenclature: taking stock of, and classifying, phenomena. By capturing natural and logical substance, the place of the speaking and thinking subject is affirmed within the order of Creation.

Humans simultaneously occupy the center, and form part, of a universe organized and governed by the Deity to suit their needs. The language of philosophy should occupy the same heights as the sublime role assigned to human *being*.[13]

Needless to say, the practical implementation of a project like this presented difficulties. A universal language could take the form of a written code (so-called pasigraphy) or be articulated. Leibniz's first effort yielded a language that was easy to speak thanks to the transcription of numbers into letters alternating between consonants and vowels ("open syllables"); it also admitted musical notation.

Pasigraphy is easier to devise than spoken language, since it employs ideography or formal symbols. At first, Chinese writing seemed to offer a model. On closer inspection, however, most of our authors found it too complicated and looked for more rational systems based on combinations of recurrent elements such as numbers, invented signs, or symbols already in existence (such as musical notation). In one of Leibniz's dialogues, his alter ego Theophilus sums up the enterprise:

> I believe that other marks could also produce the same result—the characters of the Chinese show this. And we could introduce a Universal Symbolism—a very popular one, better than theirs—if in place of words we used little diagrams which represented visible things pictorially and invisible things by means of the visible ones which go with them, also bringing in certain additional marks suitable for conveying inflections and particles. This would at once enable us to communicate easily with remote peoples; but if we adopted it among ourselves (though without abandoning ordinary writing), the use of this way of writing would be of great service in enriching our imaginations and giving us thoughts which were less blind and less verbal than our present ones are. Of course not everyone knows how to draw, so that apart from books printed in this manner, which

> everyone would soon learn to read, some people would only be able to make use of this system by printing of a sort—by having engravings ready to use for printing the pictures on paper and then adding the marks for the inflections and particles by pen. But in time everyone would learn to draw during childhood, so as to be able to take advantage of this pictorial symbolism; it would literally *speak to the eyes*, and would be much liked by the populace. In fact peasants already have almanacs which wordlessly tell them much of what they want to know.[14]

Of course, this does not settle the matter of what, exactly, is now to be transcribed. A fundamental difference exists between truly philosophical projects that concern thought and ideas directly—that is, independent of any language in particular—and putting a language that is supposed to be structurally identical to all others into code (whether pasigraphically or phonetically). In the course of the seventeenth century, a veritable host of "numerical languages" emerged, which amounted to nothing more than dictionaries with numbers taking the place of words—an absurd undertaking, even if it was based on a logical arrangement of ideas.[15]

Philosophers came to recognize that they needed a system without ties to existing languages, all of which contain elements they considered illogical or difficult to learn, or both. The ideal language, like the one once spoken by Adam, should express the true nature of things and, accordingly, be based on a rational classification of concepts, their derivates, and combined elements. In brief, it should furnish the ideal means for philosophical reflection on the world. The roots of the idea reach back at least as far as the medieval polymath Raymond Llull and are likewise indebted to cabalistic tradition.[16]

At the age of twenty, Leibniz proposed a combinatory system which would account for all human thoughts;[17] the first level consisted of conceptual nuclei, or basic elements, that yielded complex ideas at a second level of operation—a scheme that recalls the double articulation of language in speech.[18] All he had to do was work out a scheme of figural notation enabling the representation of each basic unit and, in turn, their compounded forms.

The project's appeal derived, on the one hand, from the fascination of combinatory logic and, on the other, from the idea that there are universal categories of thought that come straight from nature, unaltered by culture. In fact, this view is true only in part. Leibniz proposed a veritable algebra of thought; like any formal, man-made code, it would function independent of any particular "content": "We could reason in metaphysics and in ethics more or less as in geometry and analysis, since the characters would fix our vague and ephemeral thoughts in these matters, in which the imagination offers no help except by means of characters."[19] Leibniz spent a good deal of his life working on a *characteristica universalis*, taking up systems of representation both arbitrary and motivated ("natural"). If the results never proved satisfactory, it is because any such system presupposes that the problems of philosophy have been resolved—that the concepts at work in all the sciences have been defined once and for all.

One of the philosopher's other projects holds greater interest for linguists. Reflecting on how Latin, properly manipulated, might yield a model for grammatical logic, Leibniz came to pose many of the questions that Noam Chomsky would try to resolve three hundred years later in terms of "deep structure." Examples include ambiguities built into comparisons and the genitive case—when the same sequence of words can be "rewritten" two ways—and, conversely, instances of synonymy despite different phrasings (e.g., "mirror" relations).[20]

The famous *Grammaire générale et raisonnée de Port-Royal* (1660) belongs to the same intellectual climate: "Grammar as understood by Port-Royal is not a collection of rules for learning to speak well, it is rather a form of reasoning about rules, designed to ground them in reason and to establish a perfect correspondence between grammatical and logical categories. General grammar results from a comparison of grammar with philosophy, especially logic."[21] At the turn from the seventeenth to the eighteenth century, it was widely held that an ideal language—the Adamic tongue reborn—would express the true nature of things, and that languages already in existence share a common, universal structure; dozens of imitations followed in the book's wake.

Grammaire générale et raisonnée de Port-Royal was first to posit linguistic universals in the modern era. Now, an actual scientific theory affirmed the link between myth and utopia. Three imaginary journeys appeared in a brief span of time, bearing witness to the evolution of theories of language.

In 1677, Denis de Vairasse (or Veyras)—whose own grammar inspired by Port-Royal came out just four years later—published his *Histoire des Sevarambes* (*A History of the Sevarambians*). In the distant Austral Lands, the kingdom of the Sevarambians has the good fortune of possessing an ideal language. Wise King Sevarias[22] has built it from the hearty stock of natural elements in accordance with a few basic considerations. First and foremost stands perfect logic: the absence of any and all ambiguity when relations are to be described; consequently, cases, tenses, moods, distinctions of gender and kind, adverbs, and prepositions are far more numerous than is the case for natural languages.[23] Absolute regularity compensates for the complex morphology.

Well before nineteenth- and twentieth-century schemes, then, a great linguistic legislator has devised a language on the basis of tongues already in existence, taking the best features from each, whatever he finds to be most harmonious and in the greatest conformity to logic. In other words, Sevarias has come up with an a posteriori language—in contrast to the a priori designs of Vairasse's contemporaries. Still, the author cannot resist introducing a Cratylist component (words with a symbolic and expressive sound) for emphasis:

> These Sounds are, as far as is possible, accommodated to the Nature of the things express'd by them, each having its particular Usage and Character. Some of them have an Air of Dignity and Gravity, and others of Softness and Delicacy; one sort serve to express base, contemptible things, another grand and sublime, according to their Position, Arrangement, and Quantity. . . .
>
> [The Sevarambians] have studied the Nature of things, which they endeavor to express by conformable Sounds; never making use of long and harsh Syllables, to express short and soft things, nor of soft delicate ones, to represent grand, strong, or rough Ideas, as do almost all other Nations, who have no regard to these Rules: tho' the Observation of them makes a principal Beauty in any Language.[24]

The same quality extends to phonetic classification, which conforms to the order of nature (or, more precisely, human vocal organs), and to grammatical categories. Nature dictates that the things and beings of the world be divided into those that are inanimate and those that are animate, male and female, and so on. Thus, a system of gender and kind holds even for verbs. (Vairasse provides the example *to love*—oddly, he chooses the form for an inanimate entity expressing the sentiment: "a thing neuter or common [says] *Ermano*.")

Émile Pons held that Vairasse was a prescriptive grammarian, interested in establishing inviolable rules.[25] In contrast, I would credit him with playing a pivotal role in the development of more flexible linguistic categories. In the way he viewed invented languages, Vairasse anticipated the concerns of the eighteenth and nineteenth centuries. With little concern for Adamic schemes, he pictured the perfect tongue as a hybrid system, rationally constructed on the basis of languages already in existence, not as something to be brought about *ex nihilo*. As such, his ideas point forward to projects for creating languages a posteriori—which eventually replaced the a priori philosophical assumptions that had been the norm.

Another work of the time, *Les aventures de Jacques Sadeur dans la découverte et le voyage de la Terre Australe* (*The Adventures of Jacques Sadeur in the voyage of discovery to the Austral Land,* 1676) by Gabriel de Foigny[26] presents a language that operates "by Voice, by Signs, and by Writing." As a rule, the narrator observes, the Australians prefer gestures for everyday affairs, and they reserve speech for abstract reasoning and discussion. Articulated language in this imaginary land is entirely a priori and exhibits the traits of the most formal philosophical languages; indeed, it captures the very essence of things: "by this means a Man becomes a Philosopher, by learning the first words he pronounces, and that one can name nothing without at the same time explaining its nature."

But Foigny's conception of naturalness differs completely from Vairasse's. Instead of relying on the evocative quality of sounds, Foigny employs elements à la Leibniz, which are represented by letters (although numbers would do just as well). In this system, vowels designate simple substances: *a* = "fire," *e* = "air," *i* = "water," *o* = "salt," *u* = "earth." Consonants refer to their attributes: *b* = "clear," *c* = "hot," *d* = "unpleasant," *f* = "dry," and so on. "For example, they call the Stars *AeB*, a word which signifies in one Breath the two chief Elements, or simple Bodies, of which they are composed, and withal, that they are Luminous. . . . They call a man *Uel*, which signifies a substance, partly airy, and partly Earthy, tempered with some moisture; the same method they observe in the composition of other Names." The grammar Foigny presents is stripped-down—a feature it shares with the pasigraphical schemes proposed by any number of serious-minded contemporaries.

Foigny's "Australian" is basically a caricature of what scholars like Wilkins and Leibniz proposed in earnest. Still, it attests to the currency and influence of their thought in literary circles. Because this language consists of arbitrarily assigned vowels and consonants, it is difficult to pronounce. Moreover, since the Roman alphabet has only twenty-five characters, there's no way it could cover all the properties and meanings that combine to constitute thought, even on a primitive level.[27] It's easy to find fault with the principles the author employs by failing to note the parody at work and taking him "at his word." Although the *theoretical* number of combinations—even limited to monosyllables—that can be made with twenty-five letters exceeds the total quantity of words that exist in any natural language, the number of pronounceable and philosophically meaningful terms that can be generated is clearly inadequate.[28]

Finally, Simon Tissot de Patot's *Voyages et aventures de Jacques Massé* (1710)—another tale set on the mythical Australian continent—places formal regularity front and center. In lieu of the harmony between form and content extolled by

Vairasse or the correspondence between linguistic signs and reality prized by Foigny—in brief, the logical classification of ideas—this system is distinguished by its straightforward conception and ease of use; no philosophical preoccupations clutter up the proceedings. Simplicity, which represents an end unto itself, constitutes the beauty of language, no matter what people actually have to say. For all that, the author retains a three-case scheme of declension whose workings, to judge by appearances (see appendix, p. 259), are far from obvious. In any event, the work continues the tradition of looking for the ideal language. Here, virtue lies in economy: the fact that *it can be mastered in very little time.*

Harmony, eloquence, straightforwardness, logic, clarity of reference, musicality, symmetry, regularity, and economy are the qualities most commonly attributed to these dreamed-up languages—features set in contrast to the harshness and imperfections of natural tongues. The characterization of the latter is so uncharitable, in my estimation, that it is only right to spend some time defending them and praising their virtues (see chapters 10 and 11).

5

SCIENCE AGAINST FICTION: THE MARCH TOWARD POSITIVE FACT

The Chevalier de Béthune's *Monde de Mercure* (1750) describes inhabitants of a world who are nearly perfect. They live in harmony with their surroundings and converse with the animals in a language that is not verbal but gestural. "While refusing to give them a voice, Nature endowed them with a silent language composed of facial expressions, actions, and different postures which are scarcely less intelligible than speech,"[1] one reads.

Some two decades after this work, the Catholic priest Charles-Michel de l'Épée gave the world the first universal sign language for the deaf and dumb: *Institution des sourds et muets, par la voie des signes méthodiques; Ouvrage qui contient le projet d'une langue universelle, par l'entremise des signes naturels assujettis à une méthode* (1776). His pupil the Abbé de Sicard took up the project and completed it. In a Leibnizian spirit, both men believed that physical gestures came first in the evolution of language and sought a system of communication that would prove universal.[2] Étienne Bonnot de Condillac, author of *Essai sur l'origine des connaissances humaines* (1746) and *Cours d'études pour l'instruction du prince de Parme* (1775), also held that signs represented the original form of communication, which subsequently yielded to verbal convention: "Gestures, facial movements, and unarticulated noises—these, Monseigneur, were the first means available to men for communicating their thoughts to one another."[3]

The idea of fundamental naturalness—with whatever modifications culture may subsequently introduce—came to pervade linguistic theory: language and the universe entertain a necessary, motivated relationship that is inscribed within the very "order of the world." It is only natural for human beings in their primal condition to have exteriorized feelings and affective states by means of cries and grunts, and they did so by imitating the sounds in their environment.

The late eighteenth century witnessed any number of etymological studies on the primitive and universal roots that Nature gave to humankind. Although there were still proponents of the idea that God had granted humankind an integral tongue, more and more scholars now held that Creation represented an ongoing process, with a particular role foreseen for human beings. A broad array of opinions were in evidence: people imitate the sounds of nature; elementary units of expression and meaning occur in raw phonemes that are not yet words; gestural or musical communication precedes articulated speech, and so on. However much the details varied, these theories embraced qualitative change and growth. There were also schemes with a sociological component *avant la lettre* (from which Nikolai Marr would later draw inspiration); even the most rationalistic defenders of divine origins conceded that God had provided humankind with the capacity to create language, not a ready-made system. A notable exponent of the latter view was Johann Gottfried Herder, whose 1772 essay *Abhandlung über den Ursprung der Sprache* won the prize awarded by the Berlin Academy of Sciences on the theme of linguistic origins. In France, Charles de Brosses and Court de

Gebelin were thinking along similar lines. Evolutionary theory was in the offing.

Approaches to the facts of language, once philosophical, became increasingly pragmatic. De Brosses's 1765 work was entitled *Traité de la formation mécanique des langues*. The author hoped that exploring the phonetic and semantic workings of language would reveal its primitive elements—that is, he examined language as a physical (or physiological) phenomenon. De Brosses held that the relationship between words and things is necessary, not conventional, and that the structure of the vocal organs corresponds to the nature of objects: "The choice of articulations to be used for the construction of a word, that is to say for the name of a real object, is physically determined by the nature and quality of the object itself, in such a way as to depict the object as it actually is, without which the word would not give any idea of it."[4]

On this basis, he looked for the general laws governing linguistic evolution, proposing a nomenclature at the root of all human languages. Two centuries before Roman Jakobson,[5] de Brosses remarked that words for "father" and "mother" include labials and dentals the world over (a fact he attributed to the sucking instinct of the infant—a claim which Jakobson rejected).

Antoine Court de Gébelin also adopted a Cratylist approach, first in his *Histoire naturelle de la parole* (1772) (cf. appendix, p. 201), then in his major work, *Le monde primitif analysé et comparé avec le monde moderne* (published between 1773 and 1782, this study explores "The Origin of Language and Writing," "Universal Grammar," and "The Alphabet and Dictionary of the Primitive Tongue"). His objective was to rediscover the vanished order of the world at its first beginnings, when words and things agreed perfectly. Historical languages—chiefly Hebrew, but also Celtic—bear its traces: "Pure language, which says the thing when it says its name, still exists, then. Hebrew is not alone in preserving traces of the first tongue; all languages have done so (and Celtic, in particular)."[6] The first words were "simple and necessary," composed of monosyllables that, when combined, produced new ones. On the basis of acoustic, physiological, and psychological associations, vowels became linked with sensations, and consonants with ideas. Human beings started out by imitating the sounds of nature; expanding the process of analogy, they then were able to name abstract thoughts by metaphor. Speech was there from the outset, for it is consubstantial with, and integral to, human existence.

> There is no object which does not have a more or less direct connection with vocal sounds, and cannot be depicted by those sounds. . . . The first language was composed exclusively of monosyllables taken from nature, which depicted physical objects and were the source of all words. . . . Comparing the greatest possible number of languages is the only way to arrive at the primitive language and the true etymology of every word. . . . Universal grammar is immutable like nature, of which it is the copy.[7]

That said—and it is the case for many works before and afterward—this "universal grammar" does little but copy French.

On the one hand, Court de Gébelin and likeminded parties justified the most far-flung etymologies by appealing to observations that were often sound—for instance, the instability of vowels, consonant mutation, metathesis, epenthesis, apocope, deformation in borrowed words, semantic slippage through figures of speech, and so on. However, they applied the principles that they identified without rigor. The comparative linguistics of the next century reacted against such extravagance: when viewed outside of a system, phonetic elements can be juggled at will to forge false connections between any given word in one language and any word in another.

Antoine Destutt de Tracy (1754–1836), on the other hand, did not consider the relationship between words and ideas in Cratylist terms. For him, language originated with expressive vociferations. Humankind's first tongue was affective and served to translate sentiments, not to represent objects:

> A man utters a cry, perhaps without purpose; he recognizes that it strikes his fellow's ear, that it attracts his attention and gives him a notion of what is happening within him; he repeats the cry with the intention of making himself heard; soon he makes others, which express something else; he sets about varying these expressions, making them more distinct, more constant, more decisive; he modifies the cries with articulations; they become words, to which he introduces changes to indicate their relation to one another; from them, he forms sentences suited to the circumstances, needs, or object before him, the feeling that moves him: this is a language.[8]

Hereby, gestures assist verbal communication: "We must therefore consider as real languages the assortment of gestures through which pantomimes and mutes manage to express not just subtle feelings, but also highly abstract ideas."[9] Finally, the author contends, arbitrary cultural systems come to govern modes of expression: "All these languages, at least in their details, are absolutely conventional."[10]

James Harris (1746–1820), another notable opponent of Cratylist views of language, affirmed that signs are human inventions: "ALL LANGUAGE IS FOUNDED IN COMPACT, and not in Nature; for so are all Symbols, of which Words are a certain Species."[11] Moreover, words refer to general ideas (concepts, we would say today), not to external objects: "If Words are not the Symbols of *external particulars*, it follows of course, they must be THE SYMBOLS OF OUR IDEAS: For this is evident, if they are not Symbols of things without, they can only be Symbols of something *within*."[12] Accordingly, Harris dismisses the notion of an ideal correspondence between language and the universe:

> Hence, too, we may perceive a Reason, *why there never was a Language, nor indeed can possibly be framed one, to express the Properties and real Essences of things*, as a Mirrour exhibits their Figures and their Colours. For if Language of itself imply nothing more, than *certain Species of Sounds with certain Motions concomitant;* if to some Beings Sound and Motion are no Attributes at all; if to many others, where Attributes, they are no way essential (such as the Murmurs and Wavings of a Tree during a storm); if this is true—*it is impossible the Nature of such beings should be expressed, or the least essential Property be any way imitated, while between the Medium and themselves there is nothing CONNATURAL.*[13]

These words provide a fitting transition to the Age of Science. The nineteenth century witnessed the rise of comparative grammar and linguistic typology. Very few literary works reflected (or reflected on) this development, which makes Edward Bulwer-Lytton's *The Coming Race* (1871) all the more remarkable. Among novels to include an imaginary language, this one merits the title of "linguistic fiction." The language described here is extrapolated from scientific advances charted in the real world of the time.

As in the tradition of journeys to a mythical Australia, the Moon, or other planets, events take place in a foreign setting—here, an underground world. The Vril-ya, who inhabit this realm, are a higher race of beings with an imposing culture. Bulwer-Lytton devotes a whole chapter to describing their tongue in detail (cf. appendix, p. 248). Vril resembles philosophical languages of the seventeenth and eighteenth centuries in key respects: concise, precise, regular, economical, it translates thoughts faithfully; it also conforms to dominant theories of linguistic origins in terms of the correspondence between the sound and the sense of words. More importantly, the author has made a point of modeling it on the latest discoveries. "The philologist will have seen from the above how much the language of the Vril-ya is akin to the Aryan or Indo-Germanic," he writes.

In effect, the study of language (and languages) had shifted: linguistics was not yet being practiced in the modern sense of the word, but scholarly focus moved away from philosophical concerns toward what now generally went by the name of philology or comparative grammar.

The decisive event behind this change was the discovery of Sanskrit, which opened a new perspective by pushing back the historical frontiers of the written languages of Europe. Missionaries had been aware of Sanskrit early on, but it entered the scholarly realm thanks to the conquest of India by the British army. In 1784, Sir William Jones, who took part in the campaign, founded the Royal Asiatic Society of Calcutta. Here, in 1786, he made the declaration that would become the birth certificate of comparative grammar:

> The Sanscrit language, whatever be its antiquity, is of a wonderful structure; more perfect than the Greek, more copious than the Latin, and more exquisitely refined than either, yet bearing to both of them a stronger affinity, both in the roots of verbs and in the forms of grammar, than could possibly have been produced by accident; so strong, indeed, that no philologer

> could examine them all three without believing them to have sprung from some common source, which, perhaps, no longer exists. There is a similar reason, though not quite so forcible, for supposing that both the Gothic and the Celtic, though blended with a very different idiom, had the same origin with the Sanscrit; and the Old Persian might be added to the same family, if this were the place for discussing any question concerning the antiquities of Persia.[14]

Yet England was not destined to follow the path that one of its own had charted. From the very start, racism hobbled the Indo-European project. Hopes that Sanskrit would lead back to the lingua adamica were quashed as the British recognized the unwelcome implications of a genetic relationship between the language of the colonizers and that of the people whose lands they claimed for themselves. (The religious dogma of Hebrew as the mother tongue still carried a good deal of weight, too.) The reconstruction of the Indo-European proto-language would fall largely to Germans. And Victorian England persisted for a considerable time in rejecting the idea.[15]

In 1808, Friedrich von Schlegel (1772–1829) published *Über die Sprache und Weisheit der Indier* (*Essay on the Language and Wisdom of the Indians*). He also coined the term *Indo-Germanic* for what would later be known as *Indo-European*, when Celtic languages were included in the family. Antoine Léonard de Chézy (1773–1832) delivered the first lectures on Sanskrit at the College de France In 1815. His pupil Franz Bopp (1791–1867) has the distinction of being the real founder of comparative grammar—the field in which Jacob Grimm (1785–1863) made a name for himself; with his brother, Grimm was also responsible for the famous anthology of fairy tales, and he authored reflections on the principles to be observed when creating a universal language.[16]

On the basis of hypothetical forms extrapolated from attested ones, Indo-Europeanists sought to reconstruct the primitive roots of the language that had brought forth the tongues of Europe (with the exception of Basque and Finno-Ugrian languages) as well as a number of those in the Middle East (Hittite and the Iranian family) and parts of Asia (certain Indian languages). This enormous—and somewhat fantastical—undertaking was based on phonetic laws governing the connections between related words.[17] Since then, other families of languages have been examined by the same methods.

A Fable of Reconstruction

When linguists reconstruct proto-languages—the prime example being Indo-European in the nineteenth century—their project also represents an invention. Aiming to reconstitute something that existed in the past on the basis of "sister" languages in the present (whose kinship comparatists have established beforehand), the undertaking remains largely fanciful.

The German linguist August Schleicher (1821–1868) insisted on the reality of the Indo-European proto-language to such an extent that he made bold to compose a tale familiar to linguists past and present: "Eine Fabel in indogermanischer Ursprache," or "Fable in the Indo-Germanic Mother Tongue." About one hundred years later, in the wake of advances in comparatist scholarship, two heirs of the project updated Schleicher's fable. As the reader will readily see, the two versions are quite different:

SCHLEICHER'S VERSION (1868):

Avis akvasas ka

Avis, jasmin varna na a ast, dadarka akvams, tam, vagham garum vaghantam, tam, bharam magham, tam manum aku bharantam. Avis akvabhjams a vavakat; kard aghnutai mai vidanti manum akvams agantam.

Akvasas a vavakant krudhi avai, kard aghnutai vividvant—svas: manus patis varnam avisams karnauti svabhjam gharmam vastram avibhjams ka varna na asti.

Tat kukruvants avis agram a bhugat.

VERSION BY WINFRED P. LEHMANN AND LADISLAV ZGUSTA (1979):

[Gw&rei] owis, kwesyo wlhna ne est, ekwons espeket, oinom ghe gwrum woghom weghontm, oinomkwe megam bhorom, oinomkwe ghmenm oku bherontm. Owis nu ekwobh(y) os ewewkwet: Ker aghnutoi moi ekwons agontm nerm widntei.

Ekwos tu ewewkwont: kludhi, owei, ker aghnutoi nsmei widntbh(y) os: ner, potis, owiom r wlhnam sebhi gwhermom westrom kwrneuti. Neghi owiom wlhna esti.

Tod kekluwos owis agrom ebhuget.

LITERAL TRANSLATION:

(The) Sheep (the) Horses and

On (a) hill] (a) sheep on which no wool there was saw horses, (the) one pulling (a) heavy cart, one (other) bearing a man quickly. (The) sheep to the horses said: heart suffers me seeing (a) man leading horses.

(The) horses to the sheep said: listen, sheep, heart suffers us seeing man, (the) master, (who) makes wool of sheep for himself (a) warm coat and on sheep is no wool.

Having heard this, (the) sheep ran off into the plain.

The early successes charted by comparative philology opened the prospect of establishing the genealogy of all the world's languages by going back to a single tongue at the very origin. However, proponents of monogenesis did not acknowledge defeat when they saw the achievements of historical and comparative studies. More and more of them denounced the enterprise as vacuous fantasy.

When the Societé de Linguistique de Paris was founded in 1866, a scholarly community that had learned to work methodically on concrete data cried "Enough is enough!" The Second Article of the organization's charter declares: "The Society does not accept any communication concerning either the origin of language or the creation of a universal language."[18] In one fell swoop, the twin vision of mythical and utopian oneness had been condemned.

Although it hardly put an end to extravagant speculations—which likely will never go away—it did consign them to the realm of literal folly. Fiction separated from science, and myth from history. Whereas it was acknowledged that languages may be grouped together in families, ultimately human tongues prove as irreducible as the various kinds of people inhabiting the Earth. This new consensus accounts for why research shifted to projects of linguistic typology, pursued along lines analogous to racial "science." The scheme divided human languages into four types:[19] the *isolating* (monosyllabic) type represented by Chinese; the *agglutinative* type exemplified by Turkish; the *flexional* or *amalgamating* type that includes most Indo-European languages; and, finally, the *analytic* type, which consists of languages from the amalgamating group that have replaced declensions by prepositions over the course of their history.

Darwin's *Origin of the Species* (1859) had produced a revolution in the natural sciences comparable to the one that followed in the wake of Copernicus. Although religious dogma proved tenacious, the scientific world gradually made room for new ways of thinking. The theory of evolution extrapolated both forward and backward in time. In this framework, seeking to recover a single language was a nonstarter; research would be based on the notion of progress inherited from the eighteenth century. The theory of linguistic stages thus fits into the broader context of social and cultural evolutionism, the first manifestations of which admittedly antedate biological evolutionism in the strict sense. Darwinism, although first articulated in terms of the life sciences, gave linguists the model of evolution, of progressive stages of development.[20]

Now, despite the fact that language is a cultural phenomenon, it became tempting to situate it in the field of biology. Assimilated to living species, languages were supposed to be subject to the laws of evolution. Having charted languages geographically (not exhaustively, of course, since many remained undiscovered) and having examined them from a synchronic point of view, scholars proceeded to determine their positions in the history of humanity as a whole. A spatial map turned into a temporal one: corresponding to different dialects or tongues in a single family, which approach (or deviate from) a putative standard, stages of greater or lesser development were assigned to languages and societies. The result was "false evolutionism," which Claude Lévi-Strauss would later indict as "an attempt to wipe out the diversity of cultures while pretending to accord it full recognition. If the various conditions in which human societies are found, both in the past and in far distant lands, are treated as phases or stages in a single line of development, starting from the same point and leading to the same end, it seems clear that the diversity is merely apparent. Humanity is claimed to be one and the same everywhere, but this unity and identity can be achieved only gradually; the variety of cultures we find in the world illustrates the several stages in a process which conceals the ultimate reality or delays our recognition of it."[21]

Scholars took as their starting point modern Indo-European languages, which derived from languages of the flexional type but seemed to be evolving (or, in some cases, had already evolved) toward an analytic form. Conveniently, the last two stages of evolution were well attested and ready to hand in written form. Now, the task was to decide which of the other two types—agglutinative or isolating—was older and therefore represented the more primitive stage. Because the isolating type exemplified by Chinese seemed to be simpler, it was thought to have developed first. (As we have seen, this matched up with the role China had played in the European imagination for hundreds of years.) In the mid-nineteenth century, there was no doubt among experts that Chinese—even it was not, in fact, *the* primitive tongue of humankind—provided the model, miraculously preserved, of the primal stage through which *all* languages had passed before becoming agglutinative, flexional, and so on. Progress could only follow one path.

In brief, Chinese counted as an essentially archaic language that somehow "got stuck" in the first stage of evolution. Its modulations were held up as characteristic of primitive languages, which, in accordance with an old idea (and as we have seen), had "always been more or less intimately connected with music."[22] The thesis was taken up and defended by Léon de Rosny,[23] who taught at the École impériale des langues orientales in Paris, as well as by Louis Benloew,[24] Max Müller, Frédéric Baudry,[25] and yet again, in 1905, by Alfredo Trombetti[26]—well-respected linguists, one and all.

With ideologically disastrous consequences, another idea derived from biology was grafted onto this theoretical framework: the notion that ontogenesis recapitulates phylogenesis—in other words, the individual human being is supposed to reproduce, in the course of personal development, the evolutionary stages of the species as a whole. Hence an array of equations:

infancy	=	childhood of humankind
early language	=	infant speech
languages with demonstrable historical changes	=	adult, "civilized" languages
"primitive" languages	=	languages of peoples still at an infantile stage of culture

In this spirit, it was claimed that a mother enters a second childhood in order to speak to with her child: "She instinctively reduces language to its primitive elements; she in some sense invents it over again from the beginning by using short syllables interspersed with signs. She also contracts words, and reduces them to being no more than cries resembling interjections."[27] Rosny held the same opinion and wrote: "Children's speech is . . . an argument in favor of the simplicity of language in its primitive state: children first utter the names of objects without any grammatical marking and without any thought for phraseology."[28]

The doors were flung wide open for linguistic racism as a component of biological racism. The project of studying Indo-European language(s) flowed into the fiction of an Aryan "master race."[29]

Disagreement prevailed about the significance to be attached to the fourth, "analytic" stage of linguistic evolution. In point of fact, modern Indo-European tongues do not cohere into a single type. Some scholars held that analytic languages had achieved the highest level of evolution, to which all other languages would ultimately progress. Accordingly,

Slavic tongues (and the people who spoke them) counted as "backward." But what did this mean for the Germans—a culturally dominant nation whose language displays analogous morphological traits? Occasionally, the analytic type was taken as a sign of degeneration—a notion introduced by Mendel's discovery of the laws of heredity (1865) to account for when progress went wrong.

Earlier still, in 1853, Arthur de Gobineau's *Essai sur l'inegalite des races humaines* (*Essay on the Inequality of Human Races*) had declared that interbreeding produces inferior human specimens. The same principle could be applied to hybrid tongues, pidgins, and creoles. A controversy about English ensued. For some scholars, English stood at the forefront of evolution and was destined to be the language of the future. Others—and for the same reasons—thought it was condemned to collapse into primitive babble.[30] Baudry held that American English heralded crisis: "Imagine a state of total and prolonged barbarism: in the mouths of degenerate Yankees, English would turn back into an agglutinative language, the likes of which exist in the uncivilized parts of the world."[31]

For the moment, Europeans were busy colonizing the planet; the part that would become the Third World is precisely where isolating and agglutinative languages are spoken. The new, evolutionary scheme came made to order. Drawing on the authority of Max Müller, Bulwer-Lytton's novel positively oozes bile when agglutinative languages are at issue. In contrast, considerable indulgence is shown toward isolating languages; the author could scarcely disregard the greatness of Chinese civilization.

The paradox of Chinese for Westerners continued: on the one hand, it counted as simple and simplistic, childlike and infantile; yet at the same time, it was admirable (essentially in its written form) for *having escaped the laws of evolution*. Somehow, a living fossil served as the means by which a highly civilized nation expressed itself. Needless to say, this view was utterly incoherent.

Only agglutinative langues (exemplarily, Amerindian and African tongues) were supposed to represent a thoroughly primitive stage of culture. Once again, we have Baudry's assessment:

> At bottom, synthesis, which is the work of barbarians, is manifestly less well suited than analysis for transmitting thought; it results directly from impoverished and frequently repeated ideas: agglutination is produced by the constant association of the same words. The more a people is barbarian, the more its language is regular. It's as if instinct constructs words and reflection would spoil them. Civilization is responsible for destroying the beautiful [but primitive] harmony of language and deforming speech by forcing it to express complicated, abstract things. Barbarism, which only expresses simple things, has left the pure essence of words intact, so to speak. [32]

What's more, the expert continues, "if language is a faithful mirror of a people's spirit, the savages of America no doubt have a very rudimentary one, for as hunting nomads they occupy the lowest rung [of evolution]."

"Primitive" languages were faulted for needlessly "complicating" things on the same grounds that they were alleged to be "simple." For instance, when reviewing the models that might be employed for a new universal language, Louis Couturat affirmed that the (agglutinative) tongues of primitive peoples were too convoluted too enable clarifying generalizations; the most civilized languages, such as English, had freed themselves from excessive morphological permutations by dropping nominal and verbal inflections in the course of evolution, which made it easier to pass from concrete to abstract description.[33] From here, it would take just a step to arrive at the "primitive thinking" posited by Lucien Lévy-Bruhl.

The mind boggles at the contradictory picture. Baudry objected to the regularity of "primitive," agglutinative languages. Couturat professed admiration for analytic languages, which are notorious for exceptions, yet he appealed to the "inherent logic of our [European] languages" when considering the desirable features of a universal tongue that would be as regular and unambiguous as possible.

6

UTOPIA IN ACTION: THE ASCENT OF INTERNATIONAL AUXILIARY LANGUAGES

At the end of the eighteenth century, the idea of a philosophical language was no longer flying very high. The "ideologues" (Maine de Biran, Destutt de Tracy) put an end to plans along these lines by demonstrating their impossibility:

> Man always aspires to perfection, although he never achieves it. It is impossible to take up general grammar for even a moment without being struck by the vices of our languages and the disadvantages resulting from their multiplicity, and without conceiving the desire for a perfect language that will become universal. These ideas of perfection and universality fuse in thought, even though they are two distinct things. . . . But the reader will already have gathered that I am quite disillusioned, at least as far as universality is concerned. Surely a man who harbors no hope for general consent in the matter of a reasonable and appropriate alphabet and an orthography suited to the languages now in use will not presume that all these languages will be abandoned in favor of a single tongue, however perfect it may be. Indeed, I hold fast to what I have said elsewhere: *a universal language is as impossible as perpetual motion.* I even see an incontestable reason for this impossibility: if all the men of the earth today agreed to speak the same language, soon, by the mere fact of use, it would be altered and modified in a thousand different ways in the various countries, and would give rise to as many distinct idioms which would always draw away from one another.[1]

The project for a universal language submitted by Jean Delormel to the National Convention in revolutionary France[2]—although a handsome example of pasigraphy—was the last of its kind.

The idea of constructing a universal language did not die, however. On the contrary, it flourished. Freed from the obligation to be philosophical, the enterprise moved to more practical terrain and came to stand in the service of a new ideal: pacifism. The new wave of invented languages most often involved a posteriori designs, taking up and working with the very of stuff of tongues living or dead, especially Latin (which followed the tradition inaugurated by Leibniz). Before the advent of the systematically hybridized languages of the late nineteenth century and the "naturalist" languages of the twentieth, these projects drew sap and vigor from the most up-to-date research on ancient roots and lexical stock. After all, existing foundations could also serve ideal structures. Bit by bit, the field of *interlinguistics* emerged.

Thus, as theories about the origin of language were becoming more mechanistic and detached from religious dogma, plans for universal languages grew increasingly realistic and anchored in linguistic fact.

Comparison of International Auxiliary Languages: From Arbitrariness to Naturalism

Words in Volapük, Esperanto, Ido, and Interlingua

Volapük	Esperanto	Ido	Interlingua	English
ladet	adreso	adreso	adresse	address
vom	virino	homino	femina	woman
nedetik	maldekstra	sinistra	sinister	left
kap	kapo	kapo	testa	head
lifôn	vivi	vivar	viver	live

valik	ciu	omna	omne	all
famül	familio	familio	familia	family
nisul	insulo	insulo	insula	island
jevod	cevalo	kavalo	cavallo	horse
süperik	bonega	ecelanta	excellente	excellent
din	ajo	kozo	cosa	thing
glüg	pregejo	kirko	ecclesia	church
mot	patrino	matro	matre	mother
nemodit	malmulte	poke	pauc	little/few
tâno	tiarn	lore	alora	then

A priori designs were, and are, the most daring. They wipe the slate clean in order to transcend natural languages. It is hardly surprising, then, that they thrived in the seventeenth century—when the first principles of knowledge and the world were questioned by the likes of Pascal and Descartes—and during the eighteenth century, the Age of Enlightenment. A posteriori designs, on the other hand, fashion something new out of something old. This reformist tendency is responsible for the real-world success achieved by Volapük (if only briefly) and, even more, by Esperanto.

The nineteenth-century heyday of artificial languages conceived for practical purposes was accompanied by the disappearance of imaginary languages in fiction. This development can hardly have been a matter of chance. From here on, fiction passed from word to deed: utopia was actively implemented. It was no longer a matter of simply imagining and describing the ideal society. Instead, the goal was to make it a reality, as attested by the communities inspired by Saint-Simon and Fourier in France, or Thoreau in the United States. By the same token, the ideal language was to be made to serve actual, worldly purposes. The nascent genre of science fiction omitted linguistic themes; Bulwer-Lytton's *The Coming Race* was long the exception. The works of Jules Verne, for instance, although coeval with Volapük and Esperanto (which met with broad acclaim and nourished many hopes), did not take up questions of language at all.

Even though the Société de Linguistique de Paris, founded in 1866, declared projects for artificial languages anathema, such initiatives teemed and multiplied. As we have seen, the invention of artificial languages owes a great deal to the search for the primitive roots of language (which had been likewise "excommunicated"). Since the discovery of Sanskrit, projects did not draw on hypothetical universal roots posited by inspired (and crazy) amateurs so much as on the Indo-European *radicarium*.

Volapük

Volapük, invented in 1879, is the work of the German Catholic priest Martin Schleyer, whom God Himself inspired in a dream. It was the first artificial language to meet with real success, thanks to favorable cultural circumstances (the enlightened bourgeoisie took a keen interest in the subject). Volapük is an a posteriori language that follows a mixed system, but with many schematic features.

The Volapük alphabet consists of twenty-six letters (eight of them vowels) representing as many sounds, which have been selected on the basis of their universal diffusion. (Thus, /r/ has been eliminated for the benefit of speakers of Asian languages, who have difficulty distinguishing /l/ from /r/; the same has been done with /w/, which poses problems for Germanophones). Volapük grammar is perfectly regular, but its complex morphology makes learning and using it difficult.

There are four cases: nominative, accusative, genitive, and dative (as well as a vocative form); this system is close to the one in Indo-European languages that have preserved declensions. In turn, verbal conjugation features many tenses, plus moods not often found in world languages—for example, the optative and dubitative.

Verbal morphology is agglutinative; this means that the system of inflection is completely regular, with non-amalgamated endings and without fusion between morphemes—in other words, the opposite of what one generally finds in Indo-European tongues. For instance, the sequence *p-i-löf-ob-öv* ("I would have been loved") breaks down as follows: *p-* is the passive prefix, *i-* marks the pluperfect tense, *löf* is the root of the verb "to love," *ob* indicates the first person, singular, and *öv* is the ending of the conditional mood. In this combinatorial system, the number of forms that the verbal predicate can assume is exponential. In this respect, the language is schematic.

Trying to avoid the polysemy of natural langues, Schleyer—like many other inventors—wanted to establish an unequivocal correspondence between form and meaning. By means of a limited number of verbal forms (which, of course, vary from one language to another), all natural languages capture broad semantic categories (tense, aspect, and mood). The present in French, for example, can convey many different temporal and aspectual values, whereas English has more discrete forms. (Compare *je vais* with "I go," "I am going," and "I do go.")

The vocabulary of Volapük is derived by truncating words from several European languages (mainly German and English), but it has been deformed to such a point that the roots are hardly self-evident. (One of the reasons is the elimination of /r/, mentioned previously.) Thus, the word "volapük" itself is constructed from *vol*, from "world," and *pük*, from "speak"; "animal" produces *nim*, "compliment" becomes *plim*, "image" turns into *mag*, and so on. Words are organized in quasi-infinite families, for example:

pük	*language*	pükôf	*eloquence*
pükik	*linguistic*	pükôfik	*eloquent*
pükatidel	*language teacher*	pükôfav	*art of speaking*
pükapôk	*(language) mistake*	pükot	*talk/chat (n.)*
pükôn	*speak*	okopükot	*monologue*
motopük	*mother tongue*	gepük	*response*
pükât	*speech*	gepükôn	*respond*
pükâtil	*statement*	lepük	*affirmation*
pükatôn	*talk/speak*	lepükôn	*affirm*
telapükat	*dialogue*	libapük	*acquittal*
pükav	*philology*	lupük	*chatter*
püked	*sentence*	lupüklan	*stammering*
pükedavod	*proverb*	nepük	*silence*
pükel	*orator*	nepüken	*be silent*
pükelik	*oratory*	sepük	*pronunciation*
môpükel	*polyglot*	tapük	*contradiction*

Volapük enjoyed great success among the international intelligentsia and bourgeoisie, to whom Schleyer explicitly addressed his project. In 1887, the International Academy of Volapük (Kadem Bevünetik Volapüka) was founded. Two years later, there were 283 Volapük organizations, 384 books, and 25 journals, as well as 316 methods of instruction in 25 languages. Volapük was at its peak, but it fell as quickly as it had risen—especially as Esperanto developed.

In effect, given the inherent difficulties of Volapük—it seems that Schleyer himself spoke it quite poorly—numerous adherents began to propose reformed versions for the sake of simplicity (e.g., Dil, Dilpok, Nuvo-Volapük, Balta, Spelin, Veltparl, Idiom Neutral). Schleyer categorically opposed all of them and rejected changes, hastening the death of a movement that had counted, it seems, several hundreds of thousands of followers (and, no doubt, very few real speakers).

Esperanto

Esperanto was born in 1887, just as Volapük stood at its peak and before its precipitous decline. The name of the language comes from the pseudonym *Doktoro Esperanto* ("Doctor Who Hopes"), which Ludwik Zamenhof adopted when he published his first manual of *Lingvo Internacia*. Esperanto is an a posteriori mixed language, that is, it combines natural and (partly) artificial derivation and draws on the roots of the Indo-European radicarium.

Its alphabet of twenty-eight letters is completely phonological (each letter corresponds to a single sound, and vice versa). The nature of each word is always specified by its ending: *-o* for nouns, *-a* for adjectives, *-e* for adverbs, and *-i* for verbs in the infinitive. The definite article is la (there is no indefinite). Plurals are formed by adding *-j* (pronounced "y") to the end of words. The only oblique case is the accusative, which is marked by *-n*. Esperanto has no irregular verbs, and the conjugation has a total of twelve endings, allowing for a wide range of tenses and moods. Zamenhof avoided the excessive schematism that hobbled Volapük.

Like Volapük, Esperanto brought forth dissident progeny of sizeable dimensions (Adjuvanto, Antido, Eo, Esperanta, Esperantuisho, Esperido, Europeo, Ido, Logo, Mondlingvo, Neo, Neo-Esperanto, Nepo, Nov-Esperanto, Nuv-Esperanto, Reform-Esperanto, Romanal, Weltsprache Esperanto, Zamalo, and more). However, this has not prevented Zamenhof's creation from surviving to this day in a community limited in number (between one and ten million) but great in motivation. Now, the Esperanto movement is experiencing a remarkable revival thanks to the Internet, and the language has been recognized by international organizations (UNESCO, for instance). Doctoral theses are regularly written on Esperanto, and it is used for publications on a wide range of subjects.

In practice, Esperanto, like other languages, tends to break off into dialects. Scholarly, popular, and poetic variants also exist—a sign of vitality and, even more, of naturalization. It would seem that there are even native speakers (children exposed to Esperanto before any other tongue). All the same, Esperanto's chances for becoming the main language for international communication are insignificant compared to English.

As comparative studies and the reconstruction of "Primitive Indo-European" proceeded, the most "rational" projects of linguistic invention to date began to draw on findings in these fields. This entailed the de facto preeminence of Western languages.[3] "To be sure," Monnerot-Dumaine has observed, "a language based on the most widespread roots in Western European languages borrows little from Russian, very little from Arabic, and nothing from the languages of the Far East. But it must be considered that world trade and cultural and scientific exchanges mainly use Western languages, and that all Eastern or Far Eastern elites have at least some knowledge of a Western language."[4] The idea of a *universal* language gave way to the idea of an *international auxiliary* language. In parallel to the rise of political nationalism, it was necessary, for men of good will, to have a means of resolving differences between societies and states.

The new terrain was pragmatic; commercial, scientific, cultural, and political exchange across borders was only growing. Zamenhof was inspired to invent Esperanto by his experience in the Jewish ghetto and the ethnic hatred convulsing the Russian Empire at the end of the nineteenth century. His efforts and those of other interlinguists around 1900 should be situated in the framework of efforts to improve international relations; other projects included the Red Cross and, later, the League of Nations. From 1880 to 1914, in particular, such initiatives flourished. Monnerot-Dumaine lists 145 projects for this period alone—almost 40 percent of the 368 languages invented over the course of four centuries that he documents.

The Lord's Prayer (*Pater Noster*) in Various International Auxiliary Languages

1. AN A PRIORI EXAMPLE

Spokil—Adolphe Nicolas, 1887–1904 (symbolic phonemes)
Mael nio, kui vai o les zeal; aepseno lezai tio mita. Veze lezai tio tsaeleda. Foleno lezai tio bela, uti o zeal itu o geal. Demai da ni zaiu nio braima ulliozo. E sbilai da ni noi gelena, uti ni itu sbilai da gelenalas nio. E no spidai ni o fismena. Stu nibai ni i le sfail.

2. MIXED SYSTEMS (HALF A PRIORI, HALF NATURALIST)

Volapük—Schleyer, 1879–1880 (based on greatly altered Indo-European roots)
O fat obas, kel binol in süls, paisaludomôz nern ola! Kômomôd monargân ola! Jenomôz vil olik, âs in sül, i su tal! Bodo obsik, vâdeliki givolôs obes adelo! E pardolôs obes debis obsik, âs id obs aipardobs debeles obas. E no obis nindukolôs in tentadi; sod aidalivolôs obis de bad. Jenosôd!

Weltsprache—Volk and Fuchs, 1883 (based on modified Latin)
Not pater, vel sas in los côles, ton nomen sanctöt, ton regnon venât, ton voluntat sôt vam in le côl, tarn in le ter. Not diniv pana da mib godie. Condona mib not culpa, varn ems condonami not debitorib. Non duca mas in tentation, sed libera mas lis malot.

Spelin—Bauer and Afram, 1888 (semi-artificial roots)
Pat isel, ka bi ni sieloes! Nom el zi bi santed! Klol el zi komi! Vol el zi bi faked, kefe ni siel, efe su sium! Givi ide bod isel desel is. Fegivi doboes isel, kefe tet is fegivis tu yadoboes isel; et nen duki is ni tantoe, boet libi is de mal.

Langue bleue—Bollack, 1896–1899 (semi-artificial roots)
Nea per, ev ra seri in silu, vea nom eu santigui; vea regn eu komi; vea vil eu makui ib gev so in sil; ev givo dau nea pan taged ana, it ev solvi nae fansu ana so ne solvo aue re ufanso na; it ev nu lefti na to temt, bo ev bevri na om mal.

3. LANGUAGES WITH NATURAL ROOTS AND REGULARIZED MORPHOLOGY

Esperanto—Zamenhof, 1887(broad Indo-European base)

Patro nia kiu estas en la ĉielo, sankta estu via nomo; venu regeco via; estu volo via, kiel en la ĉielo, tiel ankaŭ sur la tero. Panon nian ĉiutagan donu al ni hodiaŭ; kaj pardonu al ni guldojn niajn, kiel ni ankau pardonas al niaj suldantoj; kaj ne konduku nia en tenton, sed liberigu nin de la malbono.

Reformed Esperanto—Zamenhof, 1894

Patro nue kvu esten in cielo, sankte estan tue nomo, venan regito tue, estan volo tue, kom in cielo, sik anku sur tero.

Adjuvanto—Louis de Beaufront, 1902–1904 (derived from Esperanto via Pido [an Esperantido])

Patro nua, kvu estas il el ĉjelo, estez honorata tua nomo; venez regno tua; estez volo tua kome in el ĉjelo, tale anke sur el tero; pano nua ĉaskajorna donez al nu hodje; ed pardonez al nu debi sua, kome nu pardonas al nua debanti; ed ne konduktez nu en tento, ma liberifez nu di el malbono.

Latinesce—Henderson, alias Hoinix, 1890–1891 (from Lingua (1888), with unchanged Latin roots.)

Nostre Patre qui esse in coelo, sanctificate esse tue nomine; veni tue regne; facte esse tue voluntate, ut in coele, ita in terre. Da ad nos hodie nostre quotidiane pane; et remitte ad nos nostre debites, sicut et nos remitte ad nostre debitores; induce nos non in tentatione, sed libera nos ab male.

4. "NATURALIST" LANGUAGES (IMITATING THE IRREGULARITIES OF NATURAL LANGUAGES)

Mundolingue—Julius Lott, 1889–1890

Patre nostri, resident in cele, tei nomine e sanctificat. Tei regne vole venir a nostri. Tei voluntate e exequer ne solu in cele ma eti in terre. Da tu a nos hodie nostri quotidian pane et pardona a nos nostri debiti, qua eti noi pardona al nostri debitores. Ne induce tu nos in tentatione, ma libera nos de omne male.

Lingua komun—F. Kürschner, 1900
Padre nose kuale tu ese in cielo, sante esa tue nomine; vena imperio tue; volunta tue esa fate sur tera komo in cielo; de a nos hodi nose pan kuotidian; perdone nose kulpas, kual nos perdona nose kulpan-tes; ni konduka nos in tentacion, ma libere nos de lu mal.

Idiom neutral—Akademi international de lingu universal, 1902
Nostr patr kel es in sieli! Ke votr nom es sanktifiked; ke votr regnia veni; ke votr volu es fasied, kuale in siel, tale et su ter. Dona sidiurne a noi nostr pan omnidiurnik; e pardona a noi nostr debiti, kuale et noi pardon a nostr debtatori e no induka noi in tentasion, ma librifika noi da it mal.

Reform neutral—Rosenberger, Pinth, de Wahl, 1912 (variant of the preceding)
Nostr Patr, qui es in cieli! Votr nômin essa sanctifiqued; votr regma venia; votr volu essa facied quale in cieli tale anque sur terr. Dona noi hodia nostr pan quotidian; e pardona nostr debitori; e no induca noi in tentation, ma libera noi del maligne.

On the occasion of the 1900 Paris Universal Exhibition, the Delegation for the Adoption of an International Auxiliary Language was formed. The group resolved that the desired language would:

- be suited to everyday activities in social life, commercial exchange, and scientific and philosophical research;
- be easy to learn for anyone with an average, elementary education, *especially people belonging to European civilization*;[5] and
- not be one of the national languages.

In 1903, Louis Couturat and Léopold Léau, interlinguists themselves and authors of the gigantic *Histoire de la langue universelle*, proposed that the International Association of Academies, founded in 1900, should take charge of choosing the international language to be used and implementing it.

As the movement became more institutionalized, teams emerged and contacts were forged. At first, however, the ranks consisted of amateurs without any real training in languages. Curiously, they included René de Saussure, the brother of the famed linguist and himself a professor of mathematics in Bern. Only after World War I, which dealt a fatal blow to idealistic projects (Zamenhof is said to have died with a broken heart), did professional linguists enter the arena. Some of the greatest minds in the field joined in—among others, Otto Jespersen (Denmark), Edward Sapir (United States), Harold Palmer (England), Nikolai Trubetzkoy (Russia), and André Martinet (France).[6] Efforts focused on reconstituting etymons[7] and ensuring greater naturalness (that is, conformity with languages already in existence) while promoting regularity, especially by eliminating allomorphs and dissymmetries. With that, the project for a universal language entered the twentieth century in earnest—at the same time that Ferdinand de Saussure was laying the groundwork for modern linguistics.

Palmer described the difference between natural and constructed languages as follows:

> By definition natural languages are extremely difficult to learn, and doing so takes a great deal of time. This is the case because of the cumulative effects of their characteristics, namely, (1) the fact that each language has its own system of sounds; (2) orthography often proves to be highly irregular; (3) vocabulary includes ambiguities, redundancies, and omissions; (4) systems of derivation are irregular and/or illogical; and (5) the syntax is complex and unpredictable.

> In contrast, artificial languages generally display (1) an efficient phonological system consisting of sounds used widely in different languages; (2) perfectly phonetic orthography; (3) a simple and straightforward lexicon; (4) morphology with a logical and regular derivation; and (5) minimal rules concerning grammar and syntax, which moreover are completely regular.
>
> Consequently, an artificial language may be mastered four to twenty times more quickly than a natural one—as observation will confirm.[8]

But in actual fact, English was well on its way to becoming the international standard. Innumerable designs based on Romance languages were followed by projects enlisting a simplified or deliberately pidginized English. The best known example is Basic English, created by Charles Kay Ogden and I. A. Richards in 1934; it featured an elementary vocabulary of 850 words, with a mere eighteen verbs that could be combined with particles or complements to create new meanings; this system capitalized on two characteristics of English grammar: aspectual particles and support verb constructions.

World War II brought the movement to a halt, at least in Western Europe. Americans continued developing Interlingua, a collective enterprise begun in 1937 by the International Auxiliary Language Association (IALA), the US counterpart to the Delegation for the Adoption of an International Auxiliary Language. Interlingua combined a Greco-Latin vocabulary with a simple grammar inspired by English but more accessible and stripped of almost all irregularities. This language amounted to a form of vehicular English based on an international lexicon.

Families of Constructed Languages

Just like natural languages, artificial languages belong to families, in keeping with points of divergence within the interlinguistic movement.

SCHLEYER'S VOLAPÜK (1879–1880) GIVES RISE TO

Balta, 1887
Esperanto, 1887
Nuvo-volapük, 1887
Spelin, 1888
Dil, 1893
Veltparl, 1896
Dilpok, 1898
Idiom neutral, 1898
Lingua european, 1907
Idiom neutral (reformed), 1907

GIUSEPPE PEANO'S INTERLINGUA (1903, ITALY), A NEW VERSION OF LATINO SINE FLEXIONE, BRINGS FORTH

Perfect (lingua), 1910
Semi-latin, 1910
Simplo, 1911
Novi latine, 1911
Nov latin logui, 1918
Latinulus, 1919
Reformed Interlingua (Semprini), 1922
Interlingua systematic, 1922
Unilingue, 1923
—> Monario, 1925
—> Mondi lingua, 1956
Interlatino, date unknown
Latino viventi, 1925
Panlingua, 1938

REFORMED ESPERANTO, ESPERANTIDOJ, AND LANGUAGES INSPIRED BY ESPERANTO

Reformed Esperanto, 1894
Perio, 1904
Lingua internacional, 1905
Ekselsioro, 1906
Ulla, 1906
Mondlingvo, 1906
Ido, 1907
Lingwo internaciona (or Antido), 1907
Mez-voio, 1908
Romanizat, 1908
Romanal, 1909
Reform-esperanto (Rodet), 1910
Reform-esperanto (Hugon), 1910
Latin-esperanto, 1911
Lingw adelfenzal, 1911
Esperanto (Stelzner), 1912
Europeo, 1914
Nepo, 1915
Hom idyomo, 1921
Néo, 1937
Espido, 1923
Esperantuisho, 1955
Olingo, date unknown
Esperilo, date unknown
Globaqo, ca. 1956 (?)
Modern espéranto, ca. 1958 (?)

ESPERANTIDOJ DEVISED BY RENÉ DE SAUSSURE

Esperantida, Switzerland, 1919
Nov-esperanto, 1929
Esperanto II, 1942

DERIVATES OF IDO

Dutalingue, 1908
Romanizat, 1908
Italico, 1909
Ispirantu and Occidental, 1909
Adjuvilo, 1910
Nuv-esperanto, 1910
Latin-ido, 1911
Esperanto (Stelzner), 1912
Etem, 1917
Unesal, 1923
Idiome federale, 1923 (from Nuv-esperanto)
Ido avancit, 1925
Esperido, 1925 (from Dutalingue)
Cosman, 1927
Novam, 1928
Mundial, 1930
Sintesal, ca. 1931 (?)
Intal, 1956
Kosmolinguo, 1956
Globaqo, ca. 1956 (?)

Behind the Iron Curtain, things went a little differently. In the Soviet Union, Esperanto enjoyed a warm welcome at first, but a cruel fate lay in store for the language and its adherents, cut off from the rest of the world in a state hostile to the Western bloc. During the second half of the nineteenth century, the libertarian and revolutionary movements that would ultimately take down the tsarist regime had welcomed the project, which promised to make the world a better place by abolishing borders and the division they entail. Tolstoy was among its first champions. In turn, at the beginning of the twentieth century, the Polish-Russian linguist Baudouin de Courtenay advocated the adoption of an international language. Finally, in the wake of the 1917 Revolution, Esperanto met with real success, gaining recognition as the future tongue of the world proletariat. Until this point, the interlinguistic movement had appealed more to the intelligentsia and members of the enlightened bourgeoisie open to pacifist and humanitarian ideas. Unlike the moneyed classes, workers had no opportunity to learn foreign languages in school. They were therefore the ideal audience for a language easy to master, which would ensure communication the world over. So long as an internationalist spirit prevailed, Esperanto seemed to provide a weapon against the supreme evil: nationalism.

But the Esperanto movement was channeled into an institutional framework subordinate to the state and communist ideology. In the 1920s and 1930s, as Soviet socialism evolved toward totalitarianism, Esperanto did not remain unaffected, coming under increasing criticism as new structures consolidated power. Adherents were accused of treason because they had foreign contacts. Within the USSR, Stalin promoted linguistic and cultural projects that were "national in form, socialist in content." In his eyes, when socialism triumphed across the globe, national languages would disappear and a universal tongue would emerge from their spontaneous fusion. According to Nikolai Marr—the lunatic whose theory Stalin endorsed—language is just a superstructural phenomenon. Ernest Drezen, the general secretary of the Union of Soviet Esperantists, was executed in the 1937 purges, and the Esperanto movement dissolved.

Of all the international auxiliary languages, only—or almost only—Esperanto has survived. It still has many advocates and a literature of its own; as a rule, few people are aware that other projects even existed. Esperanto has benefited greatly from the rise of the World Wide Web, which has increased its visibility and diffusion, facilitated relations between Esperantists, and offered an effective "showcase" for its achievements. The question of a vehicular language that can be used internationally is more topical than ever now, but an artificial language no longer forms part of the agenda, either at the UN or in European institutions, even though membership is constantly expanding. Despite long having been a fashionable subject of reflection and inspiring real hope, such linguistic voluntarism seems to be an outdated idea.

7

MYTH AT THE HEART OF SCIENCE: MODERN LINGUISTIC THEORIES AS REFLECTED IN SCIENCE FICTION

> Nice planet you have here. How many languages are spoken?
> —Ian Watson, *The Embedding*

> The limits of my language mean the limits of my world.
> —Ludwig Wittgenstein, *Tractatus Logico-Philosophicus*

In terms of its themes, science fiction belongs to the same tradition as the imaginary journeys of early modernity. The specific technologies involved are secondary to travel in space or time (or both). The old myth of other inhabited worlds and communication with aliens, now extraterrestrial, lives on. Literature of Martian inspiration plays a leading role. For instance, Alexander Bogdanov's "novelistic utopia" *Red Star* (1908), which appeared in pre-Revolutionary Russia and pursued ultra-didactic aims, is set on the red planet. In keeping with convention, the language here is unified, harmonious, musical, and easy to learn thanks to its inherent logic; without grammatical gender—deemed an arbitrary and useless category—Martian instead distinguishes between existing entities, those that existed in the past, and ones due to appear in the future. All the inhabitants of this world share a single tongue, thereby avoiding the conflict that plagues the Earth.

For his part, Edgar Rice Burroughs, the celebrated creator of *Tarzan,* wrote a series of voyages to Mars, beginning in 1917. The people here—"Barsoomians"—communicate for the most part by telepathy in a language that is common to all, even though regions have different writing systems. (Barsoom is the opposite of the mythical China, then.) The novel's hero, John Carter, masters the tongue in just one week: "This power [telepathy] is wonderfully developed in all Martians, and accounts largely for the simplicity of their language and the relatively few spoken words exchanged even in long conversations. It is the universal language of Mars, through the medium of which the higher and lower animals of this world are able to a communicate to a greater or lesser extent, depending upon the intellectual sphere of the species and the development of the individual."[1]

Burroughs's books take up themes that were fashionable in the late nineteenth and early twentieth centuries: spiritualist modes of communications and the notion of Mars's habitability (which Camille Flammarion popularized). Precisely these themes are what nourished the imagination of the famous medium Hélène Smith at exactly the same point in time (cf. chapter 9).

The ascendancy of English-speaking writers (particularly British ones) in works of fantasy and science fiction dates to the same period. Relevant titles include J. R. R. Tolkien's *The Hobbit* (1937) and *The Lord of the Rings* (1954–1955). The author was fascinated by languages even as a child and had a very good command not only of Latin and Greek, but also of Hebrew, Welsh, and Finnish. Tolkien spent most of his career at Oxford as a professor of medieval English, and he was trained as a philologist and lexicographer. Accordingly, his work draws on nineteenth-century Indo-European comparative research.

Tolkien was not a linguist in the modern sense of the word, and his novels show no concern for the academic currents of his day. The invented languages in his books defy reckoning, but the most important ones are those spoken by Hobbits and Elves. Tolkien crafted an elaborate genealogical system to account for the relationships between dialects and their stages of historical development; this is all steeped in the philology of Germanic tongues, with elements from Hungarian, Greek, and Latin. The fictional languages each have a highly detailed lexicon and grammar; as early as 1917—long before writing the *Lord of the Rings* cycle—the author published a phonological and historical description and dictionary of *High Elven*, or *Quenya*. Like his forebear, Lewis Carroll—another Oxford don and author of the famous "Jabberwocky"—Tolkien reveled in the sounds of the ancient Anglo-Saxon tongue.[2]

Indeed, languages created Tolkien's universe: the author invented them, then their speakers and their world: "Middle-earth." The tongues the author devised make the characters come to life. What's more, Tolkien claims that his narrative was translated from a manuscript written in Westron, the ancient language of the Hobbits, who tell the tale one reads. The "Hobbit English" of the books abounds in archaizing, medieval phrases that make events present and vivid.

Tolkien also had a passion for the myths and legends of Northern European cultures (Celtic, Germanic, and Scandinavian), from which he drew many of his themes. Needless to say, *rings* call the Nibelungen to mind. His work is much more akin to imaginary travel, of which the English have provided so many fine examples, than to science fiction in the commonly accepted sense; for all that, it is based on rigorous, scientific study.

In the world today, increasingly dominated by Anglo-Saxon culture, the primary, if not universal, language on planet Earth and throughout the cosmos tends to be English (or some variant of Basic English). No one seems to call this projection into question any more. Often enough, it's solemn or stilted—deliberately archaic in order to set it apart from colloquial English actually in use.[3]

Imaginary Languages in Cinema

While putting invented words in the mouths of characters in a novel is relatively easy, using them in cinematic dialogue is much more problematic: they are rarely suited for actual vocalization. All the same, a few attempts have proved successful.

When making *Quest for Fire* (1981), a film based on *La guerre du feu* (1911) by J. H. Rosny aîné, Jean-Jacques Annaud needed a language for the cavemen that would seem true to life. He enlisted the novelist Anthony Burgess, a linguist by training with a passion for both natural and invented languages. Burgess created two prehistoric tongues, the first Paleolithic and the second Neolithic; for the latter, he drew inspiration from the Indo-European radicarium.[4] Nadsat, the Anglo-Russian jargon of *A Clockwork Orange* (1962) had already appeared on screen in Stanley Kubrick's 1971 cinematic adaptation of the novel.

The best example of a fictional language coming to life is Klingon, which was created in 1984 by James Doohan and Marc Okrand for the third Star Trek movie and boasts a lexicon of 2,000 words. That's quite a lot in light of the fact that most people use some 1,500 words of their native tongue for everyday purposes (this number is also the total vocabulary of Basic English). Klingon follows grammatical rules, which one can now learn on the Web. Young fans of the Star Trek franchise evidently use it as a secret language—see, for example, Zach Braff's 2004 film, *Garden State*. Here's a sample:

nuqDaq yuch Dapol?: "Where do you keep the chocolate?"

QuchlIj vIyach vIneHs: "I'd like to stroke your forehead."

There's even a Klingon Language Institute to promote its use.

Peter Jackson's adaptation of the *Lord of the Rings* trilogy (2001–2003) likewise represents a major event. Languages play such a vital role in Tolkien's works that there was no question of not including them in the films (if only to satisfy the novels' legions of fans). A linguist, David Salo, adapted the tongues of Middle-earth for the screen, and two professional phoneticians coached actors for several months before shooting.

More recently, Sydney Pollack's *The Interpreter* (2005) has featured the Ku language (in fact, a hybrid of Shona and Swahili), supposedly spoken by the Tobosa people in the fictitious republic of Matobo.

At any rate, few recent works of science fiction have featured an original language. Here and there, traces of the myth of Babel appear in allusions to the languages of the Sun, Moon, or Mars—or there are hints of ancient Hebrew or primitive Indo-European, still in use on some distant planet. But most writers, in keeping with the spirit of the day, don't even bother and leave out the problem of language or solve it by including some all-powerful translation machine. As a rule, if their alien interlocutors don't already know English, the protagonists manage to learn extraterrestrial languages in a few minutes. Telepathy frequently comes in handy, too.

Six novels stand out, however, for granting a prominent role to language. All but one of these works are anti-utopias—in contrast to the utopias favored in earlier times. The first four display the influence of the school of thought inaugurated by Edward Sapir and Benjamin Whorf, as well as the American-style structuralism of Leonard Bloomfield. The fifth is directly inspired by Noam Chomsky's generative grammar. The sixth is intended to illustrate the feminist struggle against sexism in language. In each case, two ways of thinking about language and communication stand opposed: culturalism and universalism.

George Orwell's *1984* (1949) doesn't qualify as science fiction inasmuch as science fiction aims to entertain the reader more than anything else. Instead, the work stands in the tradition of imaginary journeys written to philosophical and didactic ends, here recast in a pessimistic mode.

The author's conception of language reflects the trends dominating linguistics in the middle of the twentieth century, which stressed the diversity of languages rather than the unity of language per se. In the simplest terms, the so-called Sapir–Whorf hypothesis claims that thought is conditioned by language—or, more precisely, by the semantic and syntactical structures of languages, which cannot be boiled down to a common denominator. In Whorf's words, "Every language is a vast pattern-system, different from others, in which are culturally ordained the forms and categories by which the personality not only communicates, but also analyzes nature, notices or neglects types of relationship and phenomena, channels his reasoning, and builds the house of his consciousness."[5] Or, as Sapir put it: "Such categories as number, gender, case, tense . . . are not so much discovered in experience as imposed upon it because of the tyrannical hold that linguistic form has upon our orientation in the world."[6]

It is not by chance that this perspective developed from the study of Amerindian languages in the United States. The languages of people long oppressed represent the last refuge of irreducible *difference*.[7] According to Whorf, the Hopi cannot perceive time in the same way as speakers of European languages because aspect plays a greater role in their language than tense.

If individual mental processes are beholden to linguistic structures, manipulating language will provide a means to gain control over its users. In this sense, Orwell's Newspeak is inspired by the Sapir–Whorf hypothesis (which itself, even in the most exaggerated form, in no way hints at using language to totalitarian ends): "The purpose of Newspeak was not only to provide a medium of expression for the world-view and mental habits proper to the devotees of Ingsoc, but to make all other modes of thought impossible. It was intended that when Newspeak had been adopted once and for all and Oldspeak forgotten, a heretical thought—that is, a thought diverging from the principles of Ingsoc—should be literally unthinkable, at least so far as thought is dependent on words."[8] In an appendix to the novel ("The Principles of Newspeak"), Orwell discusses how the problem of linguistic intervention and the construction of artificial languages prompted him to devise the gloomy caricature he presents.[9] In so doing, he demonstrates the superiority of natural languages over man-made ones.[10]

Another literary transposition of the Sapir–Whorf hypothesis occurs in Jack Vance's *Languages of Pao* (1958): "Each language is a special tool, with a particular capability. It is more than a means of communication, it is a system of thought. . . . Think of a language as the contour of a watershed, stopping flow in certain directions, channeling it into others. Language controls the mechanism of your mind. When people speak different languages, their minds work differently and they act differently."[11] So speaks one of the novel's heroes. In the galaxy where Pao is located, each planet is home to a language that reflects the temperament and behavior of its inhabitants.

Accordingly, great confusion reigns on Vale, where "language . . . is personal improvisation, with the fewest possible conventions."[12] On Breakness, the language is of the isolating type and therefore particularly suited to abstract reasoning, argument, and intellectual manipulation of various sorts; by the same token, it is "almost totally deficient in descriptives of various emotional states."[13] Herein lies its superiority over Paonese, a language with an agglutinative structure that admits a wide range of affective expressions; its speakers are correspondingly weak.

But does language determine behavior or simply reflect it? Opting for the first hypothesis, the planet's dictator enlists a group of linguists to provide his people with an array of new languages meant to fit their minds to the different functions they perform in society. The military will have Valiant, a language "rich in effort-producing gutturals and hard vowels," whose syntax embodies strength: "a number of key ideas will be synonymous; such as *pleasure* and *overcoming a resistance*—*relaxation* and *shame—out-worlder* and *rival*."[14] Industrial workers will have Technicant, intellectuals Cogitant, traders Mercantil, and commoners Batch, all in keeping with the principle of matching structure. One day, a true hero will arise and save his people by reuniting the languages of Pao into a kind of Esperanto called Pastiche, overcoming class languages that have in fact caused conflict and division.

In our own world, efforts to control minds by means of language occur in much less grotesque—but still insidious—forms of so-called "political correctness," which has been growing in recent decades in response to demands on the part of political activists.

In 1966, Samuel Delany's *Babel-17* appeared. The author works a veritable course in structural linguistics into the novel's galaxy-spanning plot. The heroine, a young linguist, faces the challenge of deciphering the language of alien invaders. When writing the book, universal theories and generative grammar weren't broadly diffused yet—Chomsky's *Syntactic Structures* dates to 1957, and *Aspects of the Theory of Syntax*, his truly groundbreaking work, to 1965—and Delany clearly boned up on Bloomfield and Whorf: the title invokes the diversity of languages rather than their unity. Incompatible languages and ways of thinking prevail among different beings inhabiting different galaxies.

Babel-17 is a musical and harmonious language of extreme concision and economy (an idea of some antiquity, as we have seen). It expresses more in a syllable than other languages can communicate in a whole sentence. Words are highly motivated and refer to their meaning naturally: "Once you learn it, it makes everything so easy. . . . A melodious torrent rippled through the room. . . . While she listened, while she understood, she moved through psychedelic perceptions. It was not only a language, she understood now, but a flexible matrix of analytical possibilities where the same 'word' defined the stresses in a webbing of medical bandage, or a defensive grid of spaceships."[15] Ultimately, our heroine deciphers Babel-17 and discovers that it is an artificial language devised by evil minds seeking to gain control over mental processes: lacking the "shifter" pronouns *I* and *you* that structure communication, the language suspends the awareness of self and other that structures conscience and consciousness, turning people into machines. Delany's novel is another anti-utopia.

In 1975, *Epepe* by Ferenc Karinthy was published in Hungary (an English translation did not appear until 2008). The novel confirms the twentieth century's penchant for negative utopias. Once more, a linguist plays the leading role. Meaning to go to Finland for a Finno-Ugric linguistics conference, he has the unpleasant surprise, when he exits the plane, of finding himself in an unknown country whose language proves utterly impenetrable. Indeed, it bears no resemblance to any tongue he has ever encountered. As a comparatist, the protagonist is well versed in uncovering points of relation between languages. (Note the irony that a Hungarian thought up this situation!) The story unfolds as a nightmare: a total lack of communication. Of course, as per the theory of linguistic universals, any person is capable of learning any human language, if circumstances so require. No natural language is irreducible to any other one, yet they share the common feature of having specific traits. But none of these rules hold in the world Karinthy describes: language constantly eludes the hero's grasp. Evidently, signs change meaning from speaker to speaker and from one utterance to the next; they resist translation into equivalent terms and any kind of pictorial or gestural symbolism. Hence the inhuman nature of this world's inhabitants. Language seems to set people against each other instead of uniting them.

Epepe provides another example of the interconnection of linguistic, mental, and social structures. Here, language is a figure for the most extreme version of an *elsewhere*, a prison world from which one never returns.

In the 1970s, the epistemological rupture of what has come to be known as the "Chomskyan revolution" occurred. The philosophical view of language that defined seventeenth-century thinking made its return.[16] Chomsky's generativism, the dominant perspective in linguistics since the preceding decade,[17] now left its mark on science fiction.

Ian Watson's *The Embedding* (1973) is a minor anti-utopian masterpiece. The "embedding" of the title—a key term in

Chomsky's generative and transformational grammar—is an active metaphor structuring the work itself. The novel's three registers—developmental linguistics, anthropology, and space travel—fit together like a Russian doll, all centered on the theme of universal grammar.

Sole, a British research scientist at a hospital specializing in language disorders, has been charged with conducting a strange experiment in utmost secrecy. He teaches three young orphans kidnapped in Pakistan to "speak badly"—in other words, to use "deep structures" (or "Chomskyan trees") to communicate. The children are being raised in a glass cage, and Sole interacts with them in English through a television screen. However, mediating their contact is a computer that transforms whatever the scientist says into embedded language—deep structures that are supposed to constitute an innate mechanism identical for all human beings. According to Chomsky's theory of universal grammar (1965), this is what enables the individual, in the course of acquiring speech, to learn the language of his or her cultural environment and operative "surface structures." In Watson's novel, the researcher is trying to implant this mechanism, which is unconscious by nature, into the children's brains directly. To this end, they are subjected to a barrage of chemical treatments so the otherwise hidden mechanism will be visible. Testing the validity of Chomsky's hypothesis will, in turn, facilitate the design of automatic translation machines.[18] Should the children undergoing the procedure manage to use what they are given as a real language, science will have experimental proof for the existence of deep structures, and the primal process by which human beings form language will at last have been discovered. The familiar parallel between phylogeny and ontogeny is evident: in the early stages of life, these children are supposed to cycle through the course completed by thousands of prehistoric generations.[19]

The account of the poor little Pakistanis (who wind up insane because their brains can't handle the treatment) is embedded in a story with a political and ethnological cast, but still focused on language. Here, one of Sole's friends, Pierre, is studying an Amazonian tribe, the Xemahoa. Their language has the peculiarity of operating on two levels. The surface level, Xemahoa A, is used under the normal conditions of everyday life. The other, Xemahoa B, is an embedded language with a magic and ritual function. Spoken only by initiates under the influence of a hallucinogenic mushroom, it serves as the vehicle for tribal myths, especially those about the origins and creation of the world. Pierre (who has been influenced by his readings of Raymond Roussel[20]) places himself at great risk both physically and mentally when he tries to get to the bottom of the phenomenon. Taken to the extreme in Xemahoa B, embedding prevents thought from being transmitted through time and space. It breaks up the essentially linear and sequential order of speech and thought. Past and future, the distance between people, places, and things, no longer exist: human experience is condensed into a *here and now* that engulfs the whole world. In this giddy moment of transport, all thought and perception belong to a universal matrix that is the *absolute truth* of language and therefore of thought.

Finally, a third plot on a galactic scale englobes these two stories. It features an alien race, the Sp'thra ("Signal Traders"), a people of linguists and communication specialists. They travel between worlds collecting brains endowed with all manner of linguistic faculties. They also have translation machines, which enable them to learn foreign tongues readily.

Thus, when they land in the United States, they speak flawless American English:

> "You can imprint a language directly into the brain, then?" Sole hazarded.
>
> "Good guess—provided it conforms to . . ."
>
> ". . . the rules of Universal Grammar! That's it, isn't it?"[21]

The Reality of the Universe is the sum total of the realities of all speech communities, which, while conditioned by different languages, have a common linguistic denominator at the galactic level. Needless to say, the Sp'thra demonstrate particular interest in acquiring Xemahoa brains, which sets off a series of events and catastrophes not to be revealed here; the curious should read the book (which nonlinguists will have no trouble following).

The novel reconciles two seemingly incompatible hypotheses, then: on the one hand, the view that the structure of a given language conditions the thought of users (the strong version of cultural relativism, which implies the impossibility of translating an experience recorded in language A into language B), and, on the other hand, the universalist position underlying not only the assorted theories and fictions of the origin of language that we have seen on the preceding pages, but also the utopia of a philosophical language capable of expressing the true nature of reality.

Chase off the idea of "nature," and it will come roaring back.

The idea of nature is precisely what generative grammar reintroduced through the notion of innateness. This also heralded the triumphant return of the philosophy of language. If language is an inherent feature of human being, this entails the universality of linguistic mechanisms across the species.

To demonstrate deep structures, generative grammarians propose to observe all available languages to find the rules by which profound semantic "content" passes to surface "forms," where other, morpho-phonological rules operate. We should note (without implying any criticism of transformational-generative grammar[22]), that another approach to linguistic universals may be taken. This method involves looking at the surface structures of different languages and identifying shared traits[23] (whereby it is understood that the results concern strong tendencies, not absolute universals).

Universals of Language

Despite their diversity, all human languages have a great deal in common, both in terms of general properties and in terms of the level of internal organization specific to each one. The objective of linguists is to discover invariants in order to reconcile unity with multiplicity.

GENERAL FEATURES

Languages are endowed with a double articulation (phonemes and morphemes) and constitute symbolic systems; a finite number of signs and rules allows for an infinite number of utterances. All languages include redundant elements and permit polysemy, synonymy, and ambiguity.

Beyond this characterization of human language as a whole, linguists have sought to formulate the most common structural features. On this basis, implicational chains have been identified—that is, rules according to which one feature (B) can only exist if another feature (A) is also given. Thus, it has been determined that every language has at least two vowels defined by extreme positions assumed by the mouth, i and a. (More often there are three, a triangle of movements: i-a-u). A given language may possess other vowels, as well. All languages have oral vowels, and some (French and Portuguese, for example) also have nasal ones, but there is no language that has nasal vowels without oral vowels. Likewise, there is no language with fricatives (f/v, s/z) that does not have occlusives (p/b, t/d, k/g).

As for morphology, when a language has verbal or nominal inflections as well as derivational morphemes, the latter are added directly to the root of the word and inflections follow; it is never the other way around: sell + er + s, not sell + s + er. Languages with postpositions (such as English) generally have adjectives prefixed to the noun and compound nouns of the determiner + determiner type, but languages that have only prepositions (French, for instance) prefer the reverse order (which also shows that genetically related languages can diverge typologically).

Noun and verb represent the principal examples of universal elements. They can be found in most known languages. This is not the case for adjectives; thus, if a language has adjectives, it necessarily has verbs, but the opposite does not hold; nor is it true of articles, which are important in French but absent in some related languages (e.g., Slavic tongues).

UNIVERSALS OF GRAMMAR

It seems there are three basic types of grammatical relation: predication (organized around a verbal nucleus), subordination, and coordination. All syntax can be reduced to these three schemes.

Linguists at UC Berkeley have introduced the concept of cognitive constraint. According to this theory, the grammaticalization of cognitive schemas (often on a metaphorical basis) ensures a relatively direct correlation between universals of cognition (for example, perception of time and space) and universals of language.

Research on universals goes hand in hand with research on typology (sets of structural universals serving to define a distinct kind of language).

As I pointed out at the very beginning of this book, the construction of languages, whether in works of fiction or to practical ends, is chiefly the province of men. But here, as in many other spheres of life, feminism has made inroads—and once again, especially in the United States. A singular and engaging (if, at points, overly didactic) work is *Native Tongue* (1984) by linguist Suzette Haden Elgin.

Native Tongue is another book of Whorfian inspiration. Its premise is that natural languages, being inherently sexist in their structure and lexicon, are unfit to express the experience of women. Accordingly, Elgin sets out to create a women's language,[24] Laadan, which will reflect the feminine universe and enable nonchauvinist thinking. Interestingly, this tongue is tonal, agglutinative, and highly regular; its many enunciative markers reflect developments in the study of discourse pragmatics toward the end of the twentieth century. At the same time, its complexity calls to mind the language Vairasse invented for the Sevarambes or Volapük; it has thirty-six personal pronouns to express different kinds of social and emotional relations—which must make it rather difficult to use.

But at least our survey can end with a genuine utopia.

The New Search for the Language of Origins: The Nostratic Hypothesis and the Return of Monogenesis

In 1903, the Danish linguist Holger Pedersen, renewing a tradition exemplified by Leibniz, claimed that languages of the Indo-European, Semitic, Finno-Ugric, and Altaic groups had a common origin. He proposed the term "Nostratic" for this superfamily. From the 1960s on, a school of Russian linguistics founded by Vladislav Illich-Svitych conducted broad-scale studies, beginning with languages belonging to what was then the Soviet Union; this territory is home to an extraordinary variety of peoples, cultures, and tongues. The field came to include the languages of the Afro-Asian, Dravidian, Eskimo-Aleut, Chukotko-Kamchatkan, and Kartvelian (Caucasus) groups. In a first step, 600 common roots were identified.

This project overlapped with work being done in the United States, especially by Joseph Greenberg, the father of universals, and Merritt Ruhlen, who specialized in the Amerindian domain (which represents a single family). English archaeologist Colin Renfrew granted their efforts the approval of his own discipline. In effect, research along these lines aims to arrive at so-called Proto-World, the mother tongue spoken by *Homo sapiens* 100,000 to 200,000 years ago in the East African cradle of humanity. Italian geneticist Luigi Cavalli-Sforza has affirmed that genetic differences between populations correspond closely to linguistic differences.

Questions of method are crucial here. Risky guesswork—like the claims advanced by amateurs in the previous centuries—is to be avoided. Proving the kinship of languages needs to be based on regular phonetic laws concerning series of words, not words taken in isolation. Before even beginning, one must eliminate all points of convergence based on borrowing, chance (say, the fact that *ker* means "house" both in Breton and in Wolof), and universal traits (words for "mother" begin with *m* in many languages spoken at great distances from each other).

Two approaches are preferred by proponents of this new version of monogenesis. The first, based on attested forms, is to find correspondences between the various proto-languages already identified by comparatists. The problem here is that gaps still exist, and many languages remain undescribed; only the Indo-European group provides a relatively solid foundation. The other option is to posit, a priori, a limited number of (supposedly) essential concepts/terms that will exist in any and every language. According to Aaron Dolgopolski, the latter include "I/me," "two/pair," "you/you" (subject and object), "who/what," "language," "name," "eye," "heart," "tooth," "finger/nail," "louse" [sic], "tear," "water," and "death." The next step is to track down words that relate to these notions in all languages, taking into account phonetic laws (insofar as they are known). One can appreciate the difficulty of the task if one considers that the French *eau* undoubtedly comes from Latin *aqua*, even though the two words do not share a single phoneme! Given the absence of forms attested in writing (and research mostly concerns languages from before it was invented), the results are questionable, to say the least.

In spite of an impressive volume of work by Dolgopolski, Sergei Starostin, Ilya Yakubovich, and others, the monogenetic hypothesis has failed to convince most linguists. Critics point out that, even if a series of matches enabled us to trace all languages back to a single tongue (which implies that everyone in the world shares common ancestors), it would still not shed any light on how, when, or why they split from each other, nor would it do anything to describe their extraordinary diversity. More still, research of this kind essentially concerns vocabulary, which is the least stable and most variable part of every language; in fact, syntax—the internal organization of each system, which allows new sentences to be constructed—is what counts for linguists. If the point is to understand human language and affirm unity in diversity, it seems more promising to highlight universals and advances in linguistic typology.

Finally, another issue seems much more pressing today: the rapid disappearance of languages as the result of globalization. It took some 100,000 years for the 5,000 to 7,000 languages that now are spoken to emerge, but they're vanishing at a much faster rate.

Here's a comparative table, based on research by Joseph Greenberg, concerning the primitive root tik/dik and the semantic field covering "one," "finger," "index," "point."

Language family	Form	Meaning
NIGER-KORDOFANIAN	"DIKE"	ONE
NILO-SAHARAN	"TEK," "DEK," "TOK"	ONE
KHOISAN	Absent	—
AFRO-ASIATIC	"TAK"	ONE
DRAVIDIAN	None	—
INDO-EUROPEAN	"DEIK"	TO POINT
URALIC-YUKAGHIR	"OTIK"	ONE
ALTAIC	"TE"	ONLY
CHUKCHI-KAMCHATKAN	Unclear	—
ESKIMO-ALEUT	"TIK"	INDEX, MIDDLE FINGER
SINO-TIBETAN	"TIK"	ONE
AUSTRIC	"TIK," "TING"	HAND, ARM
INDO-PACIFIC	"DIK"	ONE
AUSTRALIAN	Absent	—
AMERIND	"TIK"	FINGER, ONE
NA-DENE	"TIKHI"	ONE

Thus concludes our account of linguistic fancy as science and ideology have inscribed it in fiction—if not in the consciousness of the reading public. We can see that three conceptions of language emerged between the sixteenth and twentieth centuries. First, a time of myth witnessed the rise of scientific thought, distinguished by the *Grammaire générale et raisonnée de Port-Royal* and the forerunners of comparative linguistics; this period, which focused on the origins of language and its fundamental oneness across the globe, was dominated by religious dogma. Then came the scientific study of language and grammar in historical context and comparative perspective; it culminated, with Ferdinand de Saussure, in structural linguistics: the synchronic study of systems and the rejection of origins, myth, and utopia (which now stood freely available to logophiles, glossomaniacs, and other language inventors). Only in the second half of the twentieth century, with the Chomskyan revolution, did linguistics seem to stand on sufficiently scientific ground that the problem of universals could be raised again. Perhaps it marks the beginning of a new cycle.

But this hardly means that fantasy and imagination have vanished. For some time now, monogenism—the quest for the mother tongue of all humankind—has been making a comeback.

PART III TWO POLES OF LINGUISTIC FANTASY

Examination of the two case histories that follow illustrate masculine and feminine approaches to linguistic invention, the polarity of conscious and unconscious thought, and the opposition between intellect and emotion. Although separate in space, they represent twin phenomena in time. Both belong to the turn from the nineteenth century to the twentieth. This prodigiously fertile period witnessed the emergence of linguistics and psychoanalysis; meanwhile, the interlinguistic and spiritualist movements thrived, as did belief in the plurality of inhabited worlds and, finally, Pentecostalism—the supposed resurgence of the primitive Church. In brief, sciences reserved for an elite emerged against the backdrop of popular culture sending deeper and deeper roots down into the realm of the irrational.

The Georgian Nikolai Marr (1863–1933) is a prime example of the logophile as defined in chapters 2 and 3. Completely out of step with his own day and age, his work represents the continuation of a linguistic imaginary rooted in myth and justified by utopianism. In this light, a sinister farce reveals another side: instead of a (discredited) prophet who came and went, we see a system that belongs to a historical pattern.

The story of Marr's contemporary Hélène Smith (1869–1929) is the finest case of spiritualist glossolalia recorded to date. We know about this seer thanks to a remarkable book that anticipates Freud in many respects, Théodore Flournoy's *Des Indes à la planète Mars* (*From India to the Planet Mars*).

The invention of pseudo-languages in altered states draws on an innate human capacity; via the realm of fantasy, the scientific question of linguistic universals surfaces again. This is why, in formal terms, all cases of glossolalia—whether spiritualist, religious, pathological, or ludic—admit analysis along the same lines. On the level of content, they contain the variegated mythology of origins discussed in chapter 1. A continuum extends from unconsciousness and dream to waking life and visions.

8

THE EMPEROR'S NEW CLOTHES: THE CASE OF NIKOLAI MARR

> Between theory and delirium, between the scholar and the madman, between a builder of empire and a lunatic, there's always connivance that passes by way of paranoia.
>
> —Élisabeth Roudinesco, *La bataille de cent ans*

As the Darwinian theory of evolution was being adapted to the study of language, as linguistics was consolidating its status as a positive science, as Ferdinand de Saussure was starting his career in comparative philology at the École Pratique des Hautes Études in Paris—that is, just as the fantasy of a primitive tongue was being banished to the murky depths of prescientific speculation—Nikolai Marr laid the foundations for a theory that, under the patronage of Joseph Stalin, would come to stand as one of the biggest scientific impostures of all time.

Marrism's final period (1930–1950) is most familiar in the West—in other words, its afterlife, as its creator died in 1934. Born in 1863, Nikolai Marr was essentially a man of the nineteenth century, and his ideas represent a continuation of the linguistic thought that prevailed some fifty years before his birth. The seeds of his madness are not to be sought in the ideas themselves. Marr was fifty-four in 1917; he conducted most of his work in tsarist Russia—a land that, counter to what one might expect, then stood *at the forefront* of linguistics. Here, two Polish researchers, Jan Baudoin de Courtnay and Mikołaj Kruszewski, had made a name for themselves (the former by theorizing verbal aspect in Slavic tongues). The great Ferdinand de Saussure—whose work was to become known very early on in Russia[1]—acknowledged his debt to them. The next generation of linguists born on Russian territory included Nikolai Trubetzkoy, the founder of phonology, the mighty Roman Jakobson, and Alexei Polivanov, the authority on the Eastern languages of the USSR. The reason for the success of Marr's doctrine does not lie with Russian "backwardness" (which was real enough in other respects). Instead, one should look to the curious story of how two forms of madness—both of them embodied by men from Georgia—came to meet.

Marr began his studies in 1866. It took twenty years of unremitting struggle before, in 1908, the first version of a theory sketched in 1888 finally was published. In the interim, Marr had stood at odds with the scientific community of both Moscow and Saint Petersburg. Inexplicably, he was elected to the Russian Academy of Sciences in 1912. His real change of fortune occurred with the 1917 Revolution. Taking advantage of the "sociological" bent of his work, Marr spent the next ten years retooling his theory with the trappings of ad hoc Marxism. (Meanwhile, authentic and legitimate Marxist linguistics was being developed, in particular by Bakhtin and Polivanov.)

Marr was not a Marxist gone bad: he was a crackpot who used an alibi when he found one. The Soviet regime would speak of him as a "spontaneous Marxist." From this point on, his destiny belonged to a higher power. His theory's singular success, which only grew after his death, had nothing to do with him as an individual or the merits of his thinking (which, for what it's worth, was cheerfully distorted later on). Marr became the instrument of a political program to control and, eventually, kill off Russian linguistics—which, given its status at the turn of the century, should by rights occupy the summit of global learning today. This occurred at the price of human lives, languages, and cultures.

Still, biography does shed light on his unlikely career and luck. When Marr was born in Koutais (Georgia), his father, a Scotsman, was already eighty-seven years old; he died eight years later. Marr's formative years followed the classic scenario: a beautiful, young mother with a son she worshipped and adored—and whose genius she would never presume to doubt.

Marr's father, on the other hand, took his leave from earthly existence by telling his child, "'You'll never amount to anything."[2] Twenty years later, Marr found a father figure in Viktor von Rosen, a scholar of Arabic and the only university instructor to take kindly to him (even though he, like his colleagues, predicted that his pupil would fail as a scholar). In his autobiography, Marr tells how he sought out Rosen on his deathbed to obtain the latter's approval when he finally managed, after twenty years, to get his thesis on the relationship between Caucasian and Semitic languages published.

From childhood on, Marr seems to have roused hostile sentiments on all sides; clearly, he held a very high opinion of himself. Poor, without a father, and foreign (although his native tongue was Georgian, he was registered as "English" at school), he was always left out by others. Aggressive, arrogant, and spiteful, Marr displayed (at least in embryonic form) all the traits of textbook paranoia: repressed homosexuality, the tendency to consider himself persecuted, and megalomania.[3]

He was already a workaholic as a boy, and his sole belief, for all his life, was in the virtue of labor. (According to his official hagiographer V. A. Mikhankova, he spent an average of eighteen hours a day toiling away.) At secondary school in Koutais, he joined the ranks of anti-religious and anti-Russian protest. In Saint Petersburg, where he enrolled in the department of Oriental Languages and studied Arabic, Georgian, and Armenian, Marr was active in the push for Georgian independence, dreaming that his homeland would one day be free from Russian domination.

Given his youthful convictions, Marr naturally took interest in his mother tongue—which, in this case, was no metaphor: Georgian was his mother's language, whereas his father spoke English and French. The domestic pidgin he encountered in his earliest years was surely one of the sources for the theory of linguistic hybridization he later elaborated. Researching the origins of Caucasian languages is what prompted Marr to track down the origins of speech itself.

As a member of an oppressed linguistic minority, Marr rushed to defend "minor" languages, dialects, unwritten idioms, and so-called backward groups against the "great languages of culture" for which his contemporaries, especially comparatists, reserved all their attention.[4] Hence his contempt for recent scholarship: "Indo-European linguistics is the flesh of the flesh and blood of the blood of bourgeois society, built on the oppression of the peoples of the East by murderous colonial policy."[5] Indeed, when "enlightened Europe" set out to study the language of Ireland, it did not devote "one-hundredth of the material resources to learning [the language] that it spent on destroying it, along with the Irish themselves."[6] Marr held the same view of the treatment meted out to the sole "Japhetic" people of Europe, the Basques, and he deplored

Imperial Russia's treatment of ethnic minorities such as the Chuvash of the Volga, whose "language was studied only to missionizing ends, for propagating Russian Orthodoxy."[7]

This champion of minority languages also heralded the right of women and the uneducated classes to have a voice. He observed disparagingly that "ethnologists . . . are . . . experts on peoples deprived of their rights, like women, who do not have equal rights with men."[8]

In fact, Marr first set out to compare Arabic and Georgian, claiming to be a comparative philologist of a new breed. He wanted to contest the Indo-European school of thought; doing so on his own terms would allow him to take advantage of his background and direct access to the languages of the Caucasus, which were unknown to Western Europeans. There was no risk, then, of being contradicted—unless one of the few professors of Georgian or Armenian in Russia happened to speak up. For a spell, the trick worked well enough to earn invitations to lecture in France and Germany.

Not content to compete with Indo-Europeanists, Marr sought to integrate their field and subordinate it to his own theory, hoping eventually to extend its scope to *all* the world's languages. The conceptual tool he employed to dismantle Indo-European linguistics was the notion of linguistic *crossing* and *hybridization*. Such a framework prohibits genealogies depicting the fragmentation of a "parent language" into successive branches. In point of fact, comparative linguists did not wish to declare Indo-European the root stock of a single, primitive language—as we have seen, advances in comparative philology led them to be abandon this idea once and for all—but an uncharitable and/or unscientific outsider could take figural images another way. Accordingly, Marr pretended that his opponents were enthralled by monogenism. This distortion was vital for demonstrating his own innovation: polygenesis, in lieu of monogenesis.

For Marr, the idea of a single parent language was nothing but a biblical legend, with as little basis in fact as the notion that the first human beings believed in One God. The Indo-European proto-language, supposedly the continuation of a single tongue, was a fiction blocking the correct view of how human languages emerged.

Marr took up the problem of origins by enlisting concrete data provided by the nascent fields of ethnography and paleontology. In theory, this approach represented an advance over old-fashioned schemes based on the story of Genesis and the myth of Babel, but in fact what he had to say hardly differed from mechanistic theories already on record.[9]

All the same, Marr did reject the hypothesis, often voiced by his forebears, that primitive language had developed out of onomatopoeia. In his estimation, the latter represented a fairly advanced stage of linguistic evolution. Instead, he contended, prehistoric human beings expressed themselves through gestures and mimicry—symbolism incapable of communicating abstract ideas. (This argument wasn't new, either). By his account, the shift to vocal language occurred with the invention of tools and was the work of *Homo faber*—a relatively late event in prehistory. It follows that language did not emerge in a single place, but developed simultaneously at multiple sites around the Mediterranean and beyond. The various languages appeared through a process of crossing that took different forms as the same words from primitive tribes combined in different ways. From the outset, then, multiple languages existed: "he sounds of speech have nothing to do with animal sounds emitted naturally. Of course, animal sounds still were made by man in his animal state. But the sounds of speech, so-called phonemes, are the result of human work . . . ; they were obtained as the result of collective labor—by all appearances, collective or choral song. At first, complexes of sounds were brought forth: the first sounds all were complex, all of them affricates with semi-vowels, abundantly preserved in Japhetic tongues."[10]

Marr proposed a theory of semantic derivation alongside his theory of phonology. At first, there were very few linguistic elements, and they exhibited a broad range of meaning. Over time, speech and communication evolved toward greater differentiation: "Contemporary linguistic paleontology enables us, in its [method of] research, to reach back to that epoch when there was just one word available . . . to use for all meanings of which human beings then were aware."[11] Like many logophiles before and after him, Marr appealed to metonymy, metaphor, and antiphrasis to explain the "semantic diffusion" of primitive words that once meant many things at the same time. For example, he claimed that *nebo* ("sky," in Russian) originally referred to clouds, light, stars, birds, the color blue, mountains, the head, both up and down, beginning and end, and more still.[12]

In this framework, the development of speech and language is tied to the prevailing view of the world: at the outset it is cosmic, then it is ethnic (tribal), and, later still, a matter of class (social). This scheme forms a succession of stages—which, over time, Marr emphasized and progressively "Marxified." Ultimately, linguistic evolution is supposed to culminate in a single language spoken by the members of a classless society.

Parallel to incorporating more and more languages into his system, Marr tried to reduce the number of basic semantic elements. The two sides of his project were totality and the smallest possible unit—the nucleus, or atom, of language. Between

1919 and 1926, Marr boiled these units down from twelve to four. From this point on, it would be possible to analyze all the world's languages on the basis of four elements: "sal," "ber," "yon," and "rosh." These four monosyllables correspond to four primitive tribal designations—which, by means of any number of phonetic tricks, Marr found in the names of ethnicities across the globe. Triumphantly, he announced: "Most recently, we have witnessed it established as fact that, from Japan and China to the coasts of the Atlantic Ocean, the fundamental terms of cultural and prehistoric life are one and the same. All the words of all languages come down to four elements."[13] These words are oddly reminiscent of a pronouncement made by Leibniz (whose inspiration was monogenetic, however): "Over much of our continent, in languages spoken today, there survive traces of an ancient language which spread far and wide; for a large number of names extends from the Atlantic Ocean to the Sea of Japan."[14]

In sum, Marr offered a theory of the birth, crossing, and evolution of languages along lines that form a pyramid. Its broad base comprises a host of embryonic tongues; pursuant to a series of typological changes, it narrows as it approaches the summit,[15] where the formerly diverse languages of the world merge into one. This last point, we should note, represents a late addition; initially, Marr was only interested in origins. (The Indo-European family can be pictured as the mirror image, but in reverse: an upside-down pyramid that extends from unity to multiplicity.)

In spite of his focus on hybridization and rejection of progressive diversification, Marr recognized that families of languages do exist. He even accepted the biblical scheme for the purposes of classification, borrowing the name of Noah's third son, Japheth, for the group of languages in which he claimed special expertise. This group initially consisted of Caucasian languages, but subsequently Marr delivered Basque from the clutches of Westerners and added it, too. Noah's other two sons, Shem and Ham, had already lent their names to the Semitic languages (Arabic, Hebrew, Aramaic, Syriac, and so on) and the Hamitic languages (Coptic, Ancient Egyptian, etc.). The reader will recall that when he was still pursuing his university studies, Marr had attempted to strike a bridge between Georgian and Arabic.

Indeed, in seeking to outmaneuver Western linguists, Marr took pains to show that Indo-European languages had in fact emerged from the Japhetic group. Given the latter's preeminence, he named his theoretical endeavor "Japhetidology" and set the Japhetides in opposition to "Aryans" (whose racial pedigree he rightly contested).

The Japhetic languages are supposed to represent a particularly early stage of development, now miraculously preserved in a few isolated pockets of Europe, Africa, and Asia—for instance, the Pyrenees, Caucasia, and the Pamir mountain range. Although "denied by the obscurantists of bourgeois European linguistics," they offer "striking proof" of Marr's theory.

Yet again, it would seem that our author was retailoring ideas articulated by Leibniz two centuries earlier in order to fit his own purposes. The latter had written:

> The languages derived from a large common stock are divided, and not without reason, into two types: so-called Japhetic languages and Aramaic languages, the one group covering the regions of the North and the other those of the South. As for our own Europe, I assign the whole of it to the North. If one relates the languages of the North to Japheth, it would only be right to attribute those of the South to the descendants of

> his brothers Shem and Ham. Mythologists have located Japetus and his son Prometheus, the maker of men, *near the Caucasus*, and Homer already equated the Arameans with Syrians. . . . *Persian, Armenian, and Georgian* seem to come from a mixture of languages—very archaic ones that these people's descendants would not recognize—[that is,] from Scythian and Aramaic tongues, as if they used to share the same territory.[16]

When critics confronted him with counterevidence—the documents that are the very stuff of comparative research—Marr would reply that he was working on the living material of languages still in use and making extrapolations from oral data. After all, the oldest of written languages, which go back a few millennia, aren't that old at all in comparison to tongues which never were written down. "Indo-European linguistics, having an object of study already established and long formalized—namely, the Indo-European languages of recorded history, based almost exclusively on rigid written norms, indeed, first and foremost dead languages—was unable, on its own, to illuminate the process of the emergence of speech in general or the origin of its species."[17]

This classification led Marr to devise a theory of stages to his own liking. In addition to the *prehistoric* stage, he assigned a handful of languages to an *intermediary* stage: Albanian, Chuvash, and Berber, which, he claimed, emerged as latter-day versions of the original Japhetic tongues.[18] The *historic* stage followed, which, as we have seen, is exemplified by Indo-European tongues. Once upon a time, pure, Japhetic languages were more abundant, and the entire landmass of Europe–Africa–Asia was peopled by Japhetides (who, however—and this point is important—did *not* constitute a race). Needless to say, the oldest cultures in the Mediterranean Basin and Asia Minor (the Getae, Sumerians, and so on) were

Japhetic. Over the course of millennia, their language evolved in keeping with social instinct, basic needs, and economic organization. Only material factors—not matters of physiology or racial typology—played a role in the process. Marr took a firm stand against the cult of heredity and Darwinism that prevailed among his contemporaries.

We have noted the central role of linguistic crossing for Marr, according to whom hybridization fuels not just evolution but also progress. The greater the cross-pollination that feeds it, the more "developed" a language will be.[19] Ultimately, mixing will bring forth the ideal language of humankind. Marr did not hold out hope for Esperanto, Volapük, or any other project arising from individual initiative. But since Esperanto had met with widespread interest in Eastern Europe, he saw fit, on various occasions, to make clear that he considered it a bourgeois invention:

> Humankind passes from plurilingualism to monolingualism. But no particular language, no matter how broad imperialist expansion may be, will be the language of the future. All former world languages have fallen, as will languages now flourishing or on the way to full diffusion, whether great or small in terms of speakers, both the class creations of the upper strata of society and . . . productions from the grassroots of the masses. Nor will they be replaced by the substitutes for human speech now pullulating like mushrooms: Esperanto, Ido, and whatever else individual initiative contrives. The common language of future humanity will combine all the wealth, all the positive qualities, of dead languages and those yet to die, languages that are still alive. The unified, universally-expressive language of the future is the posulate of a society encompassing all people, irrespective of class or nation. But is it possible to imagine . . . that such a process of utmost importance, communally creating a new means of communication, a new universal language, whether spoken or other in kind . . . , will flow forth unconsciously and

> instinctively, as occurred . . . when the man-animal first became human through the advent, growth, and evolution of speech? Obviously not. Humankind, now wiser, needs to step in and intervene. Having recognized this necessity and commanding the science of the origin and development of spoken language, it will strive, if not to create a single tongue, then to accelerate and steer the process. . . . Linguists have already been called upon to play this creative and active role, for which they need, above all, . . . real knowledge of human speech, not omitting any detail or element.[20]

Indeed, the nature of language itself may well be entirely renewed in the future, thanks to technologies that make speaking obsolete. To give credit where credit is due, Marr was ahead of the times in anticipating machine languages.

Clearly, Marr had no intention of promoting the hegemony of Russian. If, all the same, he acknowledged the importance of its study, this was not because Russian forms a branch of the Indo-European family or the lingua franca of the Soviet Union. Rather, its significance lies in its historical and material connections—disclosed by archeology and ethnography—with the tongues spoken by other peoples inhabiting the same territory.

In spite of his claims to be working on the living substance of language (and languages), Marr directed his gaze toward the future and the past—the realm of vision and prophecy, where concrete verification is impossible. At the same time, this aspect of his project was secondary, because he always developed his hypotheses after the fact and ad hoc, using data ready to hand that had not been collected with any rigor. Marr never worried about laws and systems, and a coherent synchronic or diachronic perspective held no interest for him. Marr's realm of election was pure fantasy. As such, one may ask about the content, origin, and even value of his ideas (which was occasionally positive), or explore the historical role that they played. It is bewildering, however, to find out that a serious-minded American linguist saw fit to devote an entire volume to refuting his linguistic analyses point by point.[21]

As we have noted, Marr's career began thirty years before the Revolution—in which he seems to have taken no part. It ended seventeen years later, and Marr died ten years after Lenin. The culminating phase of his theory, when it became a kind of state religion, lasted from 1930 to 1950; in essence, it witnessed its greatest triumph after its creator no longer wandered the Earth.

For years on end, the scorn and mockery of academics strengthened Marr's conviction that he was right and everyone else was wrong. From 1920 on, his position became increasingly secure in institutional terms, and he managed to obtain support from institutions outside the university. Marr's megalomania became more pronounced on every score, and his written output assumed demented proportions. The texts that make up his selected works, which appeared from 1933–1937, fill five large volumes. The author's complete bibliography consists of fifteen pages of small print and lists 507 publications! (Needless to say, there's quite a bit of repetition.) In spite of poor health, Marr ran himself ragged doing fieldwork (mainly in the Caucasus, but also in Basque country and Northern Africa), sacrificing every last bit of his private life to the cause. In 1930, as his son lay dying, he went to his bedside with a pile of work to keep himself occupied.

As the scope of his project grew bigger and bigger, Marr's ambitions exceeded the force any single human being can muster. The scholar needed disciples, and they could never be numerous or devoted enough. Marr ceaselessly trained collaborators and set up new research teams and institutes—all of which stood under his personal supervision. In a word, he was always looking for *more*: more languages to integrate into his designs, more publications, more financial support, more sites of inquiry, more commissions, and more distinction. From 1924 on, in addition to the obligations of his university position, Marr was busy directing the Leningrad Library and *six* research institutes. After 1930, as the cult of personality thrived, the "Japhetic" institutions he headed were simply named after him. He stood at the height of fame when he expired from exhaustion, but surely he died a happy man.

Marr, a full-blooded glossomaniac, might well have met with the same fate as someone like Jean-Pierre Brisset. However, it was his good fortune that his folly came into the orbit of another kind of madness: Stalinism. Even as he was eclipsed as a speaking subject, what he said met with approbation, which made him a useful instrument for political machination.

By 1928, Marr held an academic position; he was crowned with honors and incomparably busy. For all that, he hardly enjoyed the recognition of his peers. When he delivered lectures at the Academy of Sciences, linguists guarded a prudent silence—which he found exasperating. Mocking him behind his back, a "cabal" periodically purged his circle of his faithful followers. The so-called *Yazykfront* ("Linguistic Front") formed, which attacked him for substituting Marrism for Marxism. Mortal combat ensued. Marr retaliating by accusing opponents of trying to reintroduce the tenets of bourgeois linguistics under Marxist cover. Members of the Linguistic Front, he maintained, could not fathom the government's policy or the new structure of Soviet society—hence their erroneous claims. When Evgeny Polivanov sought to demolish Japhetic theory in the name of Marxism at a debate at the Communist Academy in 1929, he was banished from scholarly institutions.

The partisans of real languages took to the field against a fantasist who had dreamed up a language out of thin air. Soon, the dream would turn into a nightmare—and without the dreamer even recognizing what was happening.

Having been challenged on doctrinal grounds and feeling vulnerable on account of his "spontaneous" Marxism, Marr, between 1928 and 1930, devoted himself to mastering the finer points of dialectical materialism, altering his theory from top to bottom so it would conform to orthodoxy. Now, he introduced the concept of language as a superstructure and claimed that linguistic change occurs in "leaps" when there are shifts to the economic base. This perspective, the best-known feature of Marrism, led him to posit the priority of class over nationality in matters of language. Absurdly, proletarians speaking different languages were supposed to understand each other better than proletarians and members of the bourgeoisie using the same language; moreover, all national and class languages would one day fuse and bring forth a single, unified tongue.

In 1930, although "unaffiliated," Marr headed the delegation of scientific and technical workers at the 16th Congress of the Soviet Communist Party, where he delivered a speech that commanded notice: merely a fellow traveler, nevertheless he had always, etc. . . . At the same gathering, Comrade Stalin held forth on the culture of the USSR, where diverse nationalities were evolving toward socialism and a single language.

For the first time, the thinking of the two Georgians converged. Stalin recognized the utility of a theory that posited the progressive unification of different languages as national ways of life merged. For his part, Marr saw that his glory was finally assured. (Alas, he wouldn't have much time to reap the benefits in person.) Immediately following the congress, he joined the Party and became vice president of the Academy of Sciences, which he set about "reorganizing." More than ever, the linguists in the Academy bit their tongues—and soon, they wouldn't be able to say anything, even if they tried. In her account of his difficulties with the Yazykfront, written some twenty years later, Marr's official biographer V. A. Mikhankova modestly refrains from mentioning names; the sole exception is Polivanov, who devoted his life to transcribing the unwritten languages of the Soviet Union and did not belong to the Linguistic Front (and wound up being liquidated in the 1930s). Luckily for them—and for linguistics—his friends Trubetzkoy and Jakobson had moved abroad in 1926 and reformed their Moscow group, which would achieve renown as the Circle of Prague. Bakhtin, the author of *Marxism and the Philosophy of Language,* probably survived because he borrowed, for publication, the names of Valentin Nikolaevich Voloshinov and Pavel Nikolaevich Medvedev (although they also were purged).

Marr succeeded in getting his protégé Ivan Meshchaninov elected to the Academy in 1932, thereby ensuring the continuation of his project. Shortly before his death in 1933, he published the results of his efforts over the previous five years, *Marx and the Problems of Language,* as well as an autobiography; the delight the author takes in vindication over the enemies he faced since childhood is evident.

Marrist doctrine remained ascendant until 1950, when Stalin reoriented policies involving "the National Question." Recognizing that language is a simple tool of power—not a matter of social class and superstructure—he sent Marrism packing. It was clear to all and sundry that the emperor had no clothes.[22]

The meeting of minds might have been a misunderstanding, but Stalin cannily exploited it. In the end, Marr's theory provided cover for the project of Russification that the General Secretary ramped up at the end of the 1930s—in complete contradiction to the scholar's vision of a single language uniting all others. At the very moment that the policy of Russification paid off, relegating national languages to secondary status once and for all, Stalin summarily killed off Marrism. In so doing, he even managed to avoid going back on his word. At the 16th Congress of the Soviet Communist Party, and in line with Marr's ideas, Stalin had defended the thesis that when socialism finally triumphed, a single tongue would emerge from the mixing of all languages. Retaining this formulation, he simply postponed its advent to a later date. In 1950, then, Stalin took up the program of 1930 as it stood: (1) unified socialist culture among diverse nationalities; and (2) a single, new language—but for the very distant future. What went missing along the way was the means for bringing about such change. Now, language would evidently transform of its own accord. The dynamic between "superstructure" and "infrastructure" fueling changes in leaps and bound was gone. Once strife had been banished from society, linguistic sublimation would finally occur.

In spite of everything that has been written about this period,[23] the relationship between Marr and Stalin remains obscure. Did Stalin really need Marr and his followers to be able to implement his political designs? If nothing else, it is certain that Stalin's policy toward national languages (which was not consistent, either) did not leave clear, explicit traces anywhere in the Marrist project. What's more, although Stalin discarded, in 1950, everything in Marr's theory concerning the origin of languages (its mythical dimension) as well as its ideological component (the idea of class languages and of language as a superstructure)—for which he no longer had any use—he held fast to its utopian dimension. Whereas the first component of Marrist theory made Soviet linguistics look ridiculous, and the second did the same to Marxism, the third was easy to retain without running any risks: analysis and facts are irrelevant to faraway promises.

As is the case with any "reasoning madman," Marr's thought has sensible and even positive aspects. Everyone knows how easy it is to arrive at mistaken conclusions by way of images or quotations taken out of context, and it's particularly easy to distort the thinking of someone whose works are not directly accessible. Not everything that Marr says is off the mark; by picking and choosing passages, one might present him as a brilliant precursor of sociolinguistics or ethnolinguistics. Without going quite that far, it seems only honest to me to try to bring out his merits. In *Marxism and the Philosophy of Language*, Bakhtin quotes Marr on five occasions, and in a way that makes him appear eminently reasonable. One cannot fail to be intrigued by this fact. Bakhtin was writing in 1928. Did opportunism or prudence motivate him? It was impossible for him not to know that Marr, as Trubetzkoy put it, was "mad, utterly mad." Surely Bakhtin referred to him because he saw a glimmer of reason.

Marr was quite right that the philological method had long kept linguists from devoting attention to the living evidence of spoken languages. He was also right that the latter require a different approach than written languages. Likewise, if one proposes to study human communication, it would be remiss not to take social factors into account. After all, social dialects exist, as do class-based ways of using language (which, *contra* Saussure's homogenizing view, is never neutral or homogeneous). Marr was right that workers don't speak like people who have attended private schools, and that elites have always managed to come up with forms of interaction inaccessible to "ordinary mortals": once upon a time it was Greek, then Latin, then French (in the early modern period); now it's English. He was right that every language includes hybridized elements to one degree or another (as is evident in regionalisms, for example, or forms resulting from colonizers imposing their language on native populations). It's quite true that efforts to reconstruct Indo-European facilitated the emergence of racial doctrine, whose ruinous effects are notorious. Finally, recent research in the field of paleontology would seem to confirm that gestures really did precede the emergence of spoken language.[24]

So the reader may arrive at a more accurate view of the various aspects of Marr's thinking, the appendix includes a number of excerpts from his works.

9

THE QUEEN OF THE NIGHT: LANGUAGE AND THE UNCONSCIOUS—SPIRITUALIST AND RELIGIOUS GLOSSOLALIA

1. ON EARTH AS IT IS IN HEAVEN

1890–1900: the turn of the century. In Vienna, Sigmund Freud, just back from Paris, was hard at work inventing psychoanalysis. In Geneva, Ferdinand de Saussure, also newly returned from Paris, was beginning his journey across the desert: a distinguished scholar of Sanskrit, he had just turned down Michel Bréal's chair at the Collège de France and withdrawn to elaborate what, from 1906 on, would become the celebrated *Course in General Linguistics*, the foundation of modern work in the field. Freud was not yet Freud,[1] and Saussure was not yet Saussure, but both men were in the process of becoming who they would be.

Meanwhile, in Paris, Camille Flammarion was publishing book after book—with stupendous print runs for the time—defending the thesis of the plurality of inhabited worlds. Keenly interested in extraterrestrial life and communication with beings on other planets, the general public developed a taste for science fiction. The suggestion that there are channels of water on Mars fired the imagination: "In . . . 1877," Flammarion wrote, "the planet being in its greatest proximity, straight lines resembling canals were discovered, and the question of possible inhabitants of this new country and future communication with them were raised."[2] Not only did Flammarion believe that thinking and speaking beings inhabited the red planet; he thought they formed a single nation, without dialects or other tongues, a civilization more advanced than those of the Earth.

More or less everywhere in the world, from Armenia to California, from Sweden to Switzerland, and England to India, Christians renewed a tradition of the primitive Church: "speaking in tongues," or *glossolalia*. At the same time, the spiritualist movement, which believed in reincarnation and communication with disembodied spirits, was attracting a growing number of adherents, who grouped around famous mediums; most often, the latter were women.

In brief, in parallel to the rise of scientific thought—empiricism, materialism, and positivism—the Western world witnessed the resurgence of the irrational, which evidently represented a kind of defense mechanism against excessive rationality. The same age that was so committed to progress and modernity—so eager to renounce superstition in all its forms—brought forth literature and music that delighted in supernatural themes, magic, fantasy, and myth. Aren't the visions of Freud already there, in germinal form, in Wagner (and, before him, in the works of the German Romantics)?

Twin sisters, linguistics and psychoanalysis might well have shared a womb in Paris as early as 1885. Freud and Saussure were both in the French capital, but they did not meet. It was not in Paris or Vienna, but Geneva, that two sciences destined to exercise decisive influence on the twentieth century first crossed paths—before the world at large, or even their founders, had recognized them as such. Saussure did not encounter Freud here, but Théodore Flournoy. A physician, philosopher, and professor of psychology at the University of Geneva (where a chair had been specially created for him in 1891), Flournoy was an innovator with a particular passion for subliminal mental processes.

A mediator facilitates every meeting. In this case, the role was played by a medium with exceptional gifts, Hélène Smith (real name: Catherine-Élise Müller, b. 1861 in Martigny [Valais]), whom Flournoy would make the stuff of legend. In January 1900, just as Freud's *Interpretation of Dreams* appeared in print, Flournoy published *From India to the Planet Mars*. The book would sound like a work of science fiction, were it not for the subtitle: *A Study of a Case of Somnambulism with Glossolalia*.

The subject matter is six years of unconscious creative activity—not a novel so much as an account of how Hélène Smith created three novels of her own. In each one, she is the star. The first is an Oriental tale set in the fifteenth century; Hélène is a Hindu princess, and Flournoy her husband. The second takes place on Mars, with later episodes on Uranus and the Moon; the heroine communicates with spirits that have taken refuge on these planets (in keeping with a tradition we have noted). Finally, the third, "historical" novel draws inspiration from the works of Alexandre Dumas, with Hélène cast as Marie-Antoinette, playing opposite Joseph Balsamo, alias Cagliostro.

The story of how these "subliminal novels" came to be reads like a novel in its own right; the relationship between the medium and her observer is a romance. But that's another story: under slightly different circumstances, Flournoy might have been the founder of psychoanalysis, with a starting point different from Freud's.[3]

Belief in reincarnation corresponds, in terms of time, to belief in extraterrestrial beings, which involves space. It was only natural for Hélène Smith that dreams of previous lives existed alongside dreams of other planets, just as journeys beyond the Earth compete with voyages into the past or future in science fiction. What made her visions interesting for linguists was the invented languages they contained, which were intended to make events seem credible. When the medium spoke of real countries, real languages—or languages that were supposed to be real—stood at issue. Her Orientalist tale features pseudo-Sanskrit, about which Saussure was asked to provide his learned opinion. Imaginary countries have imaginary languages; hence the fascination that the medium's Martian (and other planetary languages) held for Flournoy and, after him, the French linguist Victor Henry. For the seer, these tongues were genuine; the same was not true for the observer.

As a rule, the scene would play out as follows. In the evening, the drawing room (usually Flournoy's) is bathed in subdued light and the atmosphere is muted. Done with the day's work as a model employee at a commercial enterprise, Hélène Smith is "granting a séance" to a small circle of initiates. The latter include Flournoy and his friend, Professor Auguste Lemaître. The two academics occupy an exceptional and somewhat ambiguous position, insofar as they are not "believers" but neutral observers, at least in principle; in effect, they are taking part in the reality that now unfolds. Hélène knows the scholars are skeptics—"independent minds"—but she does not wish to acknowledge the fact. Typically, when a medium senses a presence of this kind, it has an inhibiting effect and "nothing happens." Fortunately, in this instance, things not only happen, but also it is clear that her mediumistic activity, which abounds in linguistic, literary, and artistic productions,[4] occurs largely for Flournoy's benefit and to meet his expectations.

The participants are seated at the round table that is the conventional setting for such meetings, resting their hands on its surface. Hélène concentrates and progressively loses touch with her surroundings. Before long, she achieves autohypnosis, culminating in a relatively deep and lengthy sleep. The medium is now in the "twilight state" conducive to contact with spirits; the latter manifest themselves through the table's motion, automatic writing on the part of the medium, messages she hears and transcribes, and direct vocalization. In this last case (alas, the tape recorder hasn't been invented yet), Flournoy or another participant feverishly takes down the torrent of words pouring forth. One day, Hélène will speak Martian; the next time, it might be Sanskrit. The various cycles of her "subliminal imagination" (in the parlance of the times) can be present simultaneously—in the course of a single séance, that is—or they might alternate. Most often, the visions are not interpreted immediately: it takes a few days, or even weeks, for the medium to provide a translation of the transmission that has taken place, which is dictated by "Léopold"—her special interpreter and guardian angel.

There is nothing inherently remarkable about Hélène Smith. Her case belongs to a long tradition of supernatural communication combining mysticism and spiritualism. The Genevan medium had a distinguished forebear in Emanuel Swedenborg, the Stockholm visionary, who published an account of his contact with other worlds in 1758: *The Earths in Our Solar System, Which Are Called Planets, and the Earths in the Starry Heaven, Their Inhabitants, and the Spirits and Angels There: From Things Heard and Seen.* Between January 23 and November 11, 1784, Swedenborg claims, he communicated by turns with the inhabitants of Mercury, Jupiter, Mars, Saturn, Venus, the Moon, and other heavenly bodies. Hereby, an ideal language was employed: "This language excels that of words, it reveals thought itself in its true form."[5] Another case that bears comparison is that of Friederike Hauffe, the "seer of Prevorst," in 1830. In a half-somnambulistic trance, she would speak a tongue "akin to the one spoken in Jacob's time," a language that all human beings supposedly bear within, and communicate with spirits. This language came from the heart, not the mind, and expressed the inherent nature and value of things; a single word could capture the sense of a whole speech in everyday German.[6]

Many other visionaries would follow Hélène Smith. According to Flammarion (who was an adherent of the movement himself, although he mocked "false spiritualist journeys"), cases of glossolalia and xenoglossia under the influence of spirits and communication with other planets, already in vogue during the second half of the nineteenth century, became all the rage in the early 1900s. Fanned by Hélène Smith's success, overheated imaginations competed to outdo each other in creating pseudo-languages. In 1906, in the United States, James H. Hyslop recorded the case of a lady he called Mrs. Smead,[7] who also constructed a Martian narrative, then another sequence of events set on Jupiter, based on visions she transformed into drawings (as the Genevan medium had done), auditory hallucinations, and messages in automatic writing.[8] Hélène Smith herself raised the stakes. Following the publication of *From India to the Planet Mars* and her break with Flournoy,[9] she expanded her repertoire of extraterrestrial tongues considerably.

For an overview of how languages invented under hypnosis flourished, one may consult a work published in 1934, *La Mediumnité polyglotte*. Unfortunately, its author, Ernesto Bozzano, adhered to spiritualism, which deprives his testimony of credibility; most accounts are also second-hand. All the same, the book provides an idea of the phenomenon's scope. From about 1920 on, glossolalia seemed to become less frequent in the spiritualist milieu. As we will see, this was not the case for religious glossolalia.

On this score, we now turn to 1980s New York: the Upper West Side, outside a small brick building in an area where social changes are in full swing. The neighborhood is home to a variety of ethnicities and intellectuals of "new bohemian" stripe; the backdrop is poverty and vigorous immigration. Stepping inside the place of worship, one encounters a dense crowd stretching back to the street. It's hard to get in, much less find a seat. Evidently, no one is presiding over events, and there's no telling whether a service is even underway. A woman stands up, raises her arms to heaven, and shouts "Praise the Lord!" Congregants include many Black, Puerto-Rican, and Latin-American people, largely of modest means; most of them are women.[10] Other members of the flock rise and perform the same gesture. Bit by bit, the right atmosphere sets in and excitement grows. There's still no sign of anybody in charge. All of a sudden, a voice announces the number of a hymn. The faithful sing in unison, linking their arms in a chain, and the emotional pitch rises. Then, abruptly, everyone freezes. A woman gets up to speak and a wave of syllables without meaning pours forth. The sound is melodious; the unknown language is strongly accentuated, like a chant—almost a song. Arms stretch into the air. When she's done, a man rises to interpret what she has said, according to the words of Saint Paul (1 Corinthians 14:26–28):

> When ye come together, every one hath a psalm, hath a teaching, hath a revelation, hath a tongue, hath an interpretation. Let all things be done unto edifying.

> If any man speaketh in an unknown tongue, let it be by two, or at the most three, and that by course; and let one interpret:
> But if there be no interpreter, let him keep silence in the church; and let him speak to himself, and to God.

What the interpreter says is conventional and banal; it holds little interest on its own. But that doesn't bother anyone—isn't the most important thing that the rite, the mediation of the divine message through the "gift of tongues," has taken place?

Let's go back to 1900, the culminating point of glossolalia in spiritualist circles. In Topeka, a small Kansas town deep in the American heartland, a group of the faithful has gathered around Pastor Charles Parham for Bible study. Now, on New Year's Eve, they are finally touched by the "tongues of fire" of which the Gospels speak. Their lips open: strange, harmonious, and unknown words issue forth, manifesting the presence of the Holy Spirit. The Pentecostalist Church is born. Parham's followers will go on to make the ability to speak in tongues a new kind of baptism, to be undergone by each new congregant. In one of those convergences that recur throughout history, similar movements are starting elsewhere in the world, especially in Armenia; a certain number of the faithful will set out from here for the United States and meet up with their counterparts in California. Today, the Pentecostalist Church has some eight million members across the globe, most of them in the United States.

Inasmuch as the sociocultural contexts for spiritualist and religious glossolalia differ markedly, inasmuch as the meaning, value, and function attached to it is far from uniform for the *speaking subject* and for others in the group, we can place such practices along a continuum for the purposes of formal analysis. Since this "threshold experience" crosses the border between the imaginary and the real, the perspectives of the subject and the observer (who is trying to be objective) cannot coincide at any level.

The space we have given to Hélène Smith is not meant to suggest that spiritualist glossolalia is superior to the religious gift of tongues. Her case is exemplary for two reasons. For one, there's the phenomenon itself. The languages she devised, especially Martian, displayed a degree of sophistication, consistency, and permanence that, in spite of their "childish" nature, had enough of a linguistic character to merit the notice of parties as distinguished as Saussure and Victor Henry. Comparable formal perfection is rarely attained by other cases on record. The second reason concerns the observer and the quality of his observations. Whereas cases of pathological glossolalia have received the attention of psychiatrists, instances involving mediums or members of religious sects have, for the most part, been described by believers alone. Only recently have researchers with a neutral view of the phenomenon of pathological glossolalia begun studying it through the lens of experimental psychology.[11] That said, these methods may not be entirely appropriate, given the difficulty of establishing objective facts under such conditions. Thus, Flournoy's study, in spite of the author's ambiguous relationship with the medium—if not because of it—remains a model of investigation. Had the scholar not been personally involved in the spiritualist séances, he would have had nothing to observe.[12]

But let's assume that the right conditions have been given for glossolalia, whether spiritualist or religious in kind. A nonbelieving observer will need to distinguish between authentic glossolalia and mere xenoglossia; as a rule, believers confuse the two because what counts for them is the *value* of the phenomenon, not its *nature*. Hélène Smith did not care about the difference between Martian and Sanskrit. From her standpoint, both languages derived from the same experience: communication with disembodied spirits. Likewise, Pentecostalists speaking in tongues do not distinguish between human language and that of angels—even though Holy Writ clearly does. (The miracle of Pentecost is a true "gift of tongues"—xenoglossia, in other words—whereas Saint Paul clearly speaks of glossolalia in his Epistle to the Corinthians.)

Glossolalia concerns the capacity to *invent* a pseudo-language that, depending on how elaborate and stable it is, resembles a real language. The subject is possessed by speech that she or he does not understand, requiring the intercession of an inspired interpreter. In Hélène Smith's case, the interpreter was a subpersonality ("Léopold")—but for her another being entirely. Language of this kind, it is claimed, emanates from the angels, God, the Holy Spirit, or an extraterrestrial intelligence. Alternatively, we have seen, it may be thought to represent the rediscovery of the original language of myth. According to Saint Paul, glossolalia is charismatic but still subordinate to interpretation (which is charismatic, too). Glossolalic expression is prayer that arises from sentiment, not the intellect. The gift of tongues never brings forth the kind of language one might hear walking down the street.

Xenoglossia, in contrast, involves miraculous knowledge of a foreign language that the speaker has never learned. Once the hypothesis of direct communication with otherworldly spirits—or a gift from God—has been eliminated, one must establish an objective order of facts and seek a rational explanation.

As a phenomenon, xenoglossia depends on the belief of participants. Such belief fosters a lifeworld that appears to be a matter of objective fact. However, it does not belong to the realm of nature so much as that of culture—that is, it is created by a culturally determined mode of perception. The spiritualist milieu, like its Pentecostalist counterpart, legitimates xenoglossia through faith, which promotes it to the status of reality. When a nonbeliever is present, as a rule nothing happens at all.

It is hardly surprising, then, that there are no reliable accounts of the miracle of someone who has had no previous contact with, or knowledge of, a language suddenly making it his or her own. But many reports share a common feature: within a closeknit community, a *stranger* will appear and recognize, in what the medium or individual with the gift of tongues is saying, his native language—one that belongs to a locale as far away as possible and is unknown to anyone at the gathering; the new arrival (if not a believer already) will promptly convert and become an ardent propagator of the faith.

Thus, in Palermo in 1853, a sixteen-year-old girl, Ninfa Filiberto, spent several months in a state of hysteria—with convulsions, cataleptic fits, and so on. At various points, she would speak in the Tuscan dialect, English, or French. Eager to behold a supernatural event, people crowded round. An observer was never found wanting. Like Hélène Smith, she displayed a different personality each time she spoke another language.[13]

Another case occurred in New York, in 1890. Laura, the daughter of Judge John Worth Edmonds, spoke in modern Greek (a language she had never learned), with the spirit of another participant's son at a spiritualist séance; the visitor formally declared that he recognized his mother tongue.[14]

The Pentecostalist tradition offers scores of similar examples. This is hardly remarkable, given that the gift of tongues is the founding article of the faith ("They . . . began to speak with other tongues, as the Spirit gave them utterance" [Acts 2: 4]). It would grow tiresome to run through all the instances on record when a Jew, upon hearing one of the faithful speaking the purest Hebrew, is said to have fallen to his knees to praise the Lord (or someone from the Philippines, China, or the Arab world recognized his mother tongue in the mouth of a child or an illiterate peasant and did the same). But I can't resist the story of the missionary who went to deepest Africa to preach the Gospel to a tribe of cannibals and found himself tied to a stake with the imminent prospect of winding up in a stew. He didn't know a word of the native tongue. Then—and just in time—God gave him the power to deliver a sermon to the tribesmen. Not only did his tormentors set him free and bow down; they converted en masse and renounced anthropophagy forever. The event is supposed to have occurred in 1922.[15]

A small Bavarian village in the 1950s was the site of another wonder. As the result of a mishap, Therese Neumann, an uneducated peasant, had been bedridden for years. With stigmata regularly appearing on her palms, she would experience visions of different times and places; usually, they involved the life and passion of Christ and were "in the original." The seer would repeat to onlookers words she had heard in Aramaic or another tongue; she herself spoke only a dialect of Low German. According to her hagiographer Ennemond Boniface,[16] some ten experts in Oriental languages took note of the phenomenon and authenticated her xenoglossic utterances. (Once again, there's no guarantee that the report is objective.)

In the 1960s, the American journalist John Sherrill, a recent convert to Pentecostalism, went to great lengths to have the gift of tongues scientifically verified. He put together a number of recordings and submitted them to six linguists. Alas, none of the experts could recognize even a fragment of any language known to exist. In keeping with his faith, Sherrill concluded that the languages of the world, past and present, are too numerous for professionals to take them all into account.

If a miracle does occur in such cases, it might concern the hearer more than the speaker. That, at any rate, is one way of interpreting the biblical story of Pentecost. Instead of the Apostles possessing linguistic gifts, it might be that the men and women who were listening to them heard (or believed to hear) words in their native tongue—a UN without interpreters! For the great Goethe the speech of the Apostles at Pentecost represented "that simple, universal language, which many a great mind has sought to no avail. Everyone thought he was hearing his own language because he understood these miracle-workers [*Wundermänner*]. . . . Yet it was not given that all should have ears to hear."[17] According to one German exegete, the event involved a kind of mystical Esperanto, a hybrid tongue: "[The Apostles] spoke the primal tongue that, in a sense, contained the elements of real, historical languages—just as the Primitive Church relates to national churches."[18] Thus did xenoglossia, through varying interpretations, become an antidote to the dispersion of Babel.

In all this, beyond the phenomenon itself, what fascinates us is the *idea* of innate competence in an unfamiliar language. As we have seen, the notion is constantly cropping up in very different times, places, and contexts. There really is a universal myth at work, then, a collective fantasy. Is there anyone who hasn't dreamed of commanding a wholly unfamiliar foreign language? Who hasn't dreamed of speaking another language without effort? A thin line separates nighttime dreams and those of waking hours, and it's readily crossed in the "twilight" states that define mystical or spiritualist experience.

Still, it seems that the phenomenon of xenoglossia cannot be reduced to dreams, autosuggestion, or collective hallucination—at least not entirely. In some cases, scraps of foreign languages really have been produced. Hélène Smith's quasi-Sanskrit, which Saussure examined at length (and to the point of fabricating a pseudo-Latin along the same lines to demonstrate what Smith was generating), contained a small share of actual Sanskrit. If her "Martian" amounted to a pseudo-language and posed no great mystery (we will return to the principles on which it was based), her Sanskrit confronted observers with a veritable enigma. The only scientifically valid hypothesis—which, needless to say, is what Flournoy advanced in his study[19]—is that unconscious assimilation of foreign languages had taken place. At some point, the medium must have had a Sanskrit grammar in her possession and committed parts of it to memory unaware. This view is all the more plausible in light of the fact that what she said during the "Hindu" séances seemed to come from visual impressions, not auditory ones. She pronounced the words in the French manner; indeed, it is difficult to imagine where she might ever have *heard* Sanskrit, given that only a handful of scholars in Geneva knew the language in the first place. Even though faithful spiritualists will reject such an explanation, it largely accounts for cases where xenoglossia can be demonstrated (for instance, the well-known story of the priest's maid who spoke Greek and Latin in a delirium because she had heard him reading aloud in these languages).

The thirteenth-century mystic, Saint Elisabeth of Schönau, seems to have spoken fluent Latin in her moments of transport. As a woman, she had not been taught the language, but it is impossible that she would never have heard it spoken. Anyone so inclined may, of course, invoke telepathy, remote reading, or even intrauterine assimilation (as a recent hypothesis would have it), but the unconscious mind and subliminal memory provide a perfectly adequate scheme of explanation that allows us to avoid obscure, supernatural forces of questionable scientific merit. What's more, specialists in foreign-language learning will hardly be surprised to hear that, under conditions where normal inhibitions are suspended, people often express themselves readily in a language they know incompletely. (And "performance," which Chomsky opposes to "competence," is marked by "slips" even in one's mother tongue.)

No direct connection, in either temporal or spatial terms, seems to exist between such phenomena, at least in the Western world. Indeed, they routinely occur all over the place. There are universal psychological roots, it would seem, but they manifest themselves when social, historical, and cultural conditions legitimate them—or, on the contrary, repress them too severely.

Whether out in the open or underground, glossolalic tradition has never really stopped. The resurgence of belief in the supernatural at the turn of the twentieth century, exemplified as much by Pentecostal revivalism as by rampant spiritualism, was a continuation of a subterranean current in popular culture reaching back to pagan times. It proved all the more vigorous inasmuch as, for the first time since the Middle Ages, the Church did not see fit to snuff it out. For centuries, the Church had acted to denounce superstition and stifle heretical practices (although claiming to be Christian, the spiritualist movement always stood at odds with official religion). Now, more and more, modern science was calling the Church's authority into question. Witches were no longer burned at the stake in the nineteenth century, but a woman speaking in tongues, even if she's a saint, was cause for worry. Was she possessed by Satan? Just think of Linda Blair talking backward in *The Exorcist.*

On the whole, the judgment that Saint Paul passed on glossolalia was rather unfavorable. He was suspicious about the excessive emotion, spontaneity, and untampered enthusiasm on display. This outlook would continue more or less uninterrupted throughout the Church's history (especially after the Montanist episode):

> For if I pray in an unknown tongue, my spirit prayeth, but my understanding is unfruitful. What is it then? I will pray with the spirit, and I will pray with the understanding also: I will sing with the spirit, and I will sing with the understanding also. [. . .]
>
> Yet in the church I had rather speak five words with my understanding, that by my voice I might teach others also, than ten thousand words in an unknown tongue (1 Corinthians 14: 14–19).

During the Middle Ages, a clear distinction came to hold between glossolalia, an elusive and unstable phenomenon, and xenoglossia, which the Acts of the Apostles had authenticated and declared legitimate. Saint Anthony of Padua and Saint Francis of Assisi were renowned for the latter. However, the official Church did not recognize the practice of glossolalia in its prophets. Once the phenomenon had been relegated to the fringes, is it surprising that it resurfaced in popular movements in the Cevennes and Wales, in the excesses of Jansenism and other dissident sects both Protestant and Orthodox (for instance, Pentecostalists and lrvingites in England, and Khlysty in Russia)?

We shouldn't make the mistake of thinking that our high-tech and ultra-rational civilization has put an end to such fantasies. If, for the time being, spiritualist glossolalia seems to have entered a dormant phase, religious glossolalia is thriving—at least in the United States. Finally, and to end on a humorous note, I'd like to point out that California, where sects abound that are open to the influence of occultism and parapsychology, is home to a group of UFO enthusiasts who have been "contacted" by extraterrestrial beings. These people, who intermarry within the community, are permanently in touch with goings-on in outer space, thanks to their mastery of alien tongues; the women are even supposed to be impregnated by visitors from the stars. Maybe their children look like E.T.

2. *SANCTA SIMPLICITAS*

When considering a case of glossolalia, a number of questions arise. Does what is said resemble a real language? How can one tell the difference by hearing alone between an unknown language and one that's made up? And since anybody can think up a pseudo-language,[20] is there such a thing as a universal and innate glossolalic "competence"? Do constants exist, independent of the speaker's mother tongue? Does glossolalia produce anything meaningful? Can we identify correspondences between stable signifiers and signifieds—in other words, is it possible to break up the flow of sounds along formal lines (pauses, tonic accents, points of demarcation[21]) and semantic units?

If all these productions are the same in nature, they must still be situated along a continuum ranging from "incomplete phonation" (cries, onomatopoeia, babble, mere noise) to the systematicity evident in elaborate creations such as Hélène Smith's Martian. At first glance, the latter looks like a real language—a genuine code of stable signs that admit analysis in terms of form and meaning, with grammatical rules enabling meaningful enunciations in relation to outside referents.[22] However impoverished its structure and lexicon, the medium's Martian would seem to perform the double function of language postulated by Émile Benveniste.[23] On the one hand, it is *semiotic:* a system with identifiable signs. On the other, it is *semantic:* signs can be combined in utterances to produce meaning. Over the course of seven years, Hélène Smith added quite a lot to her repertoire, but she changed the meaning or form of words only rarely. She really did use Martian as a language—that said, she was its only speaker (at least on Earth!).

The most intriguing feature of Martian is its vocabulary, which lies worlds apart from its inventor's native tongue. Hélène Smith's unconscious mind excelled at neological innovation. The linguist Victor Henry sought the key in the languages—English, German, Hungarian, Italian, and, of course, French—that she might have absorbed in childhood. In particular, he focused on finding traces of Hungarian, which was the language of her father (and which she had never spoken). The force of the paternal tongue—so rich in implications for psychoanalysts—had escaped Flournoy. All the same, most of the "etymologies" that Henry proposed are pretty unconvincing. At any rate, they never won over Saussure, who took exception to his colleague's fantastical derivations. In his correspondence, Saussure heaps scorn on Henry's "frivolous amusements, fantasies, and wild, almost insane conjectures."

Saussure's commitment to scientific rigor led him to neglect the dimension of dreaming: the first encounter between linguistics and psychoanalysis was a bit of a flop. Any linguist today, looking at Henry's work, would have to agree with

Saussure. All the same, it is only right, in my eyes, to look at the effort in overall terms, not in the details of its application (which often seems ridiculous). In effect, Henry set out to demonstrate that the formative process behind the Martian lexicon is, broadly speaking, the same as for natural languages; it involves shifts of meaning through figures of speech such as metonymy, metaphor, and antiphrasis; deformations through apocope, metathesis, mispronunciation, spurious etymology, portmanteaux, the reduplication common to children's speech, inversions like those that occur in slang, and so on. Henry found (or claimed to have found) modifications along these same lines: the vital interplay of sound and sense that makes languages evolve by opening up its ludic, poetic, and creative dimensions.

We should note that, at the time, the hypothesis of the parallel between ontogeny and phylogeny in language still enjoyed general acceptance in the scientific community. Ultimately, what fascinated Henry was the prospect of finding, in the unconscious project of creating one language, the key to the birth and development of human language in general—especially since he, like Flournoy, recognized the naive and primitive character of Martian.[24]

But since the task in hand is to evaluate the linguistic value of Martian, let's apply a criterion developed by two American linguists[25] to separate natural languages from artificial languages of the Esperanto variety and from pidgins. A text of a given length—say, five hundred words—in a natural language will consist between 46 percent and 48 percent of *hapax legomena,* or words that occur only once. Anything that deviates significantly from this standard cannot be a sample of a real language. A comparison document in a pidgin will contain a number of hapaxes that is lower, and the figure will grow in proportion to the text's length. But in Esperanto, the percentage reaches 63 percent. (In spite of aiming for simplicity, this artificial language is meant to eliminate the ambiguity that arises from polysemy and homonymy; hence its excessive lexical differentiation.) In other words, a pidgin is *more impoverished* than a natural language, while an artificial language is *richer*. Thus, in James Joyce's *Ulysses* the number of hapaxes rises a little above the mean, to 50.5 percent; in Basic English, on the other hand, it drops to 38 percent. As for Hélène Smith's Martian, the number of hapaxes lies at about 32 percent; this value is close to that of pidgins.

As Flournoy demonstrated, the grammatical forms of Martian are little more than "the counterpart of, or a parody upon, those of French."[26] In particular, all homophonic and homographic relations have been preserved. The Martian form *zé*, which corresponds to the French *le*, is both a definite article and a personal pronoun designating an object, and so on. Here is a list of the personal pronouns, articles, possessive adjectives, and so on, with their equivalents:

je [*I*]	cé	*moi* [*me*]	lé	*mon, ma, mes* [*my*]	êzi, êzé, éziné
tu [*you*]	dé	*te* [*you*]	di	*ton, ta, tes* [*your*]	ché, chée, chi
il [*he*]	hed	*lui* [*him*]	rès	*son, sa, ses* [*his*]	bi, bé, bée
nous [*we*]		nini			
vous [*you* (pl.)]		sini			
ils [*they*]		hed			
on [*one*]		idé			

this, this, these	tès, tês, têsé
it [pronoun]	zé
who, what	kâ, ké
which [m. and f.]	kiz, kizé
a/an [m. and f.]	mis, misé
the [article, m., f., pl.]	zé, zi zée.[27]

The poverty of Martian morphology is obvious. In terms of word order, the language follows French on every point—exemplifying the fact, well known to linguists and speech pathologists, that it's easy to invent a lexicon by means of neologism, but quite difficult to escape the syntax of one's native tongue. Moreover, a "naive" speaker will be unaware of the syntactic particularity of different languages.[28] The language of *Finnegans Wake* is still English by virtue of its phonic material and sentence structure, even if the vocabulary is completely deformed. All in all, from a historical perspective, a given language's syntax will prove far more resistant to change and borrowing than its lexicon.

Martian phonology displays the same weakness. This invented tongue actually has fewer sounds than French, and no sounds at all that do not exist in the latter. In addition, analysis reveals that 90 percent of the syllables are open. In comparison, French has an open syllable structure 80 percent of the time, but this is due to liaison and elision, which generally do not occur in Martian; here, sequences are arranged consonant-vowel-consonant-vowel, which makes it rather monotonous (in a few rare cases, however, liaisons are incorporated for euphony).

On the one hand, although the proportion of open and closed syllables varies considerably between languages, there are no languages without open syllables. On the other hand, many languages, especially in the Pacific and Indian Ocean, do not admit consonant clusters. Consequently, native speakers interject vowels to borrowed words in order to restore consonant-vowel alternations.[29]

The tendency toward open syllables and the more or less complete exclusion of consonant clusters, even at the beginning of words, are defining features of glossolalia, independent of the speaker's native tongue. These features are similarly pronounced in children's speech.

Fifty percent of words in Martian end in *-é*—a much higher rate than in French. Six percent terminate in *-iche* or *-ache,* which evokes a preferred mode of deformation in slang and children's speech (e.g., *fortiche, potache, valoche*). Half of Martian words are disyllabic, and about 20 percent are monosyllabic; approximately as many are trisyllabic, and the rest (6 percent) have four syllables—yet again, a distribution corresponding to how children talk. The typical Martian word will have two syllables, both of them open, and end in *-é,* usually with assonance or alliteration.

Because of its phonological structure and syllabic division, Martian sounds monotonous and lacks contrast. Instances of alliteration and, even more, assonance in *-i* and*-é* are numerous and give the tongue an impoverished ring. Whereas the systematic nature and stability of connections between sound and sense affiliate Martian with real languages, its "external form" sets it apart from them.

When Flournoy observed the droning and repetitive quality of Martian, Hélène Smith devised a new tongue: Ultra-Martian. Just as science fiction authors will often try to disorient their readers by inventing extraterrestrial languages with a preponderance of consonants and occlusives, the medium made a point of making Ultra-Martian abrupt and clipped—the very opposite of Martian's characteristic vocalic harmony. All the new language's words ended in an unvoiced stop, calling to mind the onomatopoeia of children's comic books (*biff, bam, boom, splat, yoink*, and so on).[30] In addition, she made a naive effort to change word order to mark a further difference from French; consequently, no syntax was left at all.

Here, in capitals, is an example of Ultra-Martian, translated word for word into Martian and English:[31]

BAK	sirima	branch
SANAK	nébé	green
TOP	viniâ-tî-mis-métiche	[man's name]
ANOK	ivré	holy
SIK	toué	in
ÉTIP	viniâ-tî-misé-bigâ	[child's name]
VANE	azâni	evil
SANIM	maprinié	entered
BATAM	imizi	under
ISSEM	kramâ	basket
TANAK	ziné	blue
VANEM	viniâ-ti-mis-zaki	[name of animal]
SÉRIM	datrinié	hidden
MAZAK	tuzé	ill
TATAK	vâmé	sad
SAKAM	gâmié	cries

Uranian, the last of Hélène Smith's astro-linguistic creations, comes even closer to infantile regression. The whole language is a series of open syllables, with *a* and *o* making up 70 percent of vowels; and there's even more assonance. It resembles singing exercises and babble: the only consonants it has are labials, dentals, and the liquid *l:*

pa lalato lito namito bo té zozoti zolota matito yoto . . .
me linito to toda pé fa ma nana tatazo ma oto do.

This time, there's no translation at all—that is, not the slightest pretense that it means anything. The end of the spectrum has been reached.

The same poverty of formal devices is found in examples of religious glossolalia,[32] which, no matter what the mother tongue of the speaker may be, display an exaggerated tendency toward repetition, reduplication of syllables, vocalic parallelism, open syllabification, excessively symmetrical contrasts, and a reduced inventory of sounds. These features tend toward the minimal system identified by Jakobson: nasal vowels (which children learn late and are uncommon in the world's languages) are reduced or suppressed, as is the set of rounded front vowels; the latter presuppose the development of primary vowels (front unrounded and back rounded); marked contrast exists between the most closed vowels and the most open vowel, at the expense of mid vowels. The whole tends toward a minimal configuration:

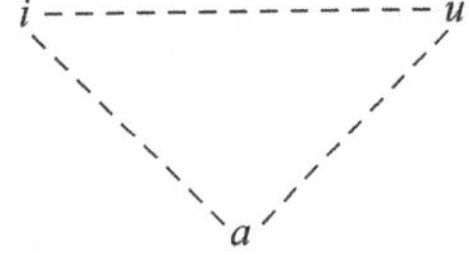

Alternatively, a reduction or elimination of back vowels is evident, tending toward a linear system of primary vowels:

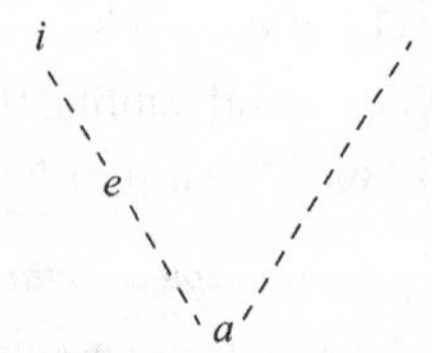

Martian and Ultra-Martian illustrate the two patterns. The former exhibits a quasi-linear system,

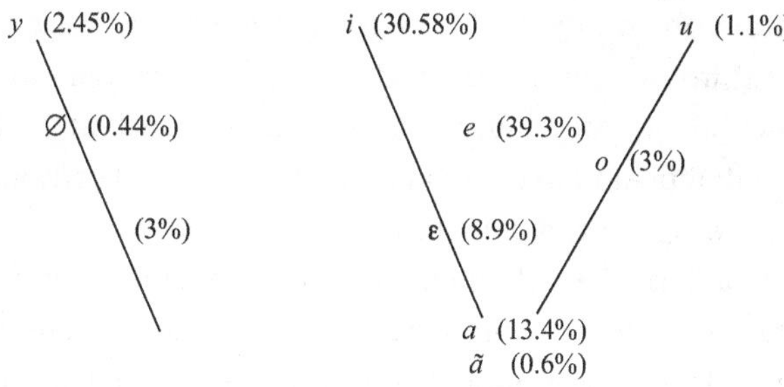

and the latter a triangular system:

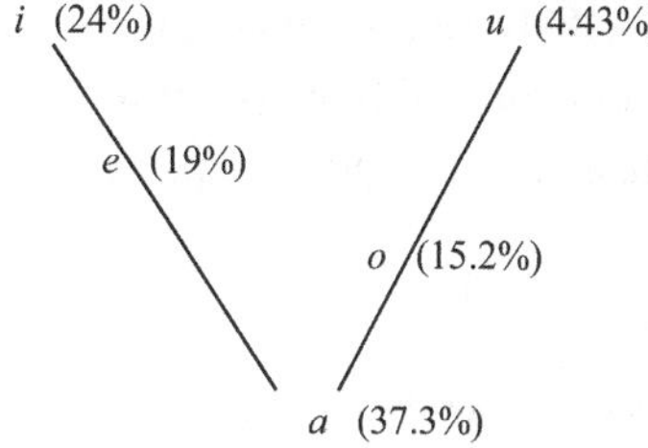

The second system is even more primitive than the first: *a* ranks first again; secondary nasal vowels (which are already very rare in Martian) have been eliminated entirely. Uranian, in turn, operates with a triangular *i-o-a* system.

In terms of consonants, both Martian and Ultra-Martian feature more occlusives than fricatives, and more of them are unvoiced than voiced. Affricates are absent. Occlusives, especially unvoiced, are the first consonants that children can make; they also form the basis of all the world's languages; /ž/ and /h/ do not occur (and are generally rare in natural languages). The absence of /f/, which is more striking, no doubt follows from Hélène Smith's unconscious desire to avoid overlapping with French, which, in a waking state, she denied had anything in common with Martian. The nasality affecting a good third of consonants in Martian and Ultra-Martian also calls children's speech to mind. In contrast, the dental articulation that predominates in Martian (54 percent of consonants are *t, d, n, s,* and *z*) represents an idiosyncratic trait.[33]

On a formal level, then, the infantile and/or universal character of the medium's astro-linguistic output cannot be denied. The rules of phonology—which today are considered the most firmly established part of the theory of linguistic universals—confirm as much.

At the beginning of the twentieth century, the Russian poet Alexander Blok (1880–1921) remarked similar characteristics in the formulas of exorcism that appear in Russian folklore[34]—for instance, the charm intended to protect against malicious water spirits:

Au, Au, šixardakavda
Šivda, vnoza, mitta, minogam
Kalandi, indi, jakutašma bitaš,
Okutomi mi nuffan, zidima.

During this same period, Jakobson, who was collecting popular beliefs and tales, developed an interest in the glossolalia of the Khlysty sect. He also had ties with Velimir Khlebnikov (1885–1922), a practitioner of *Zaum,* poetry that resembles speaking in tongues in certain respects (and translates to something like "transreasonal" [*za-um;* beyond the mind]). In this context, Jakobson was able to venture a hypothesis: "At the same time another type of pure neology in Russian oral poetry—the tongues speaking in the ecstatic practices of the Khlysty—focused my attention upon the intrinsic structure of these invocations, their semantic interpretation by the speakers themselves, and features which are shared by such frenzied utterances of different "prophets," *thus relating to a common code*."[35]

If glossolalic output is individual and spontaneous, it still is organized according to certain rules. It would seem that speakers get rid of the most idiosyncratic sounds and combinations of sounds in their mother tongue and retain only those that are first to be used by children and last to disappear in aphasia. In other words, what they keep are the sounds most widespread in the world's languages. The same principle evidently governs the reduction of phonological systems in pidgins.[36] For all that, impelled by an unconscious desire to express singularity or to hide invention, the glossolalic subject may introduce elements that are infrequent or nonexistent in his or her native tongue. Jakobson noted this tendency apropos of the vocalizations of the Khlysty, which had already been collected in the eighteenth century:

1. *kindra fendra kiraveca*;
2. *rentre fente*;
3. *natru funtru*.

The phrase that members of the sect used for spells of glossolalia—"speaking in foreign tongues"—was wholly justified: the consonant *f* and the consonant groups *ndr* and *ntr* were alien to their everyday speech.[37]

3. I IS ANOTHER

If, in its most elaborate manifestations, glossolalia has a quasi-linguistic *sense* that refuses analysis as it grows all-encompassing, it certainly has a *value* and a *function*, as well. The value attached to glossolalia by the speaker is its real *raison d'être*, and its "meaning" is in fact secondary—a "meaning-effect." Thus, Hélène Smith's Martian had the value of "proving" the soul's immortality and the possibility of communicating with spirits in other worlds. It is incumbent on the observer to identify such a function and analyze it without passing judgment on the meaning or value it has for the speaker (or anyone else). The observer's point of view and that of the subject cannot coincide where any of these three terms (sense/meaning, value, function) is concerned.

On the one hand, Hélène Smith ascribed an extraterrestrial origin to her languages. Someone with the gift of tongues, on the other hand, will point to divine origins. Such a language does not have to conform to the structures or rules that otherwise prevail. It is not there to be taken apart or translated, but to be "interpreted" as a unit. To take up (quite freely) the distinction that Émile Benveniste makes between the two modes of linguistic significance—the *semiotic* mode, which concerns the organization of signs into a system, and the *semantic* mode, which concerns how signification is organized in (a particular) discourse[38]—we might say that instances of glossolalia, like sound poetry or *Zaum*, preserve semantic significance while discarding semiotic significance: the system of stable and identifiable signs based on a consensus among speakers vanishes. Speech continues to "make sense," but it no longer constitutes a code. It approaches the realm of cryptophasia, or "private language," with expressive, ludic, and aesthetic aspects all its own.

There is still a message, but no key for it, and herein lies the paradox. "Semantic order becomes identified with the world of enunciation and with the universe of discourse," Benveniste notes, distinguishing between two conceptual universes: "Semiotics (the sign) must be recognized; semantics (the discourse) must be understood. The difference between recognition and comprehension refers to two distinct faculties of the mind: that of discerning the identity between the previous and the present, and that of discerning, on the other hand, the meaning of a new enunciation. In the pathological forms of language, these two powers are frequently dissociated."[39]

Although it would be wrong to describe religious or spiritualist glossolalia as pathological, Benveniste's observation applies perfectly to both phenomena. It is precisely its nonsemiotic character which gives glossolalia its universality. It transcends both the individual and society. Glossolalia does not transmit experience so much as nature. As such, it escapes the constraints of language, taking the form of *other speech*, which cannot be reduced to any language in particular. It emanates directly from the individual, without social mediation, and at the same time transcends the individual.

A person speaking in tongues does in fact achieve some form of communication, but linguistic communication in the strict sense does not occur. Now, structured language—which is organized semantically and syntactically—forms a screen between "man" and primitive sensibility, the pure effusion of sentiment. Like music, glossolalia conveys the ineffable. To borrow a phrase from Vladimir Jankélévitch, it "means nothing and yet means everything."[40] Like music, it "does not allow the discursive, reciprocal communication of meaning, but rather an immediate and ineffable communication."[41] In music, the production of sense also does not rest on a semiotic structure or social consensus.

"The condition of intersubjectivity . . . alone makes linguistic communication possible."[42] Language organizes subjective experience, but not for the subject alone. When the latter makes an utterance, he or she communicates personal experience, but the listener immediately interprets it in terms of his or her own experience and subjectivity, which mirror the speaker's. This "gift from God" is offered to everyone in individual variants, which are mutually incomprehensible.

In Russian, the verbal productions made in a state of religious ecstasy may be summed up in the phrase, *ya govoryu ne ot svoego uma* ("I am not speaking from my own mind"). This formula also expresses the goal of *Zaum*.

What sets the glossolalist apart from someone using his or her mother tongue, then, is that *the speaker isn't the one speaking*. Grammatically and phenomenologically, *person* is missing: no *I* stands at the center of discourse as its source; no *I* is implicated in a spatio-temporal continuity to take responsibility for the utterance. Hélène Smith spoke what spirits and extraterrestrial beings *dictated*. Those speaking in tongues bring forth the words of God or angels, and this is why their speech is a "gift." By the same token, a prophet is not an *I*. When he speaks, he isn't the person talking. He doesn't answer for what he says—he hears voices. Of course, his own unconscious gives him the words, but either he doesn't recognize as much, or he pretends not to know: it's of capital importance to ascribe this speech to an external point of origin and authority.

For all that, there is an *ego* at the heart of glossolalia, but it's not linguistic. This ego is not the same as the *I* of language, a "shifter" pronoun that can pass from one individual to another. It lies outside the social system and belongs to one who would take possession of language as a whole—whereas the opposite is what occurs. The back-and-forth that defines speech and language becomes impossible. Points of reference, indices in time and space, are abolished. The glossolalist occupies a dimension that is his or her own. If everyday language is how culture constructs the world, the individual speaking in tongues makes another one without assuming responsibility for it and is free to look into the past or the future, wherever fantasy may lead.

4. THE SONG OF INNOCENCE

> Woman carries within herself an organ susceptible to terrible spasms, disposing her to and raising in her imagination phantoms of all sorts. It is in the hysterical delirium that she returns to the past, that she throws herself into the future, that all times are present to her.[43]
>
> —Diderot

Tonight, *The Tales of Hoffmann* is on TV. The libretto is in French, but even if you know the language, it's not easy to follow dialogue when it's sung. Try cutting off the sound and picture by turns, with the remote control, to disassociate the music from what's happening on stage. As everyone knows, you can listen to an opera without watching it. But the opposite is possible, as well. Now, it seems to be something by Murnau, Pabst, or Fritz Lang: an example of German Expressionism. One doesn't expect to hear words so much as to see intertitles. Events look like a silent film with musical accompaniment, not a movie with sound, because opera is not the same thing as theater. The singers are split in two. Bodies act and mime, and faces yield to wild expression—eye rolls, flying arms, inner tension spilling outward, and exaggerated contortions—while the songs soar. The voice seems to serve a musical message, not a verbal one.

In opera, communication occurs simultaneously through body language and vocalization. The voice—that privileged instrument that finds its purest expression when it sings and says nothing in particular—marks the absolute limit of articulated sense, which, as Catherine Clément has aptly observed apropos of Mozart's "Queen of the Night," is the province of women.[44] On this score, opera and glossolalia intersect. In either case, it's communion, with a touch of hysteria. The connection has been noted on various occasions; to mark the centenary of Charcot's research, an operatic spectacle entitled *Hystérie* was staged at the Salpêtrière.[45] The Freudian heroine of D. M. Thomas's novel *The White Hotel* (1981) is an opera singer.

As far as opera is concerned, the term "hysteria" is a metaphor: a performance is being staged. Glossolalists also put on a show, for themselves and for others, but here the author is also the actor—and he or she believes the play is real. Hélène Smith, like other mediums, brought forth pseudo-language in a state of self-induced hypnosis. The séances, which Flournoy arranged to be photographed in detail, were truly theatrical, even if the role—or roles—assumed by the actress came from her unconscious mind. Flournoy may have employed the listening technique of Freud, but his gaze resembled Charcot's.

Opinion long held that a state of trance was necessary for religious glossolalia. Evidently, however, this isn't always the case. Some of the faithful affirm that they can speak in tongues at will and in a state of complete relaxation. It's as if they were simply turning a tap on and off. To be sure, one can invoke excitation or exaltation—especially when it's a group endeavor, and each individual is performing for the benefit of others so they will do the same and get carried away, too. But in Pentecostalist churches, such activity is also a matter of training and exercise.

At any rate, this kind of behavior serves to release tension. Carl Jung took a keen interest in religious glossolalia. In 1955, he wrote to an American colleague and observed, "It is probable that the strangeness of the unconscious contents not yet integrated in consciousness demands an equally strange language."[46] In Jung's eyes, these manifestations possessed therapeutic value; he even surmised that glossolalia might represent a positive step toward an integrated personality. Flournoy, for his part, thought that Hélène Smith's mediumistic creations allowed her to avoid the "bodily stigmata" that are known to occur in some cases of hysteria. According to the American specialist Morton T. Kelsey, the more a subject is cut off from his or her unconscious, the greater the attraction exerted by glossolalia—which is preferable to most ways that tension and inhibitions come out in neurotic behavior.[47] A British psychiatrist has even likened the effects of glossolalia to those of electroshock.[48] Glossolalists themselves point to the cathartic value of speaking in tongues, so it really does amount to a kind of purification—a way of resolving conflicts between the conscious and the unconscious mind.

Instead of linking glossolalia to hysteria or the splitting of the personality that occurs in psychosis, then, we should it see it in relation to dreams. Speaking in tongues represents a kind of oneiric state achieved by emptying one's mind, freeing oneself from conscious control, disregarding the surroundings, and just letting go. Such a state may be facilitated chemically or by hypnosis, but it's reversible and nonpathological—and can often be modified at will. In a word, the gift of tongues occurs when social, personal, and interpersonal barriers are broken down; hence its liberating effect, often characterized by a "high." The unconscious mind takes a plunge without surrendering, since everyday verbalization does not take place. Instead—and this brings us back to music and opera—what matters is euphony, harmony, rhyme, and rhythm that respond to needs for aesthetic expression.[49] The glossolalist perceives what she or he says as beautiful, musical, and "soaring"—a hint of paradise. The rapid cadence translates intensity of feeling, full and "rich" sounds evoke the presence of God, and melodious intonation connotes worship. The tendency toward spontaneous metric structure makes glossolalia innately poetic.

If the gift of tongues is cast in the mythological image of primal existence, then the first *Homo loquens*—as Rousseau declared—was *Homo poeticus*. Glossolalia is the living memory of the original, natural tongue of humankind. It bears witness to the ascendancy of sentiment over intellect, emotion over reason, and the uncorrupted state of being before the Fall. This is the song of innocence, not experience.

PART IV THE DEFENSE AND ILLUSTRATION OF NATURAL LANGUAGES

If languages weren't so complicated, they'd be simple.
—Zygomar de la Palice, *Oeuvres*

Language lies in the nature of man, who did not fabricate it. We tend to picture that naïve scene when one fully-formed human being encountered another one, likewise fully formed, and between them, bit by bit, language developed. That's pure fiction. We'll never get back to human life without language, and we'll never witness people inventing it. We'll never get back to man in his primal state, striving to conceive of the existence of his fellow man. We will always find a human being speaking to another human being in this world, and language teaches us the very definition of human being.
—Émile Benveniste, *Problèmes de linguistique générale II*

10

SLEEPING BEAUTY AT REST: ARTIFICIAL LANGUAGES, PRISONS OF THE MIND

> Utopia would have history, enchanted by its ministrations, show the white face of Sleeping Beauty at rest.
>
> —Gilles Lapouge, *Le singe de la montre*

The philosophy of language predates linguistics. For ages, speech and language were the business of philosophers. Is the linguist's perspective compatible with that of the philosopher? The latter was (and is) concerned with the problem of how language translates thought. For centuries, the question has been whether the imperfection of natural languages is to blame for the imperfections of human reason and discourse. A prejudice as old as the world itself is to credit one language with a "logical" nature, in contrast to another, which is declared "illogical." The matter sends us back to the two senses of the Greek word *logos*: "speech" and "reason." Logicians, in turn, are interested in the *truth* of enunciations, which is not the concern of linguists. Today, linguists examine the structure of languages as autonomous systems; whether languages match up with one philosophical view of the world or another does not matter. If the functions of language and speech receive attention, the task is to find out the means enlisted to arrive at propositions. In brief, linguists deal with language as it is, whereas philosophers (some of them, at any rate) tend to address language as it ought to be.

One of the justifications for inventing a language is often the search for naturalness. Philosophical languages aim to express the true essence of things, the order of the Universe. Paradoxically, an ultra-cultural enterprise is supposed to restore a full view of nature—which is actually a matter of fantasy: nature as it appears in a dream. In turn, speculations on the origins of language almost always credit primitive language with the power to match expression both to the material world and to humankind's physical and psychological constitution; hence the prominent role assigned to onomatopoeia—the inherent symbolism of sounds, the "natural" expressiveness of phonemes—as an explanatory principle. Such endeavors derive from a long tradition inaugurated by Plato's *Cratylus* (see appendix, p. 211). Here, the title figure maintains, "a name is not whatever people call a thing by agreement, just a piece of their own voice applied to the thing, but . . . there is a kind of inherent correctness in names, which is the same for all men, both Greeks and barbarians."

Those who speak in tongues likewise appeal to something natural when they value feeling over intellect. As we have seen, glossolalia represents, par excellence, the spontaneous and affective outpouring of language with a function that is essentially phatic and expressive.

In contrast, the cornerstone of modern linguistics is Saussure's principle that the sign is arbitrary. This thesis rules out explaining the form of language in reference to the nature of things, the way they "really are."

The opposition between natural and artificial languages does not coincide with the opposition between nature and culture. So-called "natural" languages (an infelicitous term, it has been argued[1]) belong to culture: "the symbolism of language as the power of signification is fundamental."[2] Symbolism implies culture, not nature. In fact, there is no such thing as a natural language. What is natural is the faculty of language. But even so, it must be cultivated—as has been shown by cases of children found in the wild, whose linguistic aptitude atrophies for want of exposure to human communication. Languages are only natural to the extent that people experience them as such:

> Language and society are unconscious realities for human beings, both representing nature, so to speak: the natural milieu and natural expression, which cannot be conceived of as other than they are and cannot be imagined as absent. Both [aspects of "nature"] are always inherited; at the fundamental level of using language and participating in society, no one thinks that there could ever have been a beginning for the one or the other. Nor can human will change either one. What people see changing, and what, in effect, they themselves change throughout the course of history, are institutions—sometimes the overall shape of given society, but never the principle of society itself, which is the very basis of, and condition for, collective and individual life. Likewise, what changes in language—what human beings can change—are designations, which proliferate, replace each other, and are always a conscious phenomenon; but the fundamental system of the language never changes.[3]

Natural languages contrast with artificial languages in that their origins cannot be attributed to a specific individual or group of individuals, or dated to a particular time. (That said, exception must be made for special cases such as pidgins, or languages like modern Hebrew and Bahasa Indonesia—a standardized version of Malay—which have been the object of concerted policies.) Human language entertains a dual relationship. On the one hand, it connects to thought, and through thought to the Universe on the whole. On the other hand, it connects with society. Glossolalia tries to transcend both these bonds, but it does not manage to do so entirely; instead, it reconfigures them by bringing forth an effect of global meaning that resists being broken down into discrete parts; thereby, in a phatic capacity, it affirms the community of practicing believers.

In turn, artificial languages would control these relations by reversing their direction. The rationale for philosophical languages is to mark out the boundaries of thought and make language adhere to them. Languages designed to practical ends are supposed to serve as social tools. Orwell's Newspeak is their hideous caricature. Finally, enterprising spirits who would reconstruct the primitive tongue of humankind want to find the trace of both these aspects in original and perfect form.

In so doing, what is forgotten (or never understood in the first place) is that the linguistic sign, as defined by Saussure, does not establish a relationship between words and what they serve to designate; instead, it concerns an acoustic image (the signifier) and a concept (the signified). The inventors of languages imagine that it would be enough for everyone to agree to refer to reality in the same terms. Along these lines, Harold Palmer argued that one should simply follow the principle of scientific vocabulary, which is international:

> Those who have made a study of Comparative Etymology say: "In analyzing the contents of dictionaries we find that at least 7,000 words are more or less common in spelling and meaning to the six chief European Languages: English, French, Spanish, Italian, German, and Russian, not to mention several minor languages. Most of these words have come into these languages

> not by the process of linguistic evolution from earlier forms but by deliberate acts of creation, borrowing, and adaption. We find that in certain types of texts one-third of the vocabulary is made up of these international words. Let this process of deliberate borrowing be extended to the remainder of the vocabulary—and the result will be a complete artificial language."[4]

This view takes no account of grammatical relations; what would the ideal syntax shared by all languages be—the same as Esperanto? Automated translation has long foundered on the same obstacle. In switching from one language to another, it's not enough to change vocabulary; an "interlanguage" must also exist to mediate between the "source" and "target" languages. What a human translator manages to achieve by knowing two languages, a machine can only perform if a common denominator is available. I would not presume to know what the future may bring, but anyone who has tried out the translation programs available on the Internet knows how much ground still needs to be covered.

Until then, the big issue will remain linguistic universality and diversity. The attendant debate is the very history of modern linguistics. As we have seen, the Sapir–Whorf hypothesis (which Orwell depicted in its most extreme consequences) posits that thought is shaped by language; the latter precedes and determines the former, with the result that speakers of languages with different structures do not think in the same way at all. Yet cultural differences do not mean irreducible differences. On the contrary, it seems that all human experience can be transmitted—in more or less adequate fashion, depending on the cultural distance involved—into any language. As Jakobson showed, languages are equipped to "tinker," if necessary, with equivalencies or new modes of expression; the richest of the latter is metaphor:

> All cognitive experience and its classification is conveyable in any existing language. Whenever there is a deficiency, terminology can be qualified and amplified by loanwords or loan translations, neologisms or semantic shifts, and, finally, by circumlocutions. . . . No lack of grammatical devices in the language translated into makes impossible a literal translation of the entire conceptual information contained in the original. . . . Languages differ essentially in what they *must* convey and not in what they *can* convey. . . . Any assumption of ineffable or untranslatable cognitive data would be a contradiction in terms.[5]

Here, it seems, Jakobson not only dismisses the over-rigid determinism of the Sapir–Whorf hypothesis, but also endorses the universality of conceptual thought and human experience.

Likewise, Benveniste considered it possible to abstract oneself from the limitations imposed by particular languages; in this sense, a philosophical language—while still a dream in terms of practical realization—regains its justification, if only as a theoretical abstraction. "That translation remains possible as a global process is . . . an essential fact to note. *It shows that it is possible for us to rise above language,* to abstract ourselves from it, to contemplate it while at the same time using it for reasoning and observation. The metalinguistic faculty, to which logicians have paid more attention than linguists, is proof that the mind can transcend language in its semantic capacity."[6] This means that if we are not prisoners of language, we ought to be able to conceive of it as different from the way it is. The aim of a philosophical language is to provide an interlanguage capable of uniting all languages on the basis of semantic universals. This involves codifying a universal semantics in the form of a neutral semiotics. But once there, one of the main obstacles confronting an artificial language reappears: respecting this neutrality (for each inventor cannot help but be marked by the categories imposed by his or her native tongue).

The two registers distinguished by Benveniste—semiotic and semantic—are precisely what sets language apart from other codes, such as music, which is a semantic but not a semiotic code (the units in the musical code are not signs, yet the musical "utterance" can produce meaning). "One can transpose the semantics of one language into that of another, *salva veritate*; in this sense translation is possible. However, one cannot transpose the semiotics of one language into that of another; in this sense translation is impossible. Here lies the difference between the semiotic and the semantic."[7] Being a semiotic system, on the one hand, gives language absolute autonomy with regard to the referential universe. Its semantic significance, on the other hand, comes out through the message transmitted in a given discursive situation:

> The semantic register automatically takes charge of references in their entirety, whereas the semiotic level is by definition cut off and independent from all reference.[8]
>
> The notion of semantics leads us to the realm of language in use and action; here, we see language in its mediating role between one human being and another, between man and the world, between the mind and things, transmitting information, communicating experience, ensuring belonging, provoking a response, asking, and imposing—in short, organizing the whole of human life. This is language as an instrument of description and reasoning. *Only the semantic function of language permits social integration and adequation to the world, and consequently the regulation of thought and the development of consciousness.*[9]

The trouble is, if semantics derives from semiotics through each new instance of discourse, is it legitimate, useful, or even possible to organize all conceivable semantic relations a priori? Wouldn't that amount to freezing them once and for all? Then, language would lack all flexibility, room for play, adaptive potential, and autonomy. It would truly be Sleeping Beauty at rest in the woods, and not alive.

The primordial function of language is neither to define nor express the world. Its function is to construct and reconstruct, time and again, its own universe. Language in use is symbolic, not deictic, iconic, or indexical. Inasmuch as they posit syntax to be something more or less self-evident, philosophical languages too often amount simply to nomenclatures that stress the "logical" limits and categories of concepts. When this occurs, linguistics no longer concerns signs but words (to put it uncharitably, words of the primitive, Adamic stripe); the Universe is supposed to consist of things and ideas that must each have a name once and for all, and the sole concern is to make sure that everything matches up.[10]

In practice, philosophical languages failed as much for human reasons as for theoretical ones. While they were supposed to reflect the order of the natural world, in actual fact they represented the cultural order—and often naively, at that. This shortcoming connects with the problem of understanding someone truly *other*; it took a long time for the idea of cultural relativity to gain hold, especially where language is concerned. Thus, seventeenth-century philosophers were unable to picture the world in any way that didn't include the ideas of divinity, monarchy, and absolute power granted by God—to say nothing of the other features of social organization (secular and religious) that characterized the Europe of their day.[11]

As we have seen, the notion that each language has its own way of splitting up and portioning out reality by categorizing phenomena, or that it mirrors the culture of its speakers, does not rule out the possibility of postulating supra-cultural and supra-linguistic schemes of conceptualization. The trick is to *recognize* that models operate both *on* and *through* language without succumbing to excesses of the Whorfian variety. Here, another paradox lies in store. Even though they seem to contradict each other, the hypothesis of cultural relativity and that of philosophical universalism meet up inasmuch as they both affirm the thorough-going interdependence of language and thought. In the one case, the link is a posteriori: the language of an individual's cultural environment determines his or her mental framework and view of the world; in the other, the connection is a priori: a universal mode of conceptualization is supposed to exist, which philosophers have the task of bringing to light, and the ideal language will reflect it perfectly.

In this regard, Orwell's Newspeak can be considered a kind of philosophical language; after all, anti-utopias operate along the same lines as utopias. In the nightmare world of *1984*, ideology *precedes* language; the latter is intended to be the faithful reproduction of the former (an a priori scheme). Newspeak serves the purpose of cultural engineering, guaranteeing orthodox thinking among speakers; any subversive notion should be literally unthinkable because it is inexpressible (see appendix, p. 255). By the same token, the true language of philosophy, of which early modern theorists dreamed, would make it impossible to voice a mistaken or illogical idea.

But it's not the nature of language to lock its users into a sealed and static system with no way out. Language is an adaptive symbolic system, not a list of names.

11

OPPOSING FORCES

"All the sciences of nature," Benveniste writes, "find their object already constituted. Linguistics, for its part—and this is what distinguishes it from all other scientific disciplines—is concerned with something that is not an object, not a substance: *it is form*."[1]

It is precisely because a language is *form* that *re-formers* have thought they could constrain it at will.[2] Reflecting on artificial languages necessarily entails reflecting on the formal characteristics of natural languages—which in turn leads to their "defense and illustration."

If a universal language is supposed to be sufficiently rich and exact to express "all the subtleties of human thought and activity,"[3] it must also be regular and straightforward in formal terms, so it will be easy to learn. All inventors of languages display a veritable obsession with ease of acquisition, and they try to promote it by means of an orderly and symmetrical morphology (which hasn't prevented any number of artificial tongues, especially a priori ones, from being exasperatingly difficult to learn—if not entirely unusable). That said, the category of facility is altogether meaningless in linguistics, just like "simplicity" or "naturalness"; such notions are based on subjective criteria. What's more, the core of language—its basic feature, as it were—tends to be irregularity. Thus, in Indo-European tongues, no verb displays greater variation than *to be*; it's almost as if they had a natural aversion to regularity.

Language is shaped by the play of opposing forces, from which any number of internal contradictions arise: norms and deviations, polysemy and synonymy, economy and redundancy, stability and change, ambiguity and creativity, constraint and freedom, symmetry and asymmetry, unity and fragmentation, collective traits and specific features. These factors work together to create a state of equilibrium that is constantly renewed, making sure that the language ultimately adapts to suit its many functions. Undoubtedly, this is what imparts to natural languages their richness. Already *in principle*, then, it's a mistake to tamper with the balance. Language has its own logic. Both a product and a pillar of society, its internal operations escape the latter's control. Language is governed by its own principles of evolution and creation, which resist concerted action on the part of the community and, a fortiori, the will of individuals.

For patent historical reasons, it so happens that the inventors of languages—at any rate, those whose efforts have been recorded—are almost exclusively Westerners. (De facto, the interlinguistics movement represents a colonialist enterprise.) Virtually all a posteriori artificial languages have been fashioned on Indo-European rootstock, with varying levels of hybridization. In the Indo-European family, the degree of fusion and variability in morphemes is quite high, which leads to *allomorphs* on the one hand, and to *amalgamated morphemes*[4] on the other. Consequently, and in contrast, the ideal language has often been conceived as agglutinative; indeed, the degree of fusion and the variability of morphemes stand close to zero in agglutinative languages. A priori schemes[5] apply the principle very strictly: they have a completely regular flexional system, no amalgamated endings, and no room for morpho-phonological variation. The problem of allomorphs was handled in different ways by a posteriori languages of the nineteenth and twentieth centuries. Thus, Esperanto does not allow allomorphs except for purposes of euphony; it also does not admit multiple roots for families of words associated with the same concept. So-called "naturalistic" projects (developed for the most part during the twentieth century) tried to take into account the intrinsic characteristics of languages that are not man-made and permit alternation at the level of roots; examples of such languages include Ido and Occidental.

Along such lines, Orwell's Newspeak does away with the allomorphs of English as much as possible. Likewise, its morphological regularity dictates the perfect regularity of antonyms: *good* stands opposed to *ungood, cold* to *uncold*. Strong verbs inherited from the Germanic past are also standardized. The language presented in Anthony Burgess's 1978 sequel to *1984, 1985*, represents a reaction against this contrivance. Here, Workers' English is an extremely simplified version of Bourgeois English; it shares certain qualities with Basic English (most verbs referring to specific actions have been replaced by periphrastic constructions based on *get* or *do)*. All the same, Burgess's scheme offers a realistic version of linguistic habit—for instance, the variation of vowels in plural nouns (*foot/feet*) and verbal inflection (*come/came*), which go back to Old English; likewise, the morpho-phonological constraints characteristic of Indo-European languages are in evidence.

Another problem that language inventors have often taken up is redundancy—even though it plays a functional role in natural languages by serving as a means of anticipating and circumventing misunderstandings and smoothing out communication; this system is only set aside under well-defined circumstances (e.g., telegrams). In the framework of his plans for a universal rational grammar, Leibniz sought to suppress all forms of redundancy and flexional endings (all verbs would be replaced by *to be* + adjective). It is generally accepted that the most redundant features of speech are the last ones that children acquire. And pidgins tend to lose endings when the meaning of words is already clear from context or syntax; in English-based pidgins and creoles, *-s* often goes missing for verbs in the third person, to express possession, and in the case of plural nouns. At the same time, however, creoles obey the rules of natural languages and tend to recreate other networks of redundancies.[6] Louis Couturat was quite wrong to think that the "progress" of the most "evolved" languages means lower levels of redundancy.

Ferdinand de Saussure, for his part, noted the contradiction between the particularizing (or "parochial") and unifying tendencies at work in human languages. At all times and places, people have been torn between the need to communicate with as many others as possible and the desire to cultivate an identity specific to the clan or group to which they belong.[7] This fact accounts for special languages (cryptic, ludic, ritual, and so on) and dialects, which seal communities together and protect them from outsiders. A universal tendency is at work, which runs counter to unification and uniformization. At the outer limit, it yields so-called idiolect: the language particular to a single person.[8] Language is the scene of irreducible conflict between the push for unity and the pull of individuality.

Ironically, artificial languages aiming for universality also fall victim to this conflict. A great number of them never get beyond the idiolect stage because their inventors fail to interest anyone else. Here, one enters the realm of "private languages," which, at one end of the continuum, borders on linguistic pathology—the projects of madmen. But if we stick to viable schemes, it would seem possible, by studying the four hundred-odd languages inventoried by the two "bibles" of interlinguistics, to draw up a comparative grammar of universal languages and classify them genetically, as it were, in terms of families deriving from "mother tongues"; the most important of the latter would include Esperanto, Ido, and Interlingua (see box, p. 84).

We can also superimpose a second classification on the first to account for external features (as opposed to actual affiliation). Without meaning to do so, the inventors of languages have produced a whole typology: languages with artificial or semi-artificial roots, ones with regularized or nonregularized roots, and hybrid or homogeneous tongues, which in turn can be subdivided into examples with a broad base (pan-Romance or Indo-European) or a narrow base (usually Latin, but also Slavic, Germanic, English, Franco-English, and, very marginally, Hebrew and Hungarian).

The relationships between these different "dialects" are both diachronic (when languages derive from one another through reform, sometimes on the part of the original inventor) and synchronic (when competing projects are introduced). During its heroic age, the interlanguage movement often witnessed ferocious infighting between tribes and individuals—as if a new Tower of Babel were fated to rise and fall. Indeed, the history of artificial languages seemed destined to mimic the history of natural ones, when a new language arose: Idiom Neutral (1902), combining rival schemes in a gesture of appeasement and unity.[9]

Artificial languages are not exempt from internal variation, either, and a number of interlinguists[10] have allowed for learned, popular, and poetic variants. Finally, we should note that Esperanto—the sole invented language to have enjoyed a sizeable number of speakers—tends to divide spontaneously in actual use. This "shortcoming" actually proves its dynamism and viability: in order to live and thrive, languages must change. (Of course, Zamenhof himself would have preferred his invention to stay the same once and for all.)

Whether we assume a typological perspective, examine the practice of speakers, or look at variations due to individual inventors, two abiding forces are in evidence: on the one hand, the diversity of linguistic experience, which stands opposed to unifying endeavors, and, on the other hand, features shared by all languages (natural or not) and their users, which justify the universalist hypothesis. After all, the invention of languages occurs within the bounds of the human mind. Here, there's no escaping the constant dialectic between unity and diversity.

APPENDIX 1: SYNOPTIC TABLE

History of ideas on language

	Theoretical works	Fictional works
1610	Galileo, *Nuncius sidereus*	
1615	Publication of Father Ricci's journals (first Jesuit mission to China)	
1629	Descartes's *Letter to Mersenne* (on the universal language)	
1636	Mersenne, *Harmonie universelie*	
1638	Wilkins, *The Discovery of a New World*	Godwin, *The Man in the Moone*
1641	Wilkins, *Mercury, or the Secret and Swift Messenger*	
1649 (1656)		Cyrano de Bergerac, *L'autre monde: Les états et empires de la Lune*
1652 (1662)		*Les états et empires du Soleil*
1660	*Grammaire générale et raisonnée de Port-Royal*	
1661	Dalgarno, *Ars signorum*	
1666	Leibniz, *De arte combinatoria*	

	Theoretical works	Fictional works
1668	Wilkins, *An Essay towards a Real Character* Comenius, *Via Lucis*	
1669	Webb, *An Historical Essay Endeavouring the Probability that the Language of the Empire of China is the Primitive Language*	
1676		Foigny, *Jacques Sadeur*
1677		Vairasse, *Histoire des Sévarambes*
1686	Fontenelle, *Entretiens sur la pluralité des mondes*	
1703	Leibniz, *New Essays*	
1710	Leibniz, *Brevis designatio*	Tyssot de *Patot, Jacques Massé*
1730		Desfontaines, *Le nouveau Gulliver*
1746	Condillac, *Essai sur l'origine des connaissances humaines*	
1750	Berington, *Dissertation on the Mosaical Creation*	Béthune, *Relation du monde de Mercure*
1751	J. Harris, *Hermes*	
1758		Swedenborg, *The Earths in Our Solar System*
1765	De Brosses, *Traité de la formation mécanique des langues*	
1772	Court de Gébelin, *Histoire naturelle de la parole* Herder, *Abhandlung über den Ursprung der Sprache*	
1776	De l'Épée, *Institution des sourds et muets*	
1781	Rousseau, *Essai sur l'origine des langues*	
1784	Discovery of Sanskrit	

	Theoretical works	Fictional works
1797	De Maimieux, *Pasigraphie*	
1798		Anon., *Human Vicissitudes or Travels into Unexplored Regions*
1808	Schlegel, *Über die Sprache und die Weisheit der Indier*	
1828	Nodier, *Dictionnaire raisonné des onomatopées françaises*	
1832–1852	Bopp, *Vergleichende Grammatik*	
1852	Grimm, *Über den Ursprung der Sprache*	
1853	Gobineau, *Essai sur l'inégalité des races humaines*	
1858	Renan, *De l'origine du langage*	
1859	Darwin, *The Origin of Species*	
1861	Schleicher, *Compendium*	
1863	Benloew, *De quelques caractères du langage primitif*	
1865	Mendel, *The Laws of Heredity*	
1866	Founding of the Société de linguistique de Paris	
1867	Max Müller, *Lectures on the Science of Language*	
1869	Rosny, *De l'origine du langage*	
1871		Bulwer-Lytton, *The Coming Race*
1887	Invention of Esperanto by Zamenhof	
1905	Trombetti, *L'unita d'origine del linguaggio*	
1916	Saussure, *Cours de linguistique générale*	
1921	Sapir, *Language*	

	Theoretical works	Fictional works
1929	Founding of Linguistic Circle of Prague	
1948		Orwell, *1984*
1954		Tolkien, *The Lord of the Rings*
1956	Whorf, *Language, Thought, and Reality*	
1957	Chomsky, *Syntactic Structures*	
1958		Vance, *The Languages of Pao*
1965	Chomsky, *Aspects of the Theory of Syntax*	
1966		Delany, *Babel-17*
1973		Watson, *The Embedding*
1978		Colin, *Babel* Burgess, *1985*

APPENDIX 2: SELECTED TEXTS

THE LANGUAGE OF PHILOSOPHY

René Descartes

Letter to Father Mersenne, November 20, 1629.

This project for a new language seems more commendable at first glance than I find it to be upon examination, for the only two things to learn in any tongue are the meaning of words and the grammar. Where the meaning of words is concerned, the writer promises nothing special. In his fourth proposition, he declares *linguam illam interpretari ex dictionario,* that "the language in question is to be translated from a dictionary," which is something anyone versed in languages can do without his advice; I'm sure that if you provided M. Hardy with a good dictionary of Chinese or any other language and a book in the same tongue, he will manage to work out its sense.

What prevents most people from doing so is the difficulty of the grammar. This, I wager, is your man's whole secret. But there's nothing hard about it if one devises a language with only one way to conjugate verbs, decline nouns, and arrange words while excluding defective or irregular parts of speech (which are corruptions introduced by usage); makes sure that nouns and verbs are inflected and that the syntax is constructed by means of affixes before or after the root words; and takes care to list them all in a dictionary. In such a case, it would be no wonder if ordinary people, using a dictionary, learned to use the language in less than six hours—which is the substance of the first proposition.

As for the second proposition, *cognita hac lingua coeteras omnes, ut ejus dialectos, cognoscere,* "with this language, once learned, others can be learned as its dialects"—that's just hawking the wares. The writer doesn't mention how long it would take to learn other languages, only that one would consider them dialects of the first, which, because it doesn't present the grammatical irregularities of the others, he views as their root. It's also worth noting that his dictionary could take the words used in all languages as synonyms of each other for the roots. To signify *love,* for example, one could take *aimer, amare, philein,* etc. A Frenchman would append the affix marking a noun to the verb *aimer* and obtain the word for *amour;* a Greek would do the same to the verb *philein,* and so on. The author's sixth proposition, *scripturam invenire,* "inventing a script," is easy to understand, then. He would simply need to put a single character corresponding to *aimer, amare, philein,* and synonymous terms in his dictionary, and then anyone who had the dictionary could read a book written with the characters he had invented.

Also the fifth proposition, it seems, is just advertising—any statement about an *arcanum,* or "mystery," rouses my suspicion. I think all he means is that his philosophizing on the grammars of the assorted languages he names makes it easier for him to teach them than is the case for ordinary instructors.

Then there's the third proposition, which really does pose a mystery to me. He wants to explain the thoughts of ancient authors on the basis of the words they used, whereby each one of these words is supposed to provide the true definition of the thing in question. This amounts to saying that ancient writers' thoughts will be explained by taking their words in a way they never intended—which is an offensive notion. But maybe he means something else.

This idea of reforming grammar—or, more precisely, of inventing a new one which could be learned in five or six hours and would apply to all languages—would redound to general benefit if people agreed to put it to use. I foresee two obstacles, however.

The first is that infelicitous combinations of letters would often make disagreeable sounds, if not ones intolerable to the ear. Usage has introduced the various inflections of words to remedy precisely this defect, and there's no way your author will have managed to avoid the problem in constructing a universal grammar for all nations; what sounds easy and pleasant in our tongue is coarse and intolerable to Germans, and so on. At best, bad combinations of syllables can be avoided for one or two languages: his supposedly universal language would be suited for just one country, and we hardly need to learn a new language just to talk to other Frenchmen.

The second difficulty concerns learning the vocabulary. If everyone uses the words of his own language as root words, it won't pose much of a problem, but in this case only people of the same land will understand—unless one writes down what one wishes to say and one's interlocutor takes the trouble to look up all the words in the dictionary; this is too much of a burden to become standard practice. If your author wants people to learn root words common to all languages, he'll never find anyone willing to take the trouble. It would be easier to make everyone agree to learn Latin or some other language now in use; no books have been written yet in this [new] language for practice in reading, nor are there any speakers from whom to learn the conventions of speech. Thus, the only utility I can see in the invention concerns writing. Its creator could have a big dictionary printed in all the languages in which he wanted to be understood and provide one character for each root word and not the syllables, for instance, a single sign for *aimer*, *amare*, and *philein*. Anyone with the dictionary who knew the grammar could look up each of the characters in turn and put whatever was written in them into his own tongue. But that would only be good for secret messages and disclosures (*des mystères et des révélations*); other matters would hardly warrant the bother of looking everything up in a dictionary. So I can't see much benefit to it. Maybe I'm wrong. I just wanted to share with you what I can picture on the basis of the six propositions you sent so that, when you see what I've worked out, you can tell me if I've made sense of it all.

I believe, however, that another invention might be added to this one, both for composing root words and the characters representing them, and in such a way that the language could be taught quite rapidly. Order is key, that is, establishing an order between all the thoughts which can enter the human mind in the same way that an order naturally exists between numbers. Just as one can learn, in a day, to name each of the numbers up to infinity, and to write them in an unknown language consisting of infinite different words, one could do so for all the words necessary to express all the things that occur to the human mind. If this order were found, I have no doubt the language would become common currency, because there are many people who would be glad to take five or six days to be able to make themselves understood by humankind in general.

But I don't believe your author was thinking of that, both because there's nothing in all his propositions attesting to the idea, and because the invention of a language like this is a matter of true philosophy; otherwise, it's impossible to enumerate all the thoughts of human beings and put them in order, or to make them out in a way that's clear and straightforward—which, in my opinion, is the real secret for acquiring sound knowledge. If someone were to explain well the simple ideas in the human imagination out of which all thoughts are composed, and if this explanation were generally acknowledged, I would dare hope for a universal language quite easy to learn, speak, and write—and one that, most importantly, would aid judgment by depicting all things so distinctly that error would be almost impossible. As it stands, it's quite the opposite: almost all our words have confused meanings, to which the human mind has grown so accustomed that hardly anything is understood perfectly.

I hold that such a language is possible, and that the knowledge on which it depends can be found, so that peasants would be able to assess the truth of things better than philosophers do now. But don't go hoping ever to see it in use. That would require great changes in the order of things, and the world would have to be an earthly paradise—a proposal fit only for the land of fiction.

FORERUNNERS OF SCIENTIFIC THOUGHT ABOUT THE ORIGINS OF LANGUAGE

Plato

Cratylus. Trans. Benjamin Jowett.

This text is the starting point for speculation about the motivated nature of the sign, that is, so-called Cratylist theories.

SOCRATES: That objects should be imitated in letters and syllables, and so find expression, may appear ridiculous, Hermogenes, but it cannot be avoided—there is no better principle to which we can look for the truth of first names. Deprived of this, we must have recourse to divine help, like the tragic poets, who in any perplexity have their gods waiting in the air; and must get out of our difficulty in like fashion, by saying that "the Gods gave the first names, and therefore they are right." This will be the best contrivance, or perhaps that other notion may be even better still, of deriving them from some barbarous people, for the barbarians are older than we are; or we may say that antiquity has cast a veil over them, which is the same sort of excuse as the last; for all these are not reasons but only ingenious excuses for having no reasons concerning the truth of words. And yet any sort of ignorance of first or primitive names involves an ignorance of secondary words; for they can only be explained by the primary. Clearly then the professor of languages should be able to give a very lucid explanation of first names, or let him be assured he will only talk nonsense about the rest. Do you not suppose this to be true?

HERMOGENES: Certainly, Socrates.

SOCRATES: My first notions of original names are truly wild and ridiculous, though I have no objection to impart them to you if you desire, and I hope that you will communicate to me in return anything better which you may have.

HERMOGENES: Fear not; I will do my best.

SOCRATES: In the first place, the letter rho appears to me to be the general instrument expressing all motion. But I have not yet explained the meaning of this latter word, which is just κίνησις; for the letter eta was not in use among the ancients, who only employed epsilon; and the root is κίειν, which is a foreign form, the same as ἰέναι. And the old word κίνησις will be correctly given as ἴεσις in corresponding modern letters. Assuming this foreign root κίειν, and allowing for the change of the eta and the insertion of the nu, we have κίνησις, which should have been κιείνεσις or εἶσις; and στάσις (stasis) is the negative of ἰέναι (or εἶσις), and has been improved into στάσις. Now the letter rho, as I was saying, appeared to the imposer of names an excellent instrument for the expression of motion; and he frequently uses the letter for this purpose: for example, in the actual words ῥεῖν (flow) and ῥοή (current) he represents motion by rho; also in the words τρόμος (trembling), τρέχειν (rugged); and again, in words such as κρούειν (strike), θραύειν (crush), ἐρείκειν (bruise), θρύπτειν (break), κερματίζειν (crumble), ῥυμβεῖν (whirl): of all these sorts of movements he generally finds an expression in the letter rho, because, as I imagine, he had observed that the tongue was most agitated and least at rest in the pronunciation of this letter, which he therefore used in order to express motion, just as by the letter iota he expresses the subtle elements which pass through all things. This is why he uses the letter iota as imitative of motion, ἰέναι, ἵεσθαι. And there is another class of letters, phi, psi, sigma, and xi, of which the pronunciation is accompanied by great expenditure of breath; these are used in the imitation of such notions as ψυχρόν (shivering), ζέον (seething), σείεσθαι (to be shaken), σεισμός (shock), and are always introduced by the giver of names when he wants to imitate what is windy. He seems to have thought that the closing and pressure of the tongue in the utterance of delta and tau was expressive of binding and rest in a place: he further observed the liquid movement of lambda, in the pronunciation of which the tongue slips, and in this he found the expression of smoothness, as in λεῖα (level), and in the word ὀλισθάναιν (to slip) itself, λιπαρόν (sleek), in the word κολλῶδες (gluey), and the like: the heavier sound of gamma detained the slipping tongue, and the union of the two gave the notion of a glutinous clammy nature, as in γλισχρόν, γλυκύ, γλοιῶδες. The nu he observed to be sounded from within, and therefore to have a notion of inwardness; hence he introduced the sound in ἔνδον and ἐντός: alpha he assigned to the expression of size, and nu of length, because they are great letters: omicron was the sign of roundness, and therefore there is plenty of omicron mixed up in the word γόγγυλον (round). Thus did the legislator, reducing all things into letters and syllables, and impressing on them names and signs, and out of them by imitation compounding other signs. That is my view, Hermogenes, of the truth of names; but I should like to hear what Cratylus has more to say.

Gottfried Wilhelm Leibniz

New Essays on Human Understanding, 1704. Trans. Alfred Gideon Langley (New York: Macmillan, 1896), book 3, chapter 2, "On the Signification of Words."

How Leibniz treats the problem of primitive language.

§ 1. PHILALETHES. Now as words are employed by men as signs of their ideas, we may ask in the first place how their words have been determined; and we find that it is not by any natural connection existing between certain articulate sounds and certain ideas (for in this case there would be only one language among men), but by an arbitrary institution in virtue of which a given word has been purposely made a sign of a given idea.

THEOPHILUS. I know it has been customary to say in the schools and almost everywhere else that the meanings of words are arbitrary (*ex instituto*) and it is true that they are not determined by a natural necessity, but they are nevertheless determined by reasons sometimes natural, in which chance has some share, sometimes moral, where choice enters. There are perhaps some artificial languages which are wholly of choice and entirely arbitrary, as that of China is believed to have been, or as those of George Dalgarno and the late Mr. Wilkins, bishop of Chester. But those which are known to have been coined from languages already known, are from choice mixed with what there is of nature and chance in the languages they suppose. Thus it is in the case of those languages which thieves have coined in order to be understood only by those of their gang, which the Germans call *Rothwelsch*, Italians *Lingua Zerga*, the French *Narquois*, but which they usually form upon (the basis of) the languages commonly known to them, either by changing the received significations of the words by means of metaphors, or by making new words by means of a composition or derivation in their own fashion. Languages are also formed through the intercourse of different peoples, either by mingling indifferently neighboring languages, or as most frequently happens, by taking the one as a base which is mutilated and altered, mixed and corrupted by neglecting and changing that which it observes, and even by grafting thereupon new words. The *lingua franca*, which is used in the commerce of the Mediterranean, is made from the

Italian, and no regard is paid to the rules of grammar. An Armenian Dominican, with whom I conversed at Paris, had himself made, or perhaps learned from his fellows, a kind of lingua franca, made from Latin, which I found intelligible enough, although it had neither case, nor tense, nor other inflections, and he spoke it with ease, being accustomed to it. Father Labbé, a French Jesuit, very learned, known by many other works, has made a language of which Latin is the base, which is easier and has less constraint than our Latin, but which is more regular than the Lingua Franca. He has made a book expressly of it. As for the languages which are found made a long time ago, there are but few which are not greatly altered to-day. This is evident by comparing them with their ancient books and monuments which remain. The old French approached nearer the Provençal and the Italian, and we see the Théotisque with the French or Romance rather (sometimes called *lingua Romana rustica*) as they were in the ninth century after Jesus Christ in the forms of the oaths of the sons of the Emperor Louis le Debonnaire, which Nithard, their kinsman, has preserved for us. We find little elsewhere of so old French, Italian, or Spanish. But for the Théotisque, or ancient German, there is the gospel of Otfried, a monk of Weissenburg of this same time, which Flacius has published and which Schilter wished to edit anew. The Saxons who passed into Great Britain have left us books still more ancient. They have a version or paraphrase of the beginning of Genesis and of some other parts of the Sacred History, made by a Cædmon whom Bede already mentions. But the most ancient book, not only of the Germanic languages, but of all the languages of Europe, except Greek and Latin, is that of the gospel of the Goths of the Pontus Euxinus, known by the name of Codex Argenteus, written in characters entirely peculiar, which was found in the ancient monastery of the Benedictines of Werden in Westphalia, and has been carried into Sweden, where it is preserved, as with reason it should be, with as much care as the original of the Pandects in Florence, although this version was made by the Eastern Goths and in a dialect far removed from the Scandinavian German; but it is because they believe, with some probability, that the Goths of the Pontus Euxinus came originally from Scandinavia, or at least from the Baltic Sea. Now the language or the dialect of these ancient Goths is very different from the modern German, although it has the same linguistic basis. The ancient Gallic was still more different, to judge by the language most nearly approaching the true Gallic, which is that of the country of Wales, Cornwall, and Basse-Bretagne; but the Irish differs therefrom still more and shows us traces of a Britannic, Gallic, and Germanic language, still more ancient. But all these languages come from one source, and may be taken as modifications of one and the same language, which, may be called the Keltic. Thus the ancients called both the Germans and the Gauls *Kelts*; and in going back farther in order to understand the origin both of the Keltic and the Latin and the Greek, which have many roots in common with the Germanic or Keltic tongues, we may conjecture that this fact arises from the common origin of all these peoples descended from the *Scythians*, who, having come from the Black Sea, passed the Danube and the Vistula, and of whom one part may have gone into Greece, the other have filled Germany and the Gauls; a consequence of the hypothesis which makes the Europeans come from Asia. The *Sarmatian* (supposing it to be the Sclavonic) has at least half its origin either Germanic or common with the Germanic. The case appears to be somewhat similar, indeed, in the Finnish language, which is that of the most ancient Scandinavians, before the Germanic peoples, i.e., the Danes, Swedes, and Norwegians, had taken possession of the land which is the best and nearest the sea; and the language of the Finns or of the northeast of our continent, which is also that of the Lapps, extends from the German or Norwegian Ocean even to the Caspian Sea (although interrupted by the Sclavic peoples which have been thrust in between the two) and has some relation to the Hungarian, having come from the countries which are now in part under the Muscovites. But the Tartar language, which has filled the northeast of Asia, with its variations, appears to have been that of the Huns and Cumans as it is of the Uzbeks or Turkomans, of the Kalmuks and of the Mongols. Now all these languages of Scythia have many roots common among themselves and with ours, and it is found that even the Arabic (under which the Hebrew, the ancient Punic, the Chaldee, the Syriac, the Ethiopic of the Abyssinians are to be comprised) has so great a number of them and an agreement so manifest with ours that it cannot be attributed to chance alone, nor even to commerce alone, but rather to the migrations of the peoples. So that there is nothing in this to combat and not rather to favor the view of the common origin of all nations, and of a primitive root language. If the Hebrew or the Arabic approaches the nearest to it, it must be at least much changed, and the German seems to have preserved more completely the natural and (to use the language of Jacob Boehme) the Adamic; for if we had the primitive language in its purity, or sufficiently preserved to be recognizable, the reasons of the connections whether natural or of an arbitrary institution would necessarily appear wise and worthy of the primitive author. But supposing that our languages are derivative as regards their foundation, they nevertheless have something primitive in themselves which has arisen from them in relation to new root words since formed among them by chance but upon natural grounds. Those which signify the sounds of animals or have come from them furnish examples. Such, for example, is the Latin *coaxare* attributed to the frogs, which has some relation to *couaquen* or *quaken* in German. Now it seems that the noise of these animals is the primordial root of other words of the German language. For as these animals make much noise, the term is attributed to-day to idle talk and to babblers, who are called *quakeler* in the diminutive form; but apparently this same word *quaken* was formerly understood in a good sense and signified all sorts of sounds made with the mouth not even excepting speech. And as these sounds or noises of animals are an evidence of life, and as we know thereby before we see it that there is life there, *quek* in old German has come to signify life or living, as may be observed in the most ancient books, and there are also traces of the same in the modern language, for *Quecksilber* is quicksilver (*vif-argent*), and *erquicken* is to strengthen, and, as it were, to vivify or recreate after exhaustion or some great labor. Certain weeds are called also in Low German *Quaken*, alive so to speak and running, as they say in German, which spread and propagate themselves easily in the fields to the detriment of the grain; and in English *quickly* means promptly and in a wide-awake manner. Thus we may consider that as regards these words the German language may pass as the primitive, the ancients having no need to borrow elsewhere a sound which is the imitation of that of the frogs. And there are many others in which the same thing appears. For it seems that the ancient Germans, Kelts, and other peoples allied to them have employed by a natural instinct the letter R to signify a violent movement and a noise like that of this letter. It appears in ῥέω, *fluo*, *rinnen*, *rüren* (*fluere*), *rutir* (*fluxion*), the *Rhine*, *Rhone*, *Roer*

(*Rhenus, Rhodanus, Eridanus, Rura*), *rauben* (*rapere, ravir*), *Radt* (*rota*), *radere* (*raser*), *rauschen*, a word difficult to translate into French; it signifies a noise like that which the wind or a passing animal stirs up in the leaves or the trees, or is made by a trailing dress; *reckken* (to stretch with violence), whence it comes that *reichen* is to reach; that *der Rick* signifies a long stick or perch useful for suspending anything, in this kind of Plattütsch or Low Saxon which is (spoken) near Brunswick; that *Rige, Reihe, regula, regere,* refer to length or a straight course; and that *Reck* has signified a thing or person very extended and long, and in particular a giant, and then a powerful and rich man, as it appears in the *reich* of the Germans and in the *riche* or *ricco* of the Semi-Latins. In Spanish *ricos hombres* means the nobles or chief men; and this makes it plain at the same time how metaphor, synecdoche, and metonymy have caused words to pass from one signification to another without our being able always to trace them. This noise and violent movement is noticed also in *Riss* (rupture) with which the Latin *rumpo,* the Greek ῥήγνυμι, the French *arracher,* the Italian *straccio* are connected. Now as the letter R signifies naturally a violent movement, the letter L designates a gentler one. Thus we see that children and others who find the E too harsh or too difficult to pronounce substitute for it the letter L, saying, for example, *mon lévérend pèle*. This gentle movement appears in *leben* (*vivre*—live), *laben* (*conforter*—comfort, *faire vivre*—make live), *Lind, lenis, lentus* (*lent*—slow), *lieben* (*aimer*—love), lauffen (*glisser promptement comme l'eau qui coule*—to glide quickly like flowing water), labi (*glisser*—to touch lightly, *labitur uncta vadis abies*), *legen* (mettre doucement—to place gently), whence comes *liegen* (*coucher*—to lie down), *lage* or *laye* (*un lit, comme tin lit de pierres*—a bed, as a bed of rocks), *Laystein* (*pierre à couches*, ardoise—slate), *lego, ich lese* (*je remasse ce qu'on a mis*—I collect what has been invested, it is the opposite of *mettre*—to place, and then *je lis*—I read, and finally among the Greeks *je parle*—I speak), *Laub* (*feuille*—leaf), a thing easy to stir, to which are related also *lap, lid, lenken, luo,* λύω (*solvo*), *leien* (in Low Saxon) to dissolve, to melt like the snow, whence the Leine has its name, a river of Hanover, which, rising in the mountainous countries, is greatly enlarged by the melted snows; not to speak of an infinite number of other similar appellations, which prove that there is something natural in the origin of words which indicates a relation between things and the sounds and movements of the vocal organs; and it is furthermore for that reason that the letter L joined to other nouns makes their diminutives with the Latins, the Semi-Latins, and the High Germans. But it must not be pretended that this reason can be noticed everywhere, for the lion, the lynx, the wolf, are anything but gentle. But it may be attached to another accident, the speed (*lauf*), which makes them feared or compels flight; as if the one who sees such an animal coming should cry to the others: *lauf* (*fuyez!*—fly!); besides by many accidents and changes the majority of words are very much altered and diverted from their pronunciation and original signification.

Antoine Court de Gébelin

Histoire naturelle de la parole, 1772. Extract from chapter 8, "Origine du langage."

Values Assigned to Simple, or Primitive, Intonations Ideas, being of a nature radically different from sensations, could not be depicted by the same signs; and since sounds depicted sensations, intonations were introduced to depict ideas. it would not be difficult to show that the same differences prevail between sounds and intonations as between sensations and ideas. Thus did Nature, which endowed animals with sensations but not ideas, give them sounds and deny them intonations.

However, all manner of ideas could not be depicted by just any intonation at all: that would imply that ideas have nothing to distinguish them, and that intonations all share the same properties to the same degree. These two suppositions are equally absurd.

What, then, did men undertake with respect to language? They fitted it to their ideas.

Pleasant ideas were depicted by pleasant intonations, quick ideas by quick intonations, and slow ideas by slow ones; ideas with qualities contrasting with these attributes were depicted by intonations that also contrasted with the words used for their counterparts. This was the *primum mobile* presiding over the formation of languages; hence the first words were born, which then diversified ad infinitum as they combined with one another.

The *labial* key—the easiest to play on the vocal instrument, the softest and most graceful—served to designate the first beings known to man, those he loves above all others. Hence such childish words as *papa* [father], *maman* [mother] *fanfan* [baby], *bonbon* [candy], *baiser* [kiss], *poupée* [doll], *beau* [beautiful], *bon* [good], *bien* [well].

Equally, it was used to designate the mouth and activities connected with it, such as *boire* [drinking], *manger* [eating], *parler* [speaking], *respirer* [breathing]. The same holds for all languages, for they all were drawn from nature.

In this way, a single key became the source for a prodigious quantity of words, the etymological reason for them.

The *dental* key is entirely different. Since the teeth are as firm as the lips are mobile and flexible, the intonations they produce are as powerful, sonorous, and loud as labial intonations are gentle and light. When the tongue presses against the teeth and then moves away sharply and vigorously, it makes the mouth open as wide as possible, freeing a passage for the forceful jet of air that follows.

It is natural, then, that the resulting intonations depict everything that is sonorous and loud; hence the host of primitive words drawn from nature. In this key there is *tonner* [thundering], *retentir* [resounding], *étonner* [astonishing], *donner le ton* [setting the tone/pace]. It is used to refer to noisy instruments: *les tambours* [drums] and *les tymbales* [kettledrums], *les timpanons* [timpani], *les trompettes* [trumpets]. . . . It is used to set dogs in pursuit of game, to make the voice carry and penetrate the vastness of the forest.

Thus has Nature provided for all man's needs, and he benefits from her assistance without effort or worry. Man follows impressions without doubting them. If, when he comes to reflect on the advantages thus obtained, he should fail to recognize what he owes to her—or if he imagines that these observations are simple fancy—he is an ingrate who does not deserve to be called a sentient and perceptive being.

It is not surprising that this property of the dental key brought forth the names for great and imposing objects: for masses heaped up in *tas* [piles], for *tout* [everything], *tant* [so much], *dominer* [to dominate], *dôme* [dome], *dune* [dune], *toit* [roof], and so on—for everything that *protège* [protects].

Indeed, the dental key produced the very word *dents* [teeth].

The lingual intonation *l* designates gentle movements, objects that display continuous and calm motion, all that is limpid and clear. In contrast, its forceful variant *r* designates rough and strong motion, objects that are loud or display jumping or jerky movement, or jagged edges. Such are the words *roue* [wheel], *roc* [rock], *rocher* [crag], *ravine* [ravine], *rapide* [rapid], *rude* [rough].

The *guttural* key involves the throat, a long and narrow channel. In order to make the intonations it produces audible, the voice has to plunge and then emerge from depths of the windpipe, the remotest part of the vocal organ.

Therefore, one depicts with these intonations . . . all objects that are hollow and emptied out, all objects that stretch out like channels; hence the words *canal* [canal], *canne* [cane], *col* [neck], *cours* [course], *cap* [cape], *cave* [cellar], *cavité* [cavity], and so on. The same holds for the words *gorge* [throat] and *gosier* [gullet] themselves.

On Some Other Ways of Forming Words The relationship of sounds and intonations with nature was not sufficient to depict ideas as a whole; thus it proved necessary to enlist other sources of words that were just as simple, just as natural, and which man had always imitated.

The first means was to apply names to animate or inanimate objects by imitating the cries of the ones and the noises of them all. This is what is called *onomatopoeia* or *word-formation*. Such were the names for *boeuf* [ox], *corbeau* [crow], *cigale* [cicada]. . . .

The second means was to put two or more intonations together, in order to express by this union ideas they were not adequate to express on their own. Thus, *l* and *r* can be preceded by almost all other intonations; we have words beginning with *bl*, *cl*, *gl*, *fl*, *pl*, with *br*, *er*, *gr*, *fr*, *pr*, and ones that are more or less of the same nature as *l* and *r*, such as *glisser* [to glide], *fluide* [flowing], *fieur* [flower], *pleur* [tear], *effroi* [terror], *grincement* [grinding, creaking], *cri* [cry], and so on.

Or by joining *s* and *t*, or *st*, the first of which is a hissing sound and the second a dental, which yields a highly mobile and rapid intonation together with the most rigid of intonations; by this means there forms a host of words that all refer to a permanent, or *stable*, entity.

The third means was to conjoin two or more words in a single one in order to express complex ideas: such are our words *aujourd'hui* [today], which is composed of five others, *maintenant* [now], *passe-droit* [free pass], *outremer* [overseas], *rejeter* [reject], *défaire* [undo], *parfait* [perfect]. One can lay down as a principle that any word of two syllables is a compound and brings together two different ideas to form a single one.

The fourth and final means was to designate non-material entities by the same words that already referred to material ones. Thus the word *esprit* [spirit/mind], which signified breathing, a material or sensory activity, came to designate the faculty of thought, which is not a material or sensory faculty.

The same qualities were attributed to non-material entities as to physical beings. One speaks of a mind being *vif* [lively], *ardent* [ardent], *impétueux* [impetuous], *bouché* [blocked], as if it were fire, wind, or a channel. In turn, a heart may be *tendre* [tender], *dur* [hard], or *volage* [flighty], as if it were a plant or a butterfly.

It wasn't enough to have found the means for depicting ideas representing physical, moral, or intellectual objects; the task remained of finding a way to express negative ideas, to depict objects that do not exist. Man did fail to rise to the occasion. He even found two methods instead of one.

Sometimes he would depict the object in question in the opposite sense; sometimes he was content to substitute a weak intonation for a strong one.

A, at the end of a noun, marked the existence or the possession of an object. At the beginning of the same word, it marked its non-existence or absence. The Greeks, in particular, adopted this method.

In, at the end of a word, marked existence, expanse, reality; at the beginning, it indicated non-existence, absence—as in *in-utile* [useless], *in-juste* [unjust], *im-materiel* [immaterial], *in-forme* [shapeless].

Strong intonation and strong vowels being the hallmark of positive objects, weak intonation and weak vowels came to be used for negative objects, for absence. Thus, Latin *gel-idus*, which indicates the quality of being cold or frozen, is the weak counterpart of *cal-idus* or *caldus*, which means the opposite. Our French words *gelée* [frost] and *chaleur* [heat] also derive from the same root and display the same contrast. It was necessary to have contrast between words, since there are contrasts between ideas. In consequence, this method conformed strictly to nature, and made roots available for all ideas.

Jean-Jacques Rousseau

Essay on the Origin of Languages, 1781 (posthumous). Trans. John T. Scott (Hanover, NH: University Press of New England, 1998).

Chapter II: That the First Invention of Speech Derives Not from the Needs but from the Passions It is therefore to be supposed that needs dictated the first gestures and that the passions wrested the first voices. By following the path of the facts with these distinctions in mind, it might perhaps be necessary to reason about the origin of languages altogether differently than has been done until now. The genius of the oriental languages, the most ancient known to us, absolutely contradicts the didactic course that is imagined in their formation. These languages have nothing methodical and reasoned about them; they are lively and figurative. The language of the first men is put before us as though it were the languages of Geometers, while we see that they were the languages of Poets.

This must have been so. We did not begin by reasoning but by feeling. It is claimed that men invented speech in order to express their needs; this opinion seems untenable to me. The natural effect of the first needs was to separate men and not to bring them together. This had to have been so for the species to spread and the Earth to be populated promptly, otherwise mankind would have been crammed into one corner of the world while the rest of it remained deserted.

From this alone it evidently follows that the origin of languages is not at all due to men's first needs; it would be absurd for the cause that separates them to come to be the means that unites them. From where, then, could this origin derive? From the moral needs, the passions. The passions all bring men together, but the necessity of seeking their livelihood makes them flee one another. Neither hunger nor thirst, but love, hatred, pity, anger wrested the first voices from them. Fruit does not elude our grasp, one can feed on it without speaking, one stalks in silence the prey one wishes to devour; but in order to move a young heart, to repulse an unjust aggressor, nature dictates accents, cries, complaints. The most ancient words are invented in this way, and this is why the first languages were tuneful and passionate before being simple and methodical. All this is not true without qualification, but I shall come back to it below.

Chapter III: That the First Languages Must Have Been Figurative As the first motives that made man speak were the passions, his first expressions were Tropes. Figurative language was the first to arise, proper meaning was found last. Things were not called by their true name until they were seen in their genuine form. At first, only poetry was spoken. Only long afterwards did anyone take it into his head to reason.

Now, I am well aware that the reader will stop me here, and will ask me how an expression could be figurative before having a proper meaning, since it is only in the translation of the meaning that the figurativeness consists. I admit this; but in order to understand me it is necessary to substitute the idea that the passion presents to us for the word that we transpose; for words are transposed only because ideas are also transposed, otherwise figurative language would signify nothing. I therefore respond with an example.

Upon encountering others, a savage man will at first be afraid. His fright will make him see those men as taller and stronger than himself. He will give them the name *Giants*. After many experiences he will recognize that as these supposed Giants are neither taller nor stronger than himself, their stature does not agree with the idea that he had first attached to the word Giant. He will therefore invent another name common to them and to him, such as the name man for example, and will leave that of Giant for the false object that had stuck him during his illusion. That is how the figurative word arises before the proper word, when passion fascinates our eyes and the first idea it offers us is not the true one. What I have said about words and names is applied without any difficulty to turns of phrase. The illusory image offered by the passions being presented first, the language which corresponded to it was likewise the first to be invented. It then became metaphorical when the enlightened mind, recognizing its first error, employed the expressions only with the same passions that had produced it.

Chapter IV: On the Distinctive Characteristics of the First Language and the Changes It Must Have Undergone Simple sounds issue naturally from the throat, the mouth is naturally more or less open; but the modifications of the tongue and palate that produce articulation require attention, practice;

one does not make them unless one wants to make them, all children need to learn them and some do not easily succeed in doing so. In all languages the most lively exclamations are unarticulated; cries and groans are simple voices. Mutes, that is the deaf, utter only unarticulated sounds. Father Lamy cannot even conceive how men could ever have invented others unless God had not expressly taught them to speak. Articulations are few in number, sounds are infinite in number, and the accents which mark them can be multiplied in the same way. All musical notes are so many accents; we have, it is true, only three or four in speech, but the Chinese have many more of them; on the other hand, they have fewer consonants. To this source of combinations add that of tense or quantity, and you will have not only a greater variety of words, but of syllables, than the richest language needs.

I do not at all doubt that, independent of vocabulary and of syntax, if the first language still existed it would have retained the original characteristics that would distinguish it from all the others. Not only would all the turns of phrase in this language have to be in images, in feelings, and in figures of speech; but in its mechanical aspect it would have to answer to its first object, and to present to the sense as well as to the understanding the almost inevitable impressions of the passion that is sought to be communicated.

As natural voices are unarticulated, words would have few articulations; a few interposed consonants eliminating the hiatus between the vowels would suffice to make them flowing and easy to pronounce. In contrast, its sounds would be quite varied, and the diversity of accents would multiply these same voices. Quantity and rhythm would provide further sources of combinations; in this way—since voices, sounds, accent, and number, which are from nature, would leave little to be done by articulations, which are conventional—one would sing it rather than speak it. Most of its root words would be imitative sounds, either of the accent of the passions, or of the effect of perceptible objects. Onomatopoeia would constantly make itself felt.

This language would have many synonyms to express the same being in its different relations; it would have few adverbs and abstract words to express these same relations. It would have many augmentatives, diminutives, compound words, and expletive particles to give cadence to periods and roundness to phrases. It would have many irregularities and anomalies, it would neglect grammatical analogy to stick to the euphony, number, harmony, and beauty of sounds. Instead of arguments it would have aphorisms; it would persuade without convincing, and depict without reasoning. It would resemble Chinese in certain respects, Greek in others, and Arabic in others. Develop these ideas in all their ramifications, and you will find Plato's *Cratylus* is not as ridiculous as it seems to be.

Charles Nodier

Notions élémentaires de linguistique, ou histoire abrégée de la parole et de l'écriture pour servir d'introduction à l'alphabet, à la grammaire et au dictionnaire, 1834.

Nodier was one of the last avowed defenders of the theory that language is onomatopoeic and phono-symbolic in origin; a member of the Académie Française, he witnessed the rise of comparative grammar.

Chapter II: Organic Language MAN had already expressed his thought by no other means than simple vowels, the use of which must necessarily precede the use of the other artifices of speech; and what thought it was! We know: the thought of GOD!

His moral progress would never have passed beyond these limits; he would have been limited to such effort and reduced to this achievement; and still one would have to recognize in him the crown of Creation: he would still be *man*.

But he has only reached childhood. His vocabulary will become richer from day to day, by the twofold power of growing thought and the exercise of his organs: a tongue taking form and the mystery accomplished therein.

Here, the Divine Author of speech left him to the instinct of imitation, which henceforth would be his unfailing instrument. All the organs of the human voice were granted the privilege of declaring themselves by the articulation that is their own. And, by virtue of a property still more wondrous, there was not one of these articulations that could not take on, in meaningful and vivid fashion, a share of what is to be perceived in Nature, a share of the abstract facts and figural conceptions that depict themselves to the understanding alone.

Thus do organic and intellectual speech march arm in arm as twin sisters, the one the body and the other the soul.

[. . .] Come, then, for our first lesson, and stand next to the cradle of the child making its first consonant, which leaps from its mouth in response to the kisses of the mother. The *bambin* [tot], the *poupon* [baby doll], the *marmot* [kid] has found the three labial sounds: it *bée* [gapes], *baye* [gawks], *balbutie* [stammers], *bégaye* [stutters], *babille* [babbles], *blatère* [bleats], *bêle* [brays], *bavarde* [chatters], *braille* [bawls], *boude* [sulks], *bouque* [pecks]; it *bougonne* [mumbles] about some *babiole* [bauble], *bagatelle* [trifle], *billevesée* [bit of nonsense], or *bêtise* [something silly]—a *bébé* [baby], *bonbon* [sweet], *bobo* [boo-boo], or the *bilboquet* [cup-and-ball game] hanging from the stall of the *bimbelotier* [toymaker]. The child names mother and father with affectionate acts of imitation; the simple register of the lips has only just been discovered, yet the soul already stirs in words made half by chance. This Cadmus in swaddling clothes has just glimpsed a mystery as great in itself as the rest of all Creation. He speaks his very thought.

We're quite close, you will say, to Molière's eminently philosophical Monsieur Jourdain, who proves, by reasoned argument, that one pouts when saying "U." I won't claim otherwise, but truly this is not my fault. The child we were just observing is the man at the first beginnings of human language, and it is in this way that languages were formed—if there's anything at all their history has made clear.

The child's stammer in the cradle is the speech of the first human society, before all the resources of its vocal organ have been made manifest to understanding and acquired by experience. This diction already encompasses all the fundamental ideas of civilization by a process of extension at which we have only hinted, but which will be easily explained in the following, if only we are patient or indulge our curiosity.

From there on, a society already complete is in place: a fortress towering toward God, called *Babel*, with the capital of *Biblos*, a king called *Bel* or *Belus*, the imposturous deity *Baal*, and even a mystagogue who makes the animals talk, *Balaam*. Wait a little while and, in keeping with primitive tradition, there will be the first book, *Biblion*, and the first empire, *Babylon*.

[. . .] The names of created beings were, indeed, their true names in the tongue of Adam. . . . For Adam shaped them as his senses dictated, that is, in keeping with the most obvious way things appeared to him. The sensation of sound, the first to strike the child, must have been the first to strike the family of man in its state of infancy. Today, children no longer create their language, for the lengthy task, which took a life longer than our own, and perhaps a succession of centuries whose advances finally culminated in the alphabet, is spared to them, thanks to the ability to imitate speech right away and to talk before even understanding—in contrast to primitive man, who needed to understand before speaking. But if necessity compels the child to create a word (often, when encountering something touching and new away from home), this word, without fail, is a lively onomatopoeia or evocation. There is no way for languages to enrich themselves other than by imitation or comparison. . . .

FANTASTICAL RECONSTRUCTIONS OF THE PRIMITIVE TONGUE

Father Terence Joseph O'Donnelly

Extrait de la traduction authentique des hiéroglyphes de l'Obélisque de Louqsor à Paris, 1851.

The following, from the work's introduction, is typical of how the logophile thinks: the more skepticism and mockery he encounters, the more certain he is that he is right.

Two years have passed since I announced this news, not in the public press—which has no sense of good news—but by the inadequate means at my own disposal. Since then, I have not stopped my appeal to scholars without, however, finding the satisfaction of finding a single voice that would make it heard by society.

It is clear that I am but a poor missionary. If Moses, with all the means he possessed, confessed himself unequal to his task, all the more should I not hesitate to avow my own impotence. Yet I fooled myself from the very start, and, having now recognized my error, I am changing roles. Instead of addressing my words to scholarly intuition, I would turn to the humble and meek and speak before the common people. Indeed, . . . having received what I know by way of nature, I should instead have shared it with those who have learned in her school, rather than those who are not her adepts. The philosophy of the former, whose province is common sense, would have acknowledged me upon arrival; whereas the philosophy of the latter, bounded by prejudice, took umbrage at my very approach.

From this standpoint, the way forward is certain, and I can count on the wondrous mission meeting with success. Therefore, instead of offering the public the complete translation of the Obelisk, as I should be glad to do, I am only providing an extract with the literal translation of one side, so the style of the ancients may be appreciated. Moreover, this path was the only one open to me for the following reasons:

When I sent a notice to the Asiatic Society, and likewise to all men of learning, that they should be so good as to forgather and take cognizance of my discovery and the key to it, their silence declared their opinion of me and my discovery: they were unwilling to bother themselves even to examine the matter. This trial promptly convinced me that it was not meet to provide the key for a treasure so exquisite to a society so ready to insult not only my person, but also my sacred office and God Himself, inasmuch as I am exercising the faculties He has given me to avail the universal family. The private meetings I subsequently had with scholars, with few exceptions, only strengthened this impression: *"It would take the key for me to be believed."* Granted, were it a matter of devising a mechanism or founding some kind of enterprise, it would be necessary to provide the operative principles. But to spend eighteen months composing a work that has the sole purpose or benefit of persuading one's fellow men of the truth of the issue—that was not my concern. Quite the opposite: instead of bolstering the translation I published with the Hebrew text, which would have made clear the force of particles unknown until now, I cut out [the particles] and was content to share only the results. By the light of the stern philosophy that led me to my discovery, I recognized here the immense weakness which debases humanity, and I resolved not to gratify [this weakness] by pouring forth the finest gift from God in its foul spirit—whatever it might cost me. Set back in this way from the very start, I could discern no immediate prospect of placing my humble insights in relation to pride so obstinate. Therefore I ceased all activity. From my retreat, everyone seemed to be playing blind man's bluff, not knowing where they were or where they were going. But all the same, for my own edification, I carried on with my studies, which, for want of cooperation, have not progressed beyond the frailty of infancy; last December, I applied my method of reading according to the original to the first chapter of Genesis, since it is the most ancient text. I was compelled to conduct my first experiment on the Holy Bible; otherwise, I should not have chosen, for these purposes, the sacred text I deem the very soul of humanity.

Without stopping at the *story* of Moses or the accepted meaning of words in his day—as I would have done to relate his deeds duly—I managed to bring out the sense of words at the birth of speech itself.—Well, then! This translation was enough to open the eyes of even a mole and make it plain that something extraordinary lay at the heart of my claims (and less, please note, by virtue of the explanations offered than by the unity that there prevails).

I sent copies everywhere—to Rome, to the Academy of Paris, to Oxford, to private persons, and to public figures. Was there man among them who so much as confirmed receipt of what I had sent? Not a one, and it's easy to understand why. Has ever human pride been so outflanked, cornered, and crushed as it has been by the discovery at issue? It would seem that as much was necessary before it could manifest itself to the minds of one and all.

Seeing that words and the results they yielded were being scattered to the winds, I resolved, like the man of ancient fable, to test the strength of stone. The Luxor Obelisk before me, I set to work on the hieroglyphs last Christmas, so that, if circumstances should prompt my renewed assault on the pride of society, its great mass might lend succor. I knew beforehand that, since the fall of the last pharaoh, not a single hieroglyph had been deciphered—in spite of the dictionaries and studies devoted to the subject. Truly, scholars have been led astray by a Greek inscription on the so-called Rosetta Stone; this inscription is placed beneath the hieroglyphic text in such a way that no one would doubt it is a faithful translation. This is not the case at all: it's as far from the hieroglyph as the zenith from the nadir—even though its letters copy the antiquity of the hieroglyphic script perfectly. It's a record of the vanity of Ptolemy Epiphanes; no doubt, he wanted posterity to believe that he was a great scholar—and at a time when Egyptian literature had just spent more than five hundred years in the dungeons of oblivion, about two hundred and fifty years before Christ.

Amand de Vertus

La langue primitive basée sur l'idéographie lunaire, 1868.

The work begins with a warning.

Rights Reserved All obligations imposed on authors by our laws and international treaties having been fulfilled,

I intend to prosecute any pirated edition or translation of *The Primitive Language Based on Lunar Ideography.*

This discovery is mine alone. Science has never recognized, or even suspected, that our languages and writing rest on human conventions that are based on *the moon, its course, its phases, colors, gravitational pull,* and *influence.*

Given that this extraordinary fact cannot meet with immediate acceptance, and is even likely to be rejected in the manner of all truth confounding received ideas,

I wish to ensure, at least for my children, the benefits accruing to a discovery whose merits will come to be appreciated sooner or later.

This is why, I repeat, I will prosecute any party who, on the pretext of improvement, might lay hold of the principles I set forth by altering the language, for instance, by substituting "curve" for "crescent," "circle" for "full moon," or "moonrise" for "the first light of the moon"; such a mode of expression would serve to explain a number of terms, but not *oscillation, color,* and *movement,* which are particular states of the moon.

The principles offered to the public could be expounded in more practical manner; I expressly reserve the right to do so for myself.

Every copy will bear my signature.

A. de Vertus

Brécy, by Coincy, department of Aisne (France)

A sample of the author's semantic ramblings:

Serpent This is the most extraordinary word in the Primitive Language. It expresses the moon's first crescent and a number of connected ideas. The most striking are *espérer* [to hope] and *tromper* [deceive]; in such manner that, in a wide range of tongues (which linguists do not assign to the same family), the word "crescent" signifies *cunning* and *deceit* in moral terms, and *serpent* in physical ones. Curved instruments bear the name of the crescent moon, that is, various names of the serpent. For example:

Serpè, in Italian, *serpent, serpe, croissant* (serpent, billhook, crescent); *drepani* in modern Greek, which is to be read as ***sré-pani***, or sickle; ***sherp*** [sic] in English, to trick. The elephant's *trompe* [trunk] and *trompette* [trumpet] are veritable serpents, as is the musical instrument *serpent*.

Our *faux* [scythe] and *faucille* [sickle], for harvesting, come from Latin ***falx*** and correspond to our *words fallacieux* [fallacious] and *faux* [false]: deceptive.

The god ***Hermes*** is the crescent, for ***her mès***, in Hebrew, means sickle; take the word apart, and one finds ***heri (ari)*** and ***mes***, the lunar crescent or knife, *le mois* [month], which is to be pronounced as in Italian, *mese;* ***messis***, "what is cut" in Latin lands, is *moisson* [harvest] in French. Everywhere, ***mes*** is the crescent moon, the very type and primitive image for all curved instruments, weapons, etc. fashioned by human hands.

Guivre [wyvern], as everyone knows, is a serpent. This word is composed of *gui*, "serpent," and *vere*, "shining crescent." The latter half is merely added on here, for *gui* means serpent on its own; cf. Latin *anguis*, "serpent" or "eel."

The word *tromper* [deceive] would have remained a mystery forever, like so many others, without the discovery of the fundamental laws of language; ***tor***, *tordre* [to twist], ***tor-ompa***, *hampe* [shaft, staff]; in Malagasy, ***ompa***, ***ampa***, mean "agent." The Nordic ***Tor*** is none other than the curved crescent moon, the symbol of what *acts*; the word is the suffix used in Europe to form active nouns, whereas in Madagascar ***ompe*** is placed at the beginning of the word; these two signs denoting action are combined in ***tr-ompe***, which means "twice curved," since *trompe*, in physical terms, means "siphon," and *siphon* equals ***Typhon***, who is of course a giant serpent, that is, a curved being. . . . Thus, *trompe* is a name for the crescent moon, and, in the moral sense, it means "trickery," like all the names for the lunar crescent or serpent.

The horror of the serpent which human beings have experienced at all times is a natural effect. It has nothing in common with the universal idea of hope, with the deceit and cunning that are the radically opposite meanings of the word *serpent.*

It is clear, then, that the lunar serpent—the crescent, not the terrestrial animal—stands at issue.

Sin means the Moon as a waxing crescent, *en ceinture* [belted], ***cine-tura***.

Sinus, in Latin, means "curve"; *insinuer, s'insinuer* [to insinuate (oneself)] are very close to *tromper* [deceive]; ***sinaï***, in Malagasy, means "cunning," "deceit." The Latin ***bu-cinna*** means *trompette* [trumpet] in reference to an object; ***buccina*** is also the rising of the New Moon, the crescent.

Our *doloire* [medieval axe], **dola-bera**, is a *serpe* [billhook]; the Greek **doleros**, *tromperie, fourberie* [trickery, deceit] and ***dolos*** (like Latin ***dolus***) give us *dol* [fraud].

We have just explained the pernicious influence of the crescent; its influence in the other direction yields the same words with a totally opposite sense.

The crescent, or lunar serpent, is the sign of Good and Evil. The art of determining what fortune or misfortune would occur from its appearance is the first superstition, according to our most ancient Scriptures, into which woman was drawn by her curiosity. All words are marked by the idea of the *misleading* crescent and the *beneficent* crescent.

Charles Callet

Le mystère du langage, 1928.

A champion of the natural expressivity of phonemes.

The Formation Of Language *We will be plunging into the depths of time to approach the Hominian at the epic and mysterious moment when his intelligence blossomed forth and speech was born.*

A Bimane is watching the bearing of another Bimane prowling not far away. Scenting a danger, he lows dully, "*Meu,*" or growls, "*Rre, Gre, Kre*"; or else, teeth clenched and grinding, lips spread in a savage and spiteful grin, he makes a stifled, hissing noise or a nasalized grunt—"*Ny, Gny.*"

These different sounds—manifestations of suspicion, of anger—are brought forth instinctively, but they draw the others' attention to teeth ready to bite. For the realistic minds of the watchful one's companions—the minds of those he protects: children, females, and the elderly—they could not possibly rouse ideas other than "tooth," "bite," "combat." Necessarily, then, the sounds come to be the names for these things. The same *necessity,* which it is impossible to overemphasize, we will observe in all primordial phonemes.

If we consider languages both living and dead, the bellowing sound *Meu* refers, universally, to muzzle, jaw, tooth, biting, eating, and killing. Hissing (and growling), *Ss* (or *Ff*), signifies tooth, maw, biting, eating, and killing. The guttural grunts *Rre, Kre, Gre,* and the nasalized grunt, *Ny* or *Gny,* denote tooth, maw, biting, eating, and killing.

These constant meanings follow inevitably from a single creative law.

GENERAL REMARK: *Roots, or elementary seeds, are never images; they do not depict objects, they are unconnected with onomatopoeia or the imitation of sounds, and they do not derive from any convention.*

The Hissing Language Whim, choice, convention, and onomatopoeia played no part in the production and evolution of the sound *Ny*. *Gny* or *Ny*, a sort of grunt produced by the vocal organs when making a grimace, did not announce immediate combat so much as it alerted the adversary that one was on guard, that teeth and nails were ready for action.

Hissing was more threatening; since the teeth were bared ferociously, it was inevitable that *Si*, *Shi*, and *Ffi*—natural cries and vocalizations of the species—universally became the name (or more accurately, one of the names) for tooth.

Si or *Fi*, as tooth and tip, had endless descendants.

Let us make a quick tour of such progeny over millennia and sound the deep reasons underlying the derivation of words.

S = tooth; it refers to biting, the mouth, the entire face, and, finally, physiognomic expression; the term *S* comes to designate hunger and thirst.

S will be applied to animals with fearsome teeth, sharp beaks, pointed horns, and poisonous stingers; it refers to their ferocity and the terror they inspire.

Anything pointed, or long and slender, will be named with an "S": reeds, shoots, grass, hair, eyelashes, fur, horsehair, the bristles of pachyderms; trees, stones, flint, rocks, and mountains, which often bear comparison to teeth.

As meanings expand and branch out, they register all the gains in knowledge and discoveries of the intellect: words derived from *S*, meaning "plant," are given to sowing, cultivation, crops, the harvest—to the wealth, experience, and skill of the farmer.

The Lowing Language The primary meaning of words in *N*, *G*, *R*, and *S* was, it has been established, "tooth," "biting," "killing," "eating," "saliva," "water," and so on. *Meu* brought forth a series of phonemes with identical meanings: the same law and the same logic set the course for the same developments.

Meu, as noted, rang forth plaintively. The human animal wandering over a hostile earth, convulsed by tremors, inhabited by imposing beasts, felt his weakness and, in confusion, foresaw a future of horror. As intelligence dawned, and therefore awareness of his miserable state, man lowed in desperation. Languages have preserved an echo of his lamentations, as it were. Latin *mu* is a cry of pain; in Walloon, *mus* = taciturn, sad; in Celto-Breton, *mar* = anxiety, *maritel* = suffering, and *melgre* = grief; Old French had *mari* = suffering, *marmiteux* = groan. In Hebrew, *mar* = affliction.

Let us consider the derivations, with an emphasis on the idioms of our own lands.

Some of the expressions just mentioned, as well as words for pallor, jaundice, and illness—*marrana* and *marfi* (Occitan), *morlivet* (Breton)—come from roots that refer to water, swamps. (In Walloon, *marass* = marsh, and *masi* = dirty or muddy. In the Norman patois, *marsouin* means "filthy person"; applied to the marine mammal [porpoise], it means "water boar" or "water pig." Old High German, *meri-suin*; Norrois, *mar-svin*. In Breton, *moeltr* = damp, and *morc'h* and *mastar* = stain; *mon* and *mours* = excrement, *and mouez* = stench, etc.)

The harmful influence of stagnant waters gives rise to *malaria*, "fever" and "death." *M* marks words for death in a great number of languages. Breton has *marv*, *marô*, and *marf*, the latter phoneme also occurring in Occitan. Welsh has *murv*, Hebrew *mout*, and Annamese *mot*, "drowned" and "to die." In Sanskrit, *mar a* = death; Latin has *mors*. In Assyrian, *mitu*, *marsi* = illness. In Panipat, *melar* = death. Among the Duma (Africa), *maku* = death. In Poul (Africa), *mai, maede* = death, and *moussi* = ill. Nahuatlan (Mexico) *mica* = death, and *miqui* = to die. Algic (Canada) *may, mal* = bad (cf. Latin *malus*). Australian *molwa* = corpse. Turkish *memat* = death, *maraz* = malady (cf. French *marasme*), *ma* = water, *mourdar* = corrupt. *M* signifies "muzzle" and "maw." In Occitan, *mina* = mien, face; *moufe* = muzzle, snout; *mourre, morga, mus* = nose (Fr. *se musser* = to hide, to slide); *musse,* a hunting term, refers to the narrow passage in a hedge for rabbits and hares; originally, it was a hole into which an animal could insert its muzzle or nose. In Breton, *mîn* = mien, face; *muzel* = muzzle and lip (Annamese *mep* = lip); *mannouz* = nasal-sounding, *musa* = to sniff. In French, *muser* = to sniff around. This word is associated with noses and scent.

The ascendant position of the head in man (*marré* = head) as well as the projection of the nose have served to designate elevations of terrain. In France, and particularly among the Carnutes, *mares* invariably referred to elevations or peaks. . . . *Marran* = mound, bank. In Spanish, *mare* = peak, summit; *morne* is the name given to hills in the Antilles. In Assyrian, *mah* = elevated. In Breton, *meur* = high, elevated. In Quechuan (Brazil [sic]), *mallua* and *maru* = hill. Mayan (Amer.) *mull, much* = hill; cf. Basque *mendia*, Hebrew *maros*.

Our French word *menace* reproduces the Latin *minacia* and *minari,* which have similar meaning, but the old sense is well known to have been "projecting," "prominent," "overhanging"—like the nose, *mus* or *mourr*.

Jean-Pierre Brisset

From *Le mystère de Dieu est accompli,* 1891.

No one has understood the Bible, for it is the very mystery of God, only to be known after prophecy has been fulfilled. It should be made clear as day, demonstrating, scientifically and in plain view, that a boundless spirit, the Spirit that created everything, is omnipresent, sees all, knows all, and directs all.

Behold, then, how Creation took place. Proofs irrefutable and profuse will abound and overabound as they spill forth from the analytical summary that follows; all tongues will join in and bear witness. The Word itself will speak and share what it has heard: what our ancestors did, said, and thought—and even what they didn't think, but might have been able to conceive.

God's creature is not animal man, but spiritual man, who lives by the power of the Word, which originated with our twofold arch-ancestor, the frog, more than a million—and less than ten million—years ago. The frogs of our marshes speak French. One need only listen and know how to analyze what is being said to understand them, for each articulate sound occurs in the same way in animals and human beings. . . .

So long as frogs were merely frogs, their language did not develop considerably. But as soon as sexual differences began to emerge, strange and imperious sensations forced the animal to cry out for aid; it couldn't satisfy itself or attenuate the fires which consumed it. The reason is that frogs don't have long arms, and their necks are wedged in their shoulders. Now, the emergence of sexual difference and the frog's change into an amphibious mammal capable of reproduction through sexual coupling lasted, for each individual, from the age of forty to a hundred twenty. This arch-ancestor, like the Beast of Revelation, had an average lifespan of twelve or thirteen centuries. Let no one think that this animal lacked intelligence; it was dextrous, vigilant, and clever, commanding a highly developed language. Completely obsessed with venereal and carnal desires, it gratified them by every means in its power—of which mutual licking and sucking of the genitals were the most innocent.

In effect, the frogs attending to each other in this manner had, as yet, no possibility of using fingers; they could only employ their lips, mouth, and tongue. Such activities did not offend the eyes any more than does a cow cleaning her calf or the Holy Mother suckling her Child. Over time, however, they became repellent, and the same cries that had been innocent now created spirits—or words—of aversion and disgust. Moreover, arms grew in length, and those with long arms could satisfy themselves. The neck also developed, as did the spine, which became quite flexible: now, the Ancestor could apply his maw to his own nudity. All this occurred at the banks of watering holes, swamps, ponds, and rivers. The howls of a swarm of rutting cats may provide a slight idea of the demonic uproar and racket that prevailed. It was then that the morning stars exclaimed together in joy and all the sons of God shouted in triumph (Job 38: 7).

It was fiery amorous passion, then, that loosened the ancestors' tongues. There they were, gazes fixed on their counterparts' sexual features. In this state of beatific contemplation, beckoning and stimulating each other, their spirit—the same as ours today—took form. For the spirit is born of the flesh, and for this to occur, the flesh must be tortured by all the fires of blazing love.

In light of the foregoing explanation, it is clear where Analysis of the Word will take us, for almost all syllables and phrases originated here.

Excerpts from *Les origines humaines* (1907)

When a man has announced himself as the Seventh Angel of the Apocalypse and the Archangel of the Resurrection, manifesting and bringing to fulfilment all Biblical prophecies, it is sure that no one comes before him. For none has declared himself the Angel or Archangel announced by Paul and John.

If an impostor, such a man ought to be publicly confounded. But if truly the emissary of God, presenting himself on the day appointed to explain all mysteries and raise the dead by bringing back all who have lived since the beginning of the world, he incurs great guilt, should the silence hanging over his works be charged to him.

[Thus] we will first make plain that we have cried with all our might, in a voice of thunder.

La grammaire logique faisant connaître la formation des langues et celle du genre humain [*Logical Grammar Declaring the Formation of Languages and Humankind*], which appeared in 1883 (Paris, Ernest Leroux), has spread reasonably far within the scholarly world. Submitted to the Academy for a contest, our work was rejected by M. Renan, however.

Unable to find a publisher, in 1891 we published *Le Mystère de Dieu* [*The Mystery of God*] ourselves, advertising with notices and two public lectures in Paris. This book provoked some excitement among students in Angers. Arrangements were made for a lecture there, but municipal authorities thwarted our project.

In 1900 we published *La Science de Dieu* [*The Science of God*] and a leaflet with a run of 10,000 copies, *La Grande nouvelle* [*The Great News*], summing up our work to date. Being hamstrung, as it were, our vendors did not sell this same title. We had it distributed for free throughout Paris and sent it, along with the book, more or less everywhere. Once the leaflet was distributed, the printing did sell, however we were not informed of this fact until after our agent had gone bankrupt.

These two publications made enough of a stir to induce *Le Petit Parisien* to devote a first article entirely to us (if indirectly so), "Among the Mad" (29 July 1904). We are explicitly concerned where they refer to an insane individual "who, on the basis of a system of alliteration and incoherent associations, has set forward a whole treatise on metaphysics entitled *La Science de Dieu*. For him, the Word really is everything, and the analysis of words brings out the relationship between things. For want of space, I cannot quote passages from this awful philosophy. Simply reading them, moreover, leaves one's mind truly troubled. Readers will thank me for wishing to spare them."

The madman in question—an official empowered to make arrests, whose mode of writing has nothing in common with the obscure verbiage above—was, in fact, pleased with the criticism and even expressed his gratitude. After all, isn't there reason to be satisfied when deceitful and unthinking parties grant one a place alongside Jesus, Paul, Joan of Arc, and all the others God Almighty has called to serve His purposes?

La Science de Dieu, when published, sounded the seventh trumpet of the Apocalypse, and in 1906 we published *Les Prophéties accomplies*. A fairly long prospectus was printed in two thousand copies and sent to various quarters; since our voice still needed to be heard, a lecture was held at the Hôtel de sociétés savantes on 3 June 1906. We met with a great deal of hostility, and notices prepared for the whole of Paris were posted only in the vicinity of the building. The audience numbering some fifty people, we declared that henceforth none would hear the voice of the Seventh Angel.

All the same, the goal was met far in excess of what we had hoped. The program had been sent to organs of the press individually, and *Journal des Débats* printed it almost in its entirety in the "Echoes" section: "The Archangel of the Resurrection and the Seventh Angel of the Apocalypse, being one and the same, will make their voice heard and sound the trumpet of God through the mouth of the speaker. At that moment the Seventh Angel will pour his vial into the air."

The announcement was made without a single unfavourable comment, as beseems a fact sure and true; which it was.

Our program was reproduced in full by *La Raison, L'Action, L'Aurore, Dépêche de Lyon,* and *Nouvelles d'Alger,* along with some deprecatory remarks—as newspapers have every right to make, and for which we thank them. In addition, the smaller journals *Temps, La Revue, La Liberté,* and *La Lanterne* had announced *Les Prophéties. Polybiblion* also devoted a few contemptuous lines to the work. Other attempts were frustrated and came to nothing.

Thus we fulfilled our mission, to which almost thirty years have already been devoted, spending our own savings, amidst a sea of troubles, without a single known disciple or patron other than God Almighty, in whose service we stand. All this has been, and will be, enough to complete His work, which did not end with *Les Prophéties accomplies,* as we thought it would.

Indeed, following this publication, and until the beginning of 1907, it seemed that it would take an assembly of men of all tongues to make the Analysis of the Word fully clear. Then, suddenly, as we were immersed in thought, a final revelation plunged us into a state of transport and disclosed how to analyze all speech, down to its most familiar and evident foundations—and not just in French, but in all other languages, too. For the method employed here applies to human speech the world over.

When the seventh vial is poured into the air (Revelation 16: 17), a voice from Heaven says, *It is done.* As we have explained, it is at this moment that the Seven Thunders utter their voices

(Revelation 10: 3). However, the luminous advent of the Son of Man has not yet occurred. For the Seventh Angel of the Apocalypse is not done pouring his vial into the air. Nor has the angel descended from Heaven finished crying with a great voice (Revelation 10: 3). Only after the publication of this new work will the Seven Thunders sound, announcing to all peoples that the great God Almighty rules the Earth by the voice of His only son, who is called the Word of God and is Man.

In effect, for this to occur, all must be able to enter the Temple of the Lord, and this temple, which was opened to humankind in 1891 and 1900, had remained filled with smoke from the glory of God, and from His power; and no man was able to enter into the Temple, till the Seven Plagues of the Seven Angels were fulfilled (Revelation 15:8).

Therefore, although the Temple stood open and all rules were known that made it possible to read the formation of the Word, or Man, from the very foundation of the world, none could penetrate further than we had done, and we ourselves had been stopped in our studies by the majesty of the Lord, in keeping with prophecy.

The new work at hand, scientifically and conclusively, summarizes all that we have written on human creation. He who has dictated it is the Spirit of Creation Himself. It is He who reveals Himself through our mouth, and we are but His instrument. It is He who has taught us; men have offered nothing. And as it is a simple man of no renown who writes these words, the world of priests and the learned, the Scribes and Pharisees, loathe in us the One whom Pilate delivered to them: MAN.

The Pun as Explanatory Principle The sword of fire guarding the path to the Tree of Life is punning, or word-play. The idea that there might be something hidden beneath puns could not occur to anyone, for it was forbidden to human intellect. All that was permitted was to erupt into stupid laughter. Henceforth this is the lot of the ignorant and the dullards. God has chosen the things of the world deemed mad, those most despised, to blot out that which stands.

By revelation, on the day appointed, we were brought to formulate the following Law:

> *Studying the connection between different ideas expressed by an identical sound or sequence of sounds leads the mind, naturally, to uncover the formation of words, which is the same thing as the creation of man, who is himself the Word.*

Take, for example:

> *Les dents, la bouche* [teeth, mouth]

I find:

les dents la bouchent	[the teeth close it]
l'aidant la bouche	[helping the mouth]
l'aide en la bouche	[help in the mouth]
laides en la bouche	[ugly {things} in the mouth]
laid dans la bouche	[ugly in the mouth]
lait dans la bouche	[milk in the mouth]
l'est dam le à bouche	[there's damage there, in the mouth]
les dents-là bouche	[close those teeth]

All these ideas, which are more or less different, stand in relation to one another. The teeth close off the mouth, so they lend it help [*aide*]. They are ugly [*laides*] but also white as milk [*lait*] in the mouth. *Dam* [displeasure] starts with a *dent* [tooth]; and *le mal de dents* [toothache] is linked to *le mal de dam* [pain of displeasure], or *mets à le dedans* [fodder on the inside], which is *le mal d'amour* [lovesickness]. *Les dents-là bouche* is the equivalent of "shut your mouth."

If no connections are found between two ideas, they will have something in common with a third. This Law is categorical and sure, and it extends to all languages. By way of this Law we have managed, bit by bit, to break down human speech and arrive at the language that prevailed everywhere, the world over.

The extreme simplicity of this language comes from the fact that the first beings spoke only when the ardor of the senses compelled them to do so. This is also the sole reason that frogs sing, even though they take delight in speech and are ever repeating the same sounds—as did the *prés-êtres* [pre-beings] or *prêtres* [priests].

IMAGINARY LANGUAGES IN FICTION

Francis Godwin

Excerpt from *The Man in the Moone*, 1638.

In good time, therefore, I setled my selfe immediately to the learning of the language which (a marvellous thing to consider) is one of the same throughout all the regions of the Moone, yet so much the lesse to bee wondred at, because I cannot thinke all the Earth of Moone to Amount to the fortieth part of our inhabited Earth; partly because the Globe of the Moone is much lesse then that of the Earth, and partly because their Sea or Ocean covereth in estimation Three parts of Foure, (if not more) whereas the *superficies* of our land may been judged Equivalent and comparable in Measure to that of our Seas.

The Difficulty of that language is not to bee conceived, and the reasons thereof are especially two:

First, because it hath no affinitie with any other than ever I heard.

Secondly, because it consisteth not so much of words and Letters, as of tunes and uncouth sounds, that no letters can expresse.

For you have few wordes but they signifie divers and severall things, and they are distinguished onely by their tunes that are as it were sung in the utterance of them, yea many wordes there are consisting of tunes onely, so as if they list they will utter their mindes by tunes without wordes: for Example, they have an ordinary salutation amongst them, signifying *(Verbatim)* Glorie be to God alone, which they expresse (as I take it, for I am no perfect Musitian) by this tune without any words at all.

Yea the very names of Men they will expresse in the same sort.

When they were disposed to talke of mee before my face, so as l should not perceive it; this was *Gonsales.*

By occasion hereof, I discern meanes of framing a Language (and that easie soone to bee learned) as copious as any other in the world, consisting of tunes onely, whereof my friends may know more at leasure if it please them.

This is a great Mystery and worthier the searching after then at first sight you would imagine.

Now notwithstanding the difficulty of this language, within two months space I had attained unto such knowledge of the same, as I understand most questions to be demanded of mee, and what with signes what with words, make reasonable shift to utter my mind, which thing being certified unto *Pylonas*, hee sent for mee oftentimes, and would bee pleased to give mee knowledge of many things that my *Guardians* durst not declare unto mee.

Cyrano de Bergerac

The States and Empires of the Moon, 1649 (first edition, posthumous, 1656). Trans. A. Lovell.

Musical Language Thus, all the comfort I had during the misery of my hard Usage, were the visits of this officious Spirit; for you may judge what conversation I could have with these that came to see me, since besides that they only took me for an Animal, in the highest class of the *Category* of Bruits, I neither understood their Language, nor they mine. For you must know, that there are but two Idioms in use in that Country, one for the Grandees, and another for the People in general.

That of the great ones is no more but various inarticulate Tones, much like to our Musick when the Words are not added to the Air: and in reality it is an Invention both very useful and pleasant; for when they are weary of talking, or disdain to prostitute their Throats to that Office, they take either a Lute or some other Instrument, whereby they communicate their Thoughts as well as by their Tongue: So that sometimes Fifteen or Twenty in a Company will handle a point of Divinity, or discuss the difficulties of a Law-suit, in the most harmonious Consort that ever tickled the Ear.

Gestural Language The second, which is used by the Vulgar, is performed by a shivering of the Members, but not, perhaps, as you may imagine: for some parts of the Body signifie an entire Discourse; for example, the agitation of a Finger, a Hand, an Ear, a Lip, an Arm, an Eye, a Cheek, every one severally will make up an Oration, or a Period with all the parts of it: Others serve only instead of Words, as the knitting of the Brows, the several quiverings of the Muscles, the turning of the Hands, the stamping of the Feet, the contorsion of the Arm; so that when they speak, as their Custom is, stark naked, their Members being used to gesticulate their Conceptions, move so quick that one would not think it to be a Man that spoke, but a Body that trembled.

The States and Empires of the Sun, 1652 (first edition, posthumous, 1662).

About the end of four Months Voyage, at least as near as one can reckon, when there is no Night to distinguish the Day, I came upon the Coast of one of those little Earths that wheel about the Sun, which the Mathematicians call Spots; where by reason that Clouds interposed, by Glasses now not uniting so much heat, and by consequence the Air not pushing my Shed with so much Force, what remained of the Wind could do no more, but bear up my fall, and let me down upon the top of a very high Mountain, to which I gently descended. . . .

By Gullies which seemed hollowed by the fall of Water, I descended into the Plain, where because of the thick Mud, that fatned the Earth, I had much ado to go. However, having advanced a little way, I arrived in a great Bottom, where I rencountred a little Man stark-naked, sitting and resting himself upon a Stone. I cannot call to mind whether I spoke to him first, or if it was he that put the Question to me: But it is as fresh in my Memory, as if I heard him still, that he discoursed to me three long Hours in a Language, which I knew very well I had never heard before, and which hath not the least resemblance with any of the Languages in this World; notwithstanding I comprehended it faster, and more intelligibly than my Mother Tongue. He told me, when I made enquiry about so wonderful a thing, that in Sciences there was a *true*, without which one was always far from the *easie*; that the more an Idiom was distant from this *truth*, the more it came short of the Conception, and was les easie to be understood. In the same manner, continued he, in Musick one never finds this *true;* but that the Soul immediately rises, and blindly aspires after it. We see it not, but we feel that Nature sees it; and without being able to conceive, in what manner we are swallowed up by it, it still ravishes us, tho we cannot observe where it is. It's the very same with Languages; he who hits upon that verity of Letters, Words, and Order in expressing himself, can never fall below his thought, he speaks always with congruity to his Conception; and it is because you are ignorant of this perfect Idiom, that you are at a stand, not knowing the Order, nor the Words, which might explain what you imagine. I told him, that the first Man of our World, had undoubtedly made use of that Language, because the several Names which he gave to several things, declared their Esence. He interrupted me, and went on. It is not absolutely necessary, for expressing all the mind conceives, but without it we cannot be understood at all. Seeing this Idiom is the Instinct or Voice of Nature, it ought to be intelligible to all that live under the Jurisdiction of Nature: And therefore if you understood it, you might Discourse and Communicate all your thoughts to Beasts, and the

Beasts their to you; because it is the very Language of Nature, whereby she makes her self to be understood by all Living Creatures.

Be no more surprised, then, at the facility wherewith you understand the meaning of a Language, which never sounded before in your Ear. When I speak, your Soul finds in every Word of mine, that *Truth* which it gropes after; and though her Reason understand it not, yet she has Nature with her that cannot fail to understand it.

"Ha! without doubt," cried I, it was by the means of that Emphatick Idiom, that our first Father heretofore conversed with Animals, and was by them understood; for seeing the Dominion over all the the kinds of them, was given to him, they obeyed him, because he commanded in a Language that was known to them, and it is for that Reason also, that (this Original Language being lost) they come not at present, when they are called, as heretofore they did, seeing now they do not understand us.

Gabriel de Foigny

The Adventures of Jacques Sadeur in the voyage of discovery to the Austral Land, 1676. Extract from chapter IX; 1693 translation.

The *Australians* have three ways of expressing themselves, as we have in *Europe*, that is, by *Voice*, by *Signs*, and by *Writing*. Among these, *Signs* are most familiar with them and I have observed them to converse together several hours, without declaring their minds any other way than that. They never speak but when it is necessary to make continued Discourses, and to express a long Series of Propositions: All their Words are *Monosyllables*, and they have but one *Conjugation*; as for Example, *Af* signifies to Love; which is thus conjugated in the

Present Tense: La, Pa, Ma, i.e., I Love, thou Lovest, he Loves; *Lla, Ppa, Mma,* we Love, you Love, they Love. They have but one *Tense* for the time past, *Lga, Pga, Mga, i.e.,* I have Loved, thou hast Loved, he has Loved, &c. The *Future* is *Lda, Pda, Mda,* I shall, or will Love, &c. *Llda, Ppda, Mmda,* we shall, or will Love, &c. *Uf* in the *Australian Tongue* signifies to work, which they conjugate thus, *Lu, Pu, Mu,* I work, thou workest, &c. *Lgu, Pgu, Mgu,* we Work &c. and so in the other Tenses.

They have no Declensions, nor Articles, and but very few Nouns: They express simple substances by one single Vowel, and Compound Bodies, by the Vowels that signifie the chief Elements, of which they are composed. They own but five simple Bodies or Elements, of which the first and noblest in they esteem is the Fire, which they express by the single Vowel *A,* the second is the Air, which they call *E,* the third is Salt, which they call *G,* the fourth is Water, which they call *I,* and the fifth is Earth, which they call *U.*

All their Adjectives and their Epithets are expressed by so many single Consonants, of which they have a greater number than the *Europeans*. Every Consonant signifies a Quality that belongs to the things signified by the Vowels: Thus *B* signifies Clear, *C* Hot, *D* Disagreeable, *F* Dry: and by these Explications they so perfectly form their words, that as soon as a Man hears them pronounced, he presently conceives the nature of things they signifie; as for example, they call the Stars *AeB*, a word which signifies in one Breath the two chief Elements, or simple Bodies, of which they are composed, and withal, that they are Luminous. They call the Sun *Aab*, the Birds *Oef,* which signifies at once that they are composed of a dry, salt and airy substance. They call a man *Uez,* which signifies a substance, partly airy, and partly Earthy, tempered with some moisture; the same method they observe in the composition of other Names. The advantage of this way of speaking is, that by this means a Man becomes a Philosopher, by learning the first words he pronounces, and that one can name nothing without at the same time explaining its nature, which would pass for a miraculous thing with any one that knew not their Alphabet, nor the composition of their words.

And if their way of speaking be admirable, their method of writing is much more: they use only points to express their Vowels, which points are distinguish'd only by their Situation. They have Five places for them, the uppermost signifying *A*, the Second *E*, and so forward. As for example,

A ·
E ·
I ·
O ·
U ·

And though it seems to us very difficult to distinguish them, yet use has made it very easie to them: they have 36 Consonants, 24 of which are remarkable; they are little strokes that are made round about the points, and signifie according to the order of their several places; as for example,

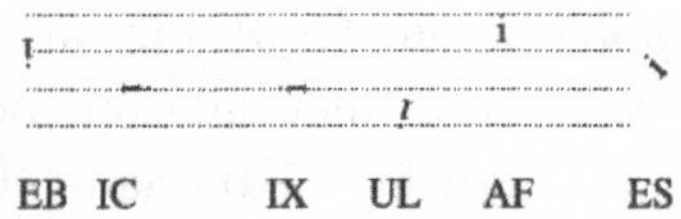

EB signifies clear Air, *IC* Hot Water, *IX* Cold Water, *UL* Moist Earth, *AF* Dry fire, *ES* White Air, and so all the rest; thy have

about 18 or 19 more, which we have no Consonants in *Europe* that can express.

The more we consider that way of writing, the more secrets we shall find in it to admire. *B* signifies clear, or bright, *C* hot, *X* cold, *L* moist, *F* dry, *S* white, *N* black, *T* green, *D* disagreeable, *P* sweet, *Q* pleasing, *R* bitter, *M* desirable, *G* evil, *Z* high, *H* low, *J* (consonant) red, *A* join'd with, peaceable. Thus as soon as they hear, or pronounce a word, they apprehend at the same time the nature of the thing signified by it; as when they write this word *Ipm* they presently understand by it an Apple, both sweet and delicious, and *Izd*, a bad and disagreeable Fruit, &c.

Denis Vairasse d'Alais

A History of the Sevarambians, 1677 (1738 translation).

Politeness of Manners ordinarily produces that of Speech; especially when there are natural Foundations which may be easily built on, without changing the first Model on which it was established. Thus *Sevarias* was perfectly well aware of at the beginning of his Reign; for foreseeing that, by his Laws, he should render the Manners of this People gentle and regular, he imagined they would want a Language conformable to their Genius, by means of which they might be able to express their Thoughts and Sentiments, in a way as polite as their Customs. He excell'd very much in Languages, being Master of several, and knowing perfectly all their Beauties and Defects. Having therefore a Design of composing a compleat one, he borrow'd from all tht he understood, every thing that was useful or beautiful in them, and rejected all that they had which was incommodious and faulty. I would not be here understood to mean, that he transferr'd the Words of other Speeches into his, but only took Notions, Idioms, and Forms of speaking, which he endeavour'd to imitate, and introduce, by accommodating them to that of the *Stroukarambians*, which he had learn'd, and intended for the Foundation of that which was to be us'd among his Subjects.

He retain'd all the Words, Phrases, and Idioms, which he thought good; contenting himself with only softening the Roughness, and retrenching the Superfluity of it; and adding to it where it wanted. These Additions, indeed, were very great' for, as the *Stroukarambians* before his time were a very barbarous People, they had but few Terms, having but few Notions to express by them; which render'd their Language very much bounded and defective, tho' otherwise it was soft and methodical, and capable of Improvement and Politeness.

Sevarias, therefore, first of all, made a Collection of all their Words, and disposed them in an alphabetical Order, like a Dictionary. After which he remark'd all their Phrases and Idioms, retrenching what was useless, and adding such things as he thought necessary; and this he did with respect to simple Sounds, as well as compound ones; Dictions, Syntax, and the Arrangement of Words and Sentences. Till his time, the Inhabitants of this Country were wholly ignorant of the Art of Writing, and wonder'd, as much as the *Americans* themselves, at the use of Letters, which gave the *Parses* an opportunity of persuading them, that the SUN had taught them this, and all the other Arts which they had brought with them out of our Continent, and that he communicated himself to them in a manner altogether particular.

Sevarias invented Characters to represent all the Sounds which he found in their Langauge, as well as those which he introduc'd into it. He taught them to write in Columns, beginning at the top the Page, and running down to the bottom, but yet inclining from the left to the right, after the manner of several of the Oriental Nations. He distinguished the Letters as we do, by the Names of Vowels and Consonants; after having invented forty Figures, which take in almost every possible Vocal Sound, which yet are perfectly distinct from one another. He contriv'd several Words, and establish'd the usage of them, in which this Variety is easily remark'd; to the end that Children might learn betimes to form all kinds of Articulations, and render their Tongues flexible and apt for the pronunciation of every sort of Sounds, without pain or difficulty.—And this is the Reason, that the *Sevarambians* learn, so easily, the Tone and Elocution of all the Languages they study, and become so quickly Masters in this part of Speech.

They have ten Vowels, and thirty Consonants, all of them distinct from one another; which gives their Language a wonderful Variety of Sounds, and renders it the most agreeable in the World. And these Sounds are, as far as is possible, accommodated to the Nature of the things express'd by them, each having its particular Usage and Character. Some of them have an Air of Dignity and Gravity, and others of Softness and Delicacy; one sort serve to express base, contemptible things, another grand and sublime, according to their Position, Arrangement, and Quantity.

In their Alphabet they have followed the Order of Nature, beginning with the *Guttural Vowels*, then going on to those of the *Palate*, and ending with the *Labial ones*. After the Vowels follow the Consonants, which, as we said, are thirty in number, and divided into Primitives and Derivatives. They subdivide the Derivatives also into the mute and the liquid; and, with respect to the Organ, that has the greatest share in uttering them, they distinguish them all into *Gutturals*, *Palaticks*, *Nasals*, *Gingivals*, *Dentals*, and *Labials*.

The first Figure which they place after their Vowels, is a Mark of Aspiration, which sounds just like the *Greek* one, or our letter *h.* Then come the Guttural Consonants, the Palaticks, and all the rest descending to the Labials, according to their natural Order.

Out of this great Number of simple Sounds, their Syllables are compos'd, which is done by a Mixture of Vowels and Consonants, in which they have studied the Nature of things, which they endeavor to express by conformable Sounds; never making use of long and harsh Syllables, to express short and soft things, nor of soft delicate ones, to represent grand, strong, or rough Ideas, as do almost all other Nations, who have no regard to these Rules: tho' the Observation of them makes a principal Beauty in any Language. They also have above thirty Dipthongs and Tripthongs, all perfectly distinct, which makes a still greater Variety of Sounds; and many of them serve to shew the Cases of Nouns, and the Tenses of Verbs. The greatest part of their Words end with Vowels, or very easy Consonants; and whenever one finds a harsh Termination, it is always used to express something of a like nature in the thing signified, and is often a Matter of choice, especially in Pieces of Eloquence. They have three Characters for each Vowel, by which they mark their Quantity, and they divide them all into the *Grave*, the *Acute*, and the *Circumflex*; to shew the kind of Accent that is to be put upon them. They never put the Circumflex but upon long and open Letters, nor the Grave but upon those which are pronounc'd by closing the Mouth, and which suppress or lower the Voice. The Acute, indeed, is indifferently plac'd on any, according to the Nature and Situation of the Word in the Discourse. They have Marks for the divers Tones and Inflexions of the Voice, as we have for the Interrogation and Admiration: nay, they go still farther in this respect, for they have Notes for almost all the several Tones us'd in Pronunciation. One sort serve to express Joy; others Grief, Anger, Doubt, Assurance, and almost every other Passion. Their Words are, for the most part, of two Syllables, when they are simple; but the compound ones are longer, tho' never so tiresome as those of the *Greeks*, which often exceed the bounds of Mediocrity, and run one quite out of breath. *Sevarias* invented several Adverbs of Time, Place, and Quality; and divers Prepositions, which, being join'd to Nouns and Verbs, express wonderfully well all sorts of Differences and Properties. The Declension of their Nouns is form'd by the different Termination of each Case, after the manner of the *Latins*, or else by the means of certain prepositive Articles, as we do; and even sometimes by both together: but then this is always emphatical, that Manner of Declension being never us'd but to express something strongly.

The Genders of Nouns are three, the masculine, the feminine, and the common. The ending *a* is peculiar to the masculine, *è* to the feminine, and *o* to the common. In their Augmentatives they affect their Letter *ou*, which frequently notes Disdain and Contempt; and in their Diminutives they use the Vowel *I*, which also signifies the same Affections, but *é*, and *I*, stand for Genteelness and Delicacy. Thus to design a Man, in their ordinary Form, they say *Amba*; and when he is a great and venerable Man, *Ambas*; but, if he is a grand Villain, they say *Ambou*, and *Ambous* when he is exceedingly remarkable. In the Diminution they say *Ambu*, when they would signify a little paltry Wretch; but if they would express a pretty little Man, 'tis *Ambé*; and when such are notable either in good or ill, they add the Letter *s*, which makes *Ambus*, and

Ambes. In like manner they call a Woman *Embé* in their ordinary Speech; but, according to the different Significations just now explain'd, they denominate them *Embés, Embeou, Embeous, Embeum Embeus, Embei,* and *Embeis*. These divers Terminations serve also to express Hatred, Anger, Contempt, Love, Esteem, and Respect, according as they are us'd in the Discourse.

They have only two Numbers, the singular and plural; which last is usually distinguished form the other, but the Addition of the Letter *I*, or *n*. Thus *Amba* makes in the plural *Ambai*; *Embé, EMbei*; and, in the common Gender, *Ero*, Light, gives the plural *Eron*, Lights.

But when they would express the Male and Female of a Species, both, by one Word, or they are doubtful of the Sex of any Animal, they change the masculine or feminine Termination into the common one, and add *i* to it. Thus *Amboi* signifies either a Man or Woman; and *Phantoi* stands for a Father or Mother, or both; for *Phanta* is a Father, and *Phanté* a Mother.

In the Verbs they also observe the three Genders, which shows the Sex of him or her who speaks; and these Verbs are also capable of Augmentation and Diminution like the Nouns. Thus to signify *to love*, in the Infinitive, they say *Ermanai*, when it is spoken of a Man; *Ermanei*, of a Woman; and if it be neither Male nor Female, or both together, *Ermanoi*. In all the Tenses and Persons, they observe also this Difference, still having a regard to the Gender of the thing which speaks or is spoken of.

For example, a Man who says he loves, uses *Ermaná*, a Woman *Ermané*, and a thing neuter or common, *Ermano*; which will be evident in all the Persons of the present Tense and indicative Mood, in the following Example.

The MASCULINE.

Ermaná, I love.	*Ermanach`*, Thou loveſt.	*Ermanas'*, He loveth.	Sing.
Ermanan, We love.	*Ermaná'chi*, Ye love.	*Erman`ſi*, They love.	Plur.

The FEMININE.

Ermané, I love.	*Ermanech`*, Thou loveſt.	*Ermenes`*, He loveth.	Sing.
Ermanen, We love.	*Ermênchi*, Ye love.	*Ermen^si*, They love.	Plur.

The COMMON.

Ermano, I love.	*Ermanôch`*, Thou loveſt.	*Ermanos`*, He *or ſhe* loves.	Sing.
Ermanon, We love.	*Ermôn`chi*, Ye lôve.	*Ermônſi*, They love.	Plur.

They observe this Difference of Genders in the Terminations, throughout all the Moods and Tenses of the Verbs; and also make use of Diminutives and Augmentatives, as in the Nouns. Thus *Ermanoui* signifies to love grossly, *Ermanui* to love little, and dishonestly, *Ermanei* to love little, but honoroubly, and *Ermané*, to love little, but with more delicacy. But to love much and nobly, they say *Ermanassai*.

Simon Tyssot de Patot

The Travels and Adventures of Jacques Masse, 1710 (1754 translation).

By hearing them talk much, we began to understand some Words of their Language: The first we retain'd was the word *Mula*, which they seldom fail'd to pronounce, when with our Eyes or Hands lifted up to Heaven, we utter'd the Name of

God. We learnt the Terms, *At*, to Eat; *Bouskin*, to Drink; *Kapan*, to Sleep; *Pryn*, to Walk; *Tian*, to Work; *Touto*, Yes; *Touton*, No; and a great many others, which we found afterwards to bear the same Meaning as we imagin'd they had at first. What very much contributed to make this Language familiar to us, was there being but three Tenses in the Indicative Mood of every Verb, *viz*. the *Present*, the *Praterperfect*, indefinite or compound, and the *Future;* and they have no *Imperative* Mood; that in their *Subjenctive* they have only the *Praeterimperfect* and Praeterplu-perfect; and that besides these they have only the *Infinitive* Mood and *Participle*. They have also but three *Persons* in both the *Singular* and *Plural Numbers;* and thus, for Instance, they conjugate the Verb *At:*

Indicative Mood, Present Tense	
Ata	I eat or We eat.
Até	Thou eatest, You eat.
Aty	He eateth, They eat.
Praeterperfect Tense	
Atài	I have eaten, We have eaten.
Atéi	Thou hast eaten, You have eaten.
Atyi	He has eaten, They have eaten.
Future Tense	
Atàio	I shall or will eat, We will eat.
Atéio	Thou wilt eat, You will eat.
Atyio	He will eat, They will eat.
Infinitive Mood	
At	To eat.

Praeterimperfect Tense of the Subjunctive Mood	
Atàin	I would eat, We would eat.
Atéin	Thou would'st eat, Ye would eat.
Atyin	He would eat, They would eat.
Praeterpluperfect	
Ataif	I would have eaten, We would have eaten.
Ateif	Thou would'st have eaten, You would have eaten.
Atyif	He or she would have eaten, They would have eaten.
Participle of the Present Tense	
Atain	Eating

FROM thence are deriv'd the Words, *Ataus*, Kitchen; *Ataias*, Food; *Atis*, Cook; *Atians*, Eater, or the Person that Eateth. . . .

It must likewise be observ'd, that their Nouns and Verbs are deriv'd from one another, like the French, *Chat*, a Boar Cat; *Chate*, a She Cat; *Chatons*, Kittlings; *Chatonner*, to Kitten. Their Declensions are also very easy, of whch this is an Example:

Nom.	*Brol*,	A Weather.
Gen.	*Brul*,	
Dat.	*Brel*,	
Nom.	*Brolu*,	An Ewe or Sheep.
Gen.	*Brula*,	
Dat.	*Brèla*,	
Nom.	*Broln*,	Weathers or Sheep.
Gen.	*Bruln*,	
Dat.	*Breln*,	

'TIS wonderful, that there is not one Exception in the Conjugations and Declensions of this Langauge; and that when we know the Variations of one Verb or Noun, it leads to the Knowledge of all the rest; which Variation consists only in adding the Letter *A* to the Infinitive Mood, to make the Present Tense of the Indicative; as from *At*, comes *Ata;* from *Baskin, Baskina*, &c. And to the Nouns they add *A*, to the Nominative Case of the Masculine Gender, to make them Feminine in *n* when they change them to the Plural Number, as is plain from the foregoing Example. From when it will not be thought strange, that at the End of six Months we understood every thing they said to us, and that they also understood what we said to them.

Edward Bulwer-Lytton

The Coming Race, 1871. Excerpt from chapter XII.

The language of the Vril-ya is peculiarly interesting, because it seems to me to exhibit with great clearness the traces of the three main transitions through which language passes in attaining to perfection of form.

One of the most illustrious of recent philologists, Max Müller, in arguing for the analogy between the strata of language and the strata of the earth, lays down this absolute dogma: "No language can, by any possibility, be inflectional without having passed through the agglutinative and isolating stratum. No language can be agglutinative without clinging with its roots to the underlying stratum of isolation."

Taking then the Chinese language as the best existing type of the original isolating stratum, "as the faithful photograph of man in his leading-strings trying the muscles of his mind, groping his way, and so delighted with his first successful grasps that he repeats them again and again,"—we have, in the language of the Vril-ya, still "clinging with its roots to the underlying stratum," the evidences of the original isolation. It abounds in monosyllables, which are the foundations of the language. The transition into the agglutinative form marks an epoch that must have gradually extended through ages, the written literature of which has only survived in a few fragments of symbolical mythology and certain pithy sentences which have passed into popular proverbs. With the extant literature of the Vril-ya the inflectional stratum commences. No doubt at that time there must have operated concurrent causes, in the fusion of races by some dominant people, and the rise of some great literary phenomena by which the form of language became arrested and fixed. As the inflectional stage prevailed over the agglutinative, it is surprising to see how much more boldly the original roots of the language project from the surface that conceals them. In the old fragments and proverbs of the preceding stage the monosyllables which compose those roots vanish amidst words of enormous length, comprehending whole sentences from which no one part can be disentangled from the other and employed separately. But when the inflectional form of language became so far advanced as to have its scholars and grammarians, they seem to have united in extirpating all such polysynthetical or polysyllabic monsters, as devouring invaders of the aboriginal forms. Words beyond three syllables became proscribed as barbarous, and in proportion as the language grew thus simplified it increased in strength, in dignity, and in sweetness. Though now very compressed in sound, it gains in clearness by that compression. By a single letter, according to its position, they contrive to express all that with civilized nations in our upper world it takes the waste, sometimes of syllables, sometimes of sentences, to express. Let me here cite one or two instances: An (which I will translate man), Ana (men); they letter *s* is with them a letter implying multitude, according to where it is placed; Sana means mankind; Ansa, a multitude of men. The prefix of certain letters in their alphabet invariably denotes compound significations. For instance, GI (which with them is a single letter, as *th* is a single letter with the Greeks) at the commencement of a word infers an assemblage or union of things, sometimes kindred, sometimes dissimilar,—as Oon, a house; Gloon, a town (that is, an assemblage of houses). Ata is sorrow; Glata, a public calamity. Aur-an is the health or well-being of a man; Glauran, the well-being of the State, the good of the community; and a word constantly in their mouths is A-glauran, which denotes their political creed,—namely, that "the first principle of a community is the good of all." Aub is invention; Sila, a tone in music. Glaubsila, as uniting the ideas of invention and of musical intonation, is the classical word for poetry,—abbreviated in ordinary conversation to Glaubs. Na, which with them is, like Gl, but a single letter, always, when an initial, implies something antagonistic to life or joy or comfort, resembling in this the Aryan root Nak, expressive of perishing or destruction. Nax is darkness; Narl, death; Naria, sin or evil. Nas—an uttermost condition of sin and evil—corruption. In writing, they deem it irreverent to express the Supreme Being by any special name. He is symbolized by what may be termed the hieroglyphic of a pyramid, Δ. In the prayer they address Him by a name which they deem too sacred to confide to a stranger, and I know it not. In conversation they generally use a periphrastic epithet, such as the All-Good. The letter V, symbolical of the inverted pyramid, where it is an initial, nearly always denotes excellence or power; as Vril, of which I have said so much; Veed, an immortal spirit; Veedya, immortality; Koom, pronounced like the Welsh Cwm, denotes something of hollowness. Koom itself is a profound hollow, metaphorically a cavern; Koom-in, a hole; Zi-koom, a valley; Koom-zi, vacancy or void; Bodh-koom, ignorance (literally, knowledge-void).

Koom-Posh is their name for the government of the many, or the ascendancy of the most ignorant or hollow. Posh is an almost untranslatable idiom, implying, as the reader will see later, contempt. The closest rendering I can give to it is our slang term, "bosh;" and thus Koom-Posh may be loosely rendered "Hollow-Bosh." But when Democracy of Koom-Posh degenerates from popular ignorance into that popular passion or ferocity which precedes its decease, as (to cite illustrations from the upper world) during the French Reign of Terror, or for the fifty years of the Roman Republic preceding the ascendancy of Augustus, their name for that state of things is Glek-Nas. Ek is strife; Glek, the universal strife. Nas, as I before said, is corruption or rot,—thus Glek-Nas may be construed, "the universal strife-rot." Their compounds are very expressive; thus, Bodh being knowledge, and Too, a participle that implies the action of cautiously app roaching, Too-bodh is their word for Philosophy. Pah is a contemptuous exclamation analogous to our idiom, "stuff and nonsense;" Pah-bodh (literally, stuff-and-nonsense-knowledge) is their term for futile or false philosophy, and is applied to a species of metaphysical or speculative ratiocination formerly in vogue, which consisted in making inquiries that could not be answered, and were not worth making,—such, for instance, as "Why does an An have five toes to his feet instead of four or six?" "Did the first An, created by the All-Good, have the same number of toes as his descendants?" "In the form by which an An will be recognised by his friends in the future state of being, will he retain any toes at all, and, if so, will they be material toes or spiritual toes?" I take these illustrations of Pah-bodh, not in irony or jest, but because the very inquiries I name formed the subject of controversy by the latest cultivators of that "science" four thousand years ago.

In the declension of nouns I was informed that anciently there were eight cases (one more than in the Sanskrit Grammar); but the effect of time has been to reduce these cases, and multiply, instead of these varying terminations, explanatory prepositions. At present, in the Grammar submitted to my study, there were four cases to nouns, three having varying terminations, and the fourth a differing prefix.

Singular		
Nom.	An,	Man.
Dat.	Ano,	to Man.
Ac.	Anam,	Man.
Voc.	Hil-An,	O Man.
Plural		
Nom.	Ana,	Men.
Dat.	Anoi,	to Men.
Ac.	Ananda,	Men.
Voc.	Hil-Ananda,	O Men.

In the elder inflectional literature the dual form existed; it has long been obsolete.

The genitive case with them is also obsolete: the dative supplies its place: they say the house *to* a man, instead of the house *of* a man. When used (sometimes in poetry), the genitive in the termination is the same as the nominative; so is the ablative, the preposition that marks it being a prefix or suffix at option, and generally decided by ear, according to the sound of the noun. It will be observed that the prefix Hil marks the vocative case. It is always retained in addressing another, except in the most intimate domestic relations; its omission would be considered rude: just as in our old forms of speech in addressing a king it would have been deemed disrespectful to say "King," and reverential to say "O King." In fact, as they have no titles of honour, the vocative adjuration supplies the place of a title, and is given impartially to all. The prefix Hil enters into the composition of words that imply distant communications, as Hil-ya, to travel.

In the conjugation of their verbs, which is much too lengthy a subject to enter on here, the auxiliary verb Ya, "to go," which plays so considerable a part in the Sanskrit, appears and performs a kindred office, as if it were a radical in some language from which both had descended. But another auxiliary of opposite signification also accompanies it and shares its labours,—namely, Zi, to stay or repose. Thus Ya enters into the future tense, and Zi in the preterite of all verbs requiring auxiliaries. Yam, I go Yiam, I may go, Yani-ya, I shall go (literally, I go to go), Zam-poo-yan, I have gone (literally, I rest from gone). Ya, as a termination, implies by analogy, progress, movement, efflorescence. Zi, as a terminal, denotes fixity, sometimes in a good sense, sometimes in a bad, according to the word with which it is coupled. lva-zi, eternal goodness; Nan-zi, eternal evil. Poo (from) enters as a prefix to words that denote repugnance, or things from which we ought to be averse. Poo-pra, disgust; Poo-naria, falsehood, the vilest kind of evil. Poosh or Posh I have already confessed to be untranslatable literally. It is an expression of contempt not unmixed with pity. This radical seems to have originated from inherent sympathy between the labial effort and the sentiment that impelled it, Poo being an utterance in which the breath is exploded from the lips with more or less vehemence. On the other hand, Z, when an initial, is with them a sound in which the breath is sucked inward, and thus Zu, pronounced Zoo (which in their language is one letter), is the ordinary prefix to words that signify something that attracts, pleases, touches the heart,—as Zummer, lover; Zutze, love; Zuzulia, delight. This indrawn sound of Z seems indeed naturally appropriate to fondness. Thus, even in our language, mothers say to their babies, in defiance of grammar, "Zoo darling;" and I have heard a learned professor at Boston call his wife (he had been only married a month) "Zoo little pet."

I cannot quit this subject, however, without observing by what slight changes in the dialects favoured by different tribes of the same race, the original signification and beauty of sounds may become confused and deformed. Zee told me with much indignation that Zummer (lover) which, in the way she uttered it, seemed slowly taken down to the very depths of her heart, was, in some not very distant communities of the Vril-ya, vitiated into the half-hissing, half-nasal, wholly disagreeable, sound of Subber. I thought to myself it only wanted the introduction of *n* before *u* to render it into an English word significant of the last quality an amorous Gy would desire in her Zummer.

I will but mention another peculiarity in this language which gives equal force and brevity to its forms of expressions.

A is with them, as with us, the first letter of the alphabet, and is often used as a prefix word by itself to convey a complex idea of sovereignty or chiefdom, or presiding principle. For instance, Iva is goodness; Diva, goodness and happiness united; A-Diva is unerring and absolute truth. I have already noticed the value of A in A-glauran, so, in vril (to whose properties they trace their present state of civilization), A-vril, denotes, as I have said, civilization itself.

The philologist will have seen from the above how much the language of the Vril-ya is akin to the Aryan or Indo-Germanic;

but, like all languages, it contains words and forms in which transfers from very opposite sources of speech have been taken. The very title of Tur, which they give to their supreme magistrate, indicates theft from a tongue akin to the Turanian. They say themselves that this is a foreign word borrowed from a title which their historical records show to have been borne by the chief of a nation with whom the ancestors of the Vril-ya were, in very remote periods, on friendly terms, but which has long become extinct; and they say that when, after the discovery of vril, they remodelled their political institutions, they expressly adopted a title taken from an extinct race and a dead language for that of their chief magistrate, in order to avoid all titles for that office with which they had previous associations.

Should life be spared to me, I may collect into systematic form such knowledge as I acquired of this language during my sojourn amongst the Vril-ya. But what I have already said will perhaps suffice to show to genuine philological students that a language which, preserving so many of the roots in the aboriginal form, and clearing from the immediate, but transitory, polysynthetical stage so many rude incumbrances, has attained to such a union of simplicity and compass in its final inflectional forms, must have been the gradual work of countless ages and many varieties of mind; that it contains the evidence of fusion between congenial races, and necessitated, in arriving at the shape of which I have given examples, the continuous culture of a highly thoughtful people.

George Orwell

"The Principles of Newspeak," *1984*, 1948.

Newspeak was the official language of Oceania and had been devised to meet the ideological needs of Ingsoc, or English Socialism. . . . It was expected that Newspeak would have finally superseded Oldspeak (or Standard English, as we should call it) by about the year 2050. . . .

The purpose of Newspeak was not only to provide a medium of expression for the world-view and mental habits proper to the devotees of Ingsoc, but to make all other modes of thought impossible. It was intended that when Newspeak had been adopted once and for all and Oldspeak forgotten, a heretical thought—that is, a thought diverging from the principles of Ingsoc—should be literally unthinkable, at least so far as thought is dependent on words. Its vocabulary was so constructed as to give exact and often very subtle expression to every meaning that a Party member could properly wish to express, while excluding all other meanings and also the possibility of arriving at them by indirect methods. This was done partly by the invention of new words, but chiefly by eliminating undesirable words and by stripping such words as remained of unorthodox meanings, and so far as possible of all secondary meanings whatever. To give a single example. The word *free* still existed in Newspeak, but it could only be used in such statements as "This dog is free from lice" or "This field is free from weeds." It could not be used in its old sense of "politically free" or "intellectually free" since political and intellectual freedom no longer existed even as concepts, and were therefore of necessity nameless. Quite apart from the suppression of definitely heretical words, reduction of vocabulary was regarded as an end in itself, and no word that could be dispensed with was allowed to survive. Newspeak was designed not to extend but to diminish the range of thought. . . .

The grammar of Newspeak had two outstanding peculiarities. The first of these was an almost complete interchangeability between different parts of speech. Any word in the language (in principle this applied even to very abstract words such as *if* or *when*) could be used either as verb, noun, adjective, or adverb. . . . There was, for example, no such word as cut, its meaning being sufficiently covered by the noun-verb *knife*. . . .

In addition, any word this again applied in principle to every word in the language could be negatived by adding the affix *un–* or could be strengthened by the affix *plus–*, or, for still greater emphasis, *doubleplus–*. Thus, for example, *uncold* meant "warm," while *pluscold* and *doublepluscold* meant, respectively, "very cold" and "superlatively cold." . . . Given, for instance, the word *good*, there was no need for such a word as *bad*, since the required meaning was equally well—indeed, better—expressed by *ungood*. . . .

The second distinguishing mark of Newspeak grammar was its regularity. Subject to a few exceptions which are mentioned below all inflexions followed the same rules. . . .

The B vocabulary consisted of words which had been deliberately constructed for political purposes: words, that is to say, which not only had in every case a political implication, but were intended to impose a desirable mental attitude upon the person using them. [. . .]

Some of the B words had highly subtilized meanings, barely intelligible to anyone who had not mastered the language as a whole. Consider, for example, such a typical sentence from a *Times* leading article as *Oldthinkers unbellyfeel Ingsoc*. The shortest rendering that one could make of this in Oldspeak would be: "Those whose ideas were formed before the Revolution cannot have a full emotional understanding of the principles of English Socialism." [. . .]

But the special function of certain Newspeak words, of which *oldthink* was one, was not so much to express meanings as to destroy them. . . .

As we have already seen in the case of the word *free*, words which had once borne a heretical meaning were sometimes retained for the sake of convenience, but only with the undesirable meanings purged out of them. Countless other words such as *honour, justice, morality, internationalism, democracy, science*, and *religion* had simply ceased to exist. A few blanket words covered them, and, in covering them, abolished them. All words grouping themselves round the concepts of liberty and equality, for instance, were contained in the single word *crimethink*. . . . [T]he party member knew what constituted right conduct, and in exceedingly vague, generalized terms he knew what kinds of departure from it were possible. His sexual life, for example, was entirely regulated by the two Newspeak words *sexcrime* (sexual immorality) and *goodsex* (chastity). . . . In Newspeak it was seldom possible to follow a heretical thought further than the perception that it was heretical: beyond that point the necessary words were nonexistent.

No word in the B vocabulary was ideologically neutral. A great many were euphemisms. Such words, for instance, as *joycamp* (forced-labour camp) or *Minipax* Ministry of Peace, (i.e. Ministry of War) meant almost the exact opposite of what they appeared to mean. . . .

So far as it could be contrived, everything that had or might have political significance of any kind was fitted into the B vocabulary. The name of every organization, or body of people, or doctrine, or country, or institution, or public building, was invariably cut down into the familiar shape; that is, a single easily pronounced word with the smallest number of syllables that would preserve the original derivation. In the Ministry of Truth, for example, the Records Department, in which Winston Smith worked, was called *Recdep*, the Fiction Department was called *Ficdep*, the Teleprogrammes Department was called

Teledep, and so on. This was not done solely with the object of saving time. Even in the early decades of the twentieth century, telescoped words and phrases had been one of the characteristic features of political language; and it had been noticed that the tendency to use abbreviations of this kind was most marked in totalitarian countries and totalitarian organizations. Examples were such words as *Nazi, Gestapo, Comintern, Inprecorr, Agitprop*. In the beginning the practice had been adopted as it were instinctively, but in Newspeak it was used with a conscious purpose. It was perceived that in thus abbreviating a name one narrowed and subtly altered its meaning, by cutting out most of the associations that would otherwise cling to it. The words *Communist International*, for instance, call up a composite picture of universal human brotherhood, red flags, barricades, Karl Marx, and the Paris Commune. The word *Comintern*, on the other hand, suggests merely a tightly–knit organization and a well–defined body of doctrine. . . .

The C vocabulary was supplementary to the others and consisted entirely of scientific and technical terms. . . . [B]ut the usual care was taken to define them rigidly and strip them of undesirable meanings. They followed the same grammatical rules as the words in the other two vocabularies. . . .

From the foregoing account it will be seen that in Newspeak the expression of unorthodox opinions, above a very low level, was well-nigh impossible. . . . A person growing up with Newspeak as his sole language would no more know that *equal* had once had the secondary meaning of "politically equal," or that *free* had once meant "intellectually free," than for instance, a person who had never heard of chess would be aware of the secondary meanings attaching to *queen* and *rook*. . . .

When Oldspeak had been once and for all superseded, the last link with the past would have been severed. History had already been rewritten, but fragments of the literature of the past survived here and there, imperfectly censored, and so long as one retained one's knowledge of Oldspeak it was possible to read them. In the future such fragments, even if they chanced to survive, would be unintelligible and untranslatable.

J. R. R. Tolkien's Elvish (An Overview)

Constructed on the basis of Anglo-Saxon Germanic languages, this is the tongue that medieval Elves would have spoken, had they been real. The grammar and morphology are modeled on Old English: three genders, two numbers (singular and plural), and four cases; adjectives, pronouns and determiners are declined; verbs have two voices (active and passive), six modes, five tenses, and so on. The alphabet calls to mind the runic writing of the ancient Celts and Gothic script.

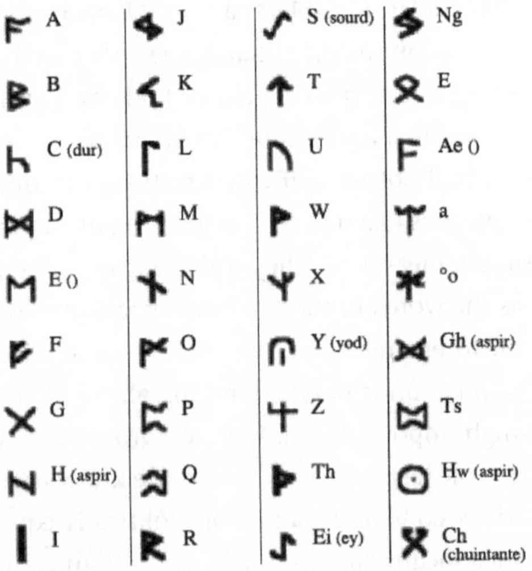

A	J	S (sourd)	Ng
B	K	T	E
C (dur)	L	U	Ae ()
D	M	W	a
E ()	N	X	°o
F	O	Y (yod)	Gh (aspir)
G	P	Z	Ts
H (aspir)	Q	Th	Hw (aspir)
I	R	Ei (ey)	Ch (chuintante)

The numbers 1–20:

1	a-n-s	11	e-l-é-f
2	t-w-e	12	t-w-é-l-f

3	th-r-i	13	th-r-i-st-é-n
4	f-e-r	14	f-e-r-st-é-n
5	f-i-n-f	15	f-i-f-st-é-n
6	s-é-x	16	s-é-c-st-é-n
7	s-é-b-é-n	17	s-é-b-st-é-n
8	a-h-t	18	a-h-st-é-n
9	n-ou-n	19	n-e-i-n-st-é-n
10	st-é-n	20	t-w-é-t-i

One of the best-known poems from The Fellowship of the Ring:

A Elbereth Gilthoniel	O Elbereth Starkindler,
silivren penna míriel	white-glittering, slanting down sparkling like a jewel,
o menel aglar elenath!	the glory of the starry host!
Na-chaered palan-díriel	Having gazed far away
o galadhremmin ennorath,	from the tree-woven lands of Middle-earth,
Fanuilos, le linnathon	to thee, Everwhite, I will sing,
nef aear, sí nef aearon!	on this side of the Sea, here on this side of the Ocean!

The Lord of the Rings *is narrated in "Hobbit English." The names for months also are clearly inspired by Old English, before words of Latin origin were adopted.*

Hobbit English	Old English	Modern English
Afteryule	*aeftergeola*, "afteryule"	January
Solmath	*solmonath*, "mire-month"	February
Rethe	*re-the*, "fierce, furious"	March
Astron	*Easter-monath*, "Easter-month"	April
Thrimidge	*thri-milce*	May
Forelithe	*lith*, "midsummer"	June

Hobbit English	Old English	Modern English
Afterlithe	*aefter-lith*	July
Wedmath	*weth*, "mild, gentle"	August
Halimath	*halig-monath*, "holy-month"	September
Winterfilth	*winter-fylleth*, "winter-fall"	October
Blotmath	*blotmonath*, "blood-month"	November
Foreyule	*geo-la*, "yule"	December

TEXTS BY NIKOLAI MARR

1. Japhetic Linguistics

Excerpts from *On the Origin of Language*, 1926.

From the prehistoric traits of Japhetic languages it emerges quite clearly that sense was made before articulated speech existed: at some point, it seems, the still-herdlike community, not distinguishing itself from physical nature, remarked faraway objects and felt the need to signify them by symbolic sound—first of all "sky," evidently the source of light and darkness, an object not yet separated in the first people's worldview from their own being. This group was not yet an ethnos, a fully established tribe, but a spatial [космическая] community. Uttering "sky" (which I am using conditionally, in the sense of the embryonic thinking of primeval man, who equated "sky" with the whole universe, including himself), the word's meaning was composed of all the elements: first "water" (+ "darkness") and consequently, as we will see, its opposite "fire" (+ "light"). Things would change when the idea of "sky"—a totem and subsequently a deity and merciful creator—combined with "creating, giving hand": "hand" was signified by the same word as "sky," and it's no coincidence that Georgian *neb* (palm) and Abkhazian *nap* (as well as its variant, *e-nap*) sound the same as Russian *nebo* (pl. *nebesa*); this consonance was preserved from the earliest epochs up to later ones, before the birth of Indo-European speech, before the hybridized forms made from the meeting of two tribes emerged—as these same words show, having been affected in Japhetic languages more than in Indo-European Russian.

Especially important for the question of the origin of language is the semantic radiance of "hand"; that is, a single word, "hand," without any change, has several dozen fundamentally different meanings—to say nothing of the fact that the hand is a part of the body and the names of parts of the body correspond to parts of the cosmos, in other words that the structure of the human body turns out to be a microcosm, and man the bearer of the title of "sky." Consequently, we see that articulated speech consists, all in all, of a few primordial words not more than seven in number.

Generally, in Japhetic semantics—which, please note, concerns articulated speech—words belonging to the objective order may be seen to precede subjective ones. Precisely what was unattainable by means of perception or by hand, it was necessary to express by articulated speech; conversely, the sense of objects goes from the multiple to the single, from what is foreign or distant to what is familiar. On this basis, one of the oldest words, if not the first, is "sky," a cosmic phenomenon—and not objects close to man which, understandably, are clearly discernible and therefore easily expressed or named by gestural language [ручным языком].

According to the data of Japhetic linguistics, "sky + water," with the split of "water" into "darkness" and "light," proves to be the prototype of the vast majority of words. Is there any need to say that there was no deity "sky," not even a totem, before the advent of tribes? It's an incontestable fact, in light of the great wealth of material, that each of the many basic words circulating daily in our earthly surroundings has, at its source, one semantic split [разрезе] or another pertaining to the notion of "sky-water," or "skies-waters." In this manner, through this exceedingly simple circumstance, straightforward to the point of naïveté, Japhetidology meets up with the newest research on the genesis of myths. This is hardly a problem, since myth-creation, of course, is word-creation. . . .

"Sky" . . . gave rise to semantic derivatives corresponding to each one of the semantic components perceived: "sky," "water," and "fire." "Water" + "sky" led to "clouds," "smoke," and "darkness"; "fire" + "sky," to "light," "brilliance," "lightning," and so on. At this point in time, so few articulated words existed (specifically, ones signifying cosmic forces experienced vividly) that they expressed a multitude of beings before gradually taking on an independent existence.

The further production of semantic derivatives—such as, for example, the transfer of the name "skies" to "heavenly bodies" ("stars," "sun," and so on) and to "birds" (which, if they were not called "skies" . . . received the designation "skylets")—takes us away from the questions associated with the origin of language, into the realm of subsequent developments created by human speech—the epochs of its refinement and enrichment, the emergence of more complete species and types via [linguistic] crossbreeding.

But if we train our gaze on the depths of the ages with the goal of illuminating the rudiments of human speech, given the conflict between macrocosm and microcosm imposed by the abundance of material, a most difficult and complex question arises about what occupied the foreground of human representation: did "sky" or "hand" come first? Japhetic linguistics brings us back . . . from "skies" to "hand," which is the elementary word, then: the hand of man at work, this creator of all our material culture, including language. The hand is the inaugural and sole instrument of speech, the sole tool of all production, until the point when the productive force that is Working Man creates its substitutes in artificial instruments, the objects of material culture; only then does the function of the tool of speech naturally pass to the tongue [язык]—which, lest we forget, the paleontology of speech shows to have the same name as "hand."

2. The Single Language of the Future

From *The Principal Achievements of Japhetic Theory*, 1925.

Humankind passes from plurilingualism to monolingualism. But no particular language, no matter how broad imperialist expansion may be, will be the language of the future. All former world languages have fallen, as will languages now flourishing or on the way to full diffusion, whether great or small in terms of speakers, both the class creations of the upper strata of society and . . . productions from the grassroots of the masses. Nor will they be replaced by the substitutes for human speech now pullulating like mushrooms: Esperanto, Ido, and whatever else individual initiative contrives. The common language of future humanity will combine all the wealth, all the positive qualities, of dead languages and those yet to die, languages that are still alive. The unified, universally-expressive language of the future is the postulate of a society encompassing all people, irrespective of class or nation. But is it possible to imagine . . . that such a process of utmost importance, communally creating a new means of communication, a new universal language, whether spoken or other in kind . . . , will flow forth unconsciously and instinctively, as occurred . . . when the man-animal first became human through the advent, growth, and evolution of speech? Obviously not. Humankind, now wiser, needs to step in and intervene. Having recognized this necessity and commanding the science of the origin and development of spoken language, it will strive, if not to create a single tongue, then to accelerate and steer the process. . . . Linguists have already been called upon to play this creative and active role, for which they need, above all, . . . real knowledge of human speech, not omitting any detail or element.

3. The Linguistic Policy of the USSR

Linguistic policy is a public question, inextricably tied to the national question. Not only has the national question in the USSR, the paramount issue for our system [строя], already been resolved ideologically, as it has nowhere else in the world; it has been resolved to provide for the full self-determination of each nation, independent of its cultural achievements under the fallen regime. In practice, the true line of our Soviet Constitution concerning the national question, and with it the question of language, has been curbed both by local nationalism and by the chauvinism of power [великодержавного шовинизма]—for the main, that of the Russian, but not just Russian, language. However, at the recent 16th All-Union Congress of the Communist Party—the party pioneering the dictatorship of the proletariat—Comrade Stalin unambiguously formulated linguistic policy in our country and, more still, on a global scale. Though a mere scientific worker, I would make bold to affirm—of course, only in terms of my own specialization—the program [Формулировку] of that Worker who bears the most responsibility in the party organization. With striking clarity and penetration, Comrade Stalin's program, as a guiding political conception, articulates the very position that was reached by Japhetic theory, a general doctrine of language on a global scale without precedent . . . through unremitting theoretical research over many decades. . . .

The passage from Comrade Stalin's speech reads: "The question of national languages vanishing and merging into one common tongue is not a domestic question, not a matter of socialism prevailing in one country, but an international question, the victory of socialism on an international scale. It is not without reason that Lenin said that national differences would remain for a long time even after the international victory of the dictatorship of the proletariat."

How is this agreement to be explained? It's not a matter of borrowing, of course. The dates and concrete facts make that impossible. The essential unity of programs proposed by a revolutionary politician, on the one hand, and a linguistic specialist, on the other, derives from the fact that Comrade Stalin arrived at his social-organizational conclusion in the same way that the Japhetidologist arrived at his own theoretical position, specifically, through . . . organizing linguistic material from all over the world by the very same Marxist method.

TEXTS ON GLOSSOLALIA

Saint Paul

First Epistle to the Corinthians (King James Version)

CHAPTER XIII—Though I speak with the tongues of men and of angels, and have not charity, I am become as sounding brass, or a tinkling cymbal. And though I have the gift of prophecy, and understand all mysteries, and all knowledge; and though I have all faith, so that I could remove mountains, and have not charity, I am nothing. And though I bestow all my goods to feed the poor, and though I give my body to be burned, and have not charity, it profiteth me nothing.

Charity suffereth long, and is kind; charity envieth not; charity vaunteth not itself, is not puffed up, doth not behave itself unseemly, seeketh not her own, is not easily provoked, thinketh no evil; Rejoiceth not in iniquity, but rejoiceth in the truth; Beareth all things, believeth all things, hopeth all things, endureth all things.

Charity never faileth: but whether there be prophecies, they shall fail; whether there be tongues, they shall cease; whether there be knowledge, it shall vanish away. For we know in part, and we prophesy in part. But when that which is perfect is come, then that which is in part shall be done away.

When I was a child, I spake as a child, I understood as a child, I thought as a child: but when I became a man, I put away childish things. For now we see through a glass, darkly; but then face to face: now I know in part; but then shall I know even as also I am known. And now abideth faith, hope, charity, these three; but the greatest of these is charity.

CHAPTER XIV—Follow after charity, and desire spiritual gifts, but rather that ye may prophesy.

For he that speaketh in an unknown tongue speaketh not unto men, but unto God: for no man understandeth him; howbeit in the spirit he speaketh mysteries. But he that prophesieth speaketh unto men to edification, and exhortation, and comfort. He that speaketh in an unknown tongue edifieth himself; but he that prophesieth edifieth the church.

I would that ye all spake with tongues, but rather that ye prophesied: for greater is he that prophesieth than he that speaketh with tongues, except he interpret, that the church may receive edifying. Now, brethren, if I come unto you speaking with tongues, what shall I profit you, except I shall speak to you either by revelation, or by knowledge, or by prophesying, or by doctrine? And even things without life giving sound, whether pipe or harp, except they give a distinction in the sounds, how shall it be known what is piped or harped? For if the trumpet give an uncertain sound, who shall prepare himself to the battle? So likewise ye, except ye utter by the tongue words easy to be understood, how shall it be known what is spoken? for ye shall speak into the air. There are, it may be, so many kinds of voices in the world, and none of them is without signification. Therefore if I know not the meaning of the voice, I shall be unto him that speaketh a barbarian, and he that speaketh shall be a barbarian unto me. Even so ye, forasmuch as ye are zealous of spiritual gifts, seek that ye may excel to the edifying of the church.

Wherefore let him that speaketh in an unknown tongue pray that he may interpret. For if I pray in an unknown tongue, my spirit prayeth, but my understanding is unfruitful. What is it then? I will pray with the spirit, and I will pray with the understanding also: I will sing with the spirit, and I will sing with the understanding also. Else when thou shalt bless with the spirit, how shall he that occupieth the room of the unlearned say Amen at thy giving of thanks, seeing he understandeth not what thou sayest? For thou verily givest thanks well, but the other is not edified. I thank my God, I speak with tongues more than ye all: Yet in the church I had rather speak five words with my understanding, that by my voice I might teach others also, than ten thousand words in an unknown tongue.

Brethren, be not children in understanding: howbeit in malice be ye children, but in understanding be men. In the law it is written, With men of other tongues and other lips will I speak unto this people; and yet for all that will they not hear me, saith the Lord. Wherefore tongues are for a sign, not to them that believe, but to them that believe not: but prophesying serveth not for them that believe not, but for them which believe. If therefore the whole church be come together into one place, and all speak with tongues, and there come in those that are unlearned, or unbelievers, will they not say that ye are mad? But if all prophesy, and there come in one that believeth not, or one unlearned, he is convinced of all, he is judged of all: And thus are the secrets of his heart made manifest; and so falling down on his face he will worship God, and report that God is in you of a truth.

How is it then, brethren? when ye come together, every one of you hath a psalm, hath a doctrine, hath a tongue, hath a revelation, hath an interpretation. Let all things be done unto edifying. If any man speak in an unknown tongue, let it be by two, or at the most by three, and that by course; and let one interpret. But if there be no interpreter, let him keep silence in the church; and let him speak to himself, and to God.

Let the prophets speak two or three, and let the other judge. If any thing be revealed to another that sitteth by, let the first hold his peace. For ye may all prophesy one by one, that all may learn, and all may be comforted. And the spirits of the prophets are subject to the prophets. For God is not the author of confusion, but of peace, as in all churches of the saints. Let your women keep silence in the churches: for it is not permitted unto them to speak; but they are commanded to be under obedience, as also saith the law. And if they will learn any thing, let them ask their husbands at home: for it is a shame for women to speak in the church.

What? came the word of God out from you? or came it unto you only? If any man think himself to be a prophet, or spiritual, let him acknowledge that the things that I write unto you are the commandments of the Lord. But if any man be ignorant, let him be ignorant.

Wherefore, brethren, covet to prophesy, and forbid not to speak with tongues. Let all things be done decently and in order.

Emanuel Swedenborg

The Earths in Our Solar System, Which Are Called Planets, and the Earths in the Starry Heaven, Their Inhabitants, and the Spirits and Angels There: From Things Heard and Seen, 1758 (Swedenborg Society translation, 1894).

It was also shown me how the thoughts are expressed by means of the face. The affections which belong to the love are manifested by means of the countenance and its changes, and the thoughts therein by variations as to the forms of the interiors there: it is impossible to describe them further. The inhabitants of the earth Jupiter have also verbal speech, but not so loud as with us. The one speech aids the other, and life is insinuated into the verbal speech by the speech of the face. I have been informed by the angels that the very first speech in every earth was speech by the face, and from two origins there, the lips and the eyes. The reason this kind of speech was the first is, that the face was formed to effigy forth whatever a man thinks and wills; in consequence of which the face is also called the effigy and index of the mind *(animus)*. Another reason is, that in the Most Ancient or primeval times sincerity prevailed, and no one cherished or wanted to cherish a thought which he was not willing should shine forth out of his face.

Spirits from thence came to me, and applied themselves to my left temple, where they breathed their speech upon me, but I did not understand it. As to its flow it was very soft: I had never before perceived any softer; it was like a very gentle breeze. It breathed first upon the left temple, and upon the upper part of the left ear; the breathing proceeded thence to the left eye, and by degrees to the right, and flowed down afterwards, especially from the left eye, to the lips; and when at the lips it entered through the mouth, and through a way within the mouth, and, indeed, through the Eustachian tube, into the brain. When the breathing arrived there, I understood their speech, and was enabled to speak with them. When they spoke with me, I observed that my lips were moved, and my tongue also slightly, which was owing to the correspondence of interior with exterior speech.

Theodore Flournoy

From India to the Planet Mars, 1900.

The Martian tongue, as spoken by Hélène Smith.

1. métiche C.	**médache C.**	**métaganiche S.**	**kin't'che**
Monsieur C.	*Madame C.*	*Mademoiselle S.*	*quatre*
Mr. C.	Mrs C.	Miss S.	Four.

2. dodé né ci haudan té mess métiche astané ké dé mé véche.
Ceci est la maison du grand homme Astané que tu as vu.
This is the house of the great man Astané, whom thou has seen.

3. mode iné cé di cévoitche ni êvé ché kiné liné.
Mère adorée, je te reconnais et suis ton petit Linet.
Adored mother, I recognize thee, and am thy little Linet.

4. o modé mété modé modé ine palette is ché péliché ché chiré né ci ten ti vi.
O mère, tendre mère, mère bien-aimée, calme tout ton souci, tons fils est près de toi.

Oh mother, tender mother, dearly loved mother, calm all thy care, thy son is near thee.

5. ikiché ten ti si ké di êvé dé étéche mêné izé bénêzée.

Oh! pourquoi près de moi ne te tiens-tu toujours, amie enfin retrouvée!

Oh! Why dost thou not keep thyself always near me, friend, at last found again?

6. ti iche cêné éspênié ni ti êzi atêv astané êzi érié vize é vi . . .

De noire belle "Éspénié" et de mon être Astané, mon âme descend à toi . . .

From our beautiful "Éspénié" and from my being Astané, my soul descends to thee . . .

> **i kiché ten ti si ké di êvé dé étéche mêné izé bénézée**
>
> *oh! pourquoi prèes de moi ne te tiens-tu toujours, amie enfin retrouvée!*
>
> —Oh! Why dost thou not keep thyself always near to me, friend, at last found again?

7. cé êvé plêva ti di bénèz éssat riz tès midée durée cé ténassé riz iche éspênié

Je suis chagrin de le retrouver vivant sur cette laide terre; je voudrais sur notre Éspénié

I am sorry to find you again living on this wretched earth; I would on our Éspénié

> **vétéche ié ché atev hêné ni povê ten ti si éni zée métiché oné gudé ni zée darié grêvé**
>
> *voir tout ton être s'élever et rester près de moi; ici Les hommes sont bons et les coeurs larges.*
>
> see all thy being raise itself and remain near me; here men are good and hearts large.

8. amès mis tensée ladé si—amès ten tivé avé men—koumé ié ché pélésse—amès some têsé

Viens un instant vers moi, viens près d'un vieil ami fondre tout ton chagrin; viens admirer

Come towards me a moment, come near an old friend to melt away all thy sorrow; come to admire

misaîmé—ké dé surès pit châmi—izâ méta ii borêsé ti finalimé—iâ izi dé séimiré

ces fleurs, que tu crois sans parfum, mais pourtant si pleines de senteurs! . . . Mais si tu comprendras!

these flowers, which you believe without perfume, but yet so full of fragrance! But if thou couldst understand.

9. ané éni ké érédutè cé ilassuné té imâ ni bétiné chée durée

C'est ici que, solitaire, je m'approche du ciel et regarde la terre.

It is here that, alone, I bring myself near to heaven and look upon the earth.

10. simandini lé lâmi méné kizé pavi kiz atimi

Simandini, me voici! amie! Quelle joie, quel bonheur!

Simandini, here I am! Friend! What joy! What happiness!

11. i modé duméiné modé kévi cé mache povini poénezé mûné é vi saliné éziné rnimâ

O mère, ancienne mère, quand je peux arriver quelques instants vers toi j'oublie mes parents

Oh, mother, former mother, when I can arrive a few instants near thee, I forget my parents,

nikainé modé—i men.

Nikaine, mère!—ô ami!

Nikainé, mother!—Oh friend!

12. lassunée ké nipuné ani tis dé machir mirivé iche manir sé dé évenir toué

Approche, ne crains pas; bientôt tu pourras tracer notre écriture, et tu posséderas dans

Approach, fear not; soon thou wilt be able to trace our writing, and thou willt possess in

chi amiché zé forimé ti viche tarviné

tes mains les marques de notre langage.

thy hands the signs of our language.

13. (adèl) ané sini (yestad) i astané cé fimès astané mirâ

C'est vous, ô Astané, je meurs! Astané, adieu!

It is you, oh Astané, I am dying! Astané, farewell!

14. eupié zé palir né amé arvâ nini pédriné évai diviné lâmée ine vinâ té luné

Eupié, le temps est venu; Arva nous quitte; sois heureux jusqu' au retour du jour

Eupié, the time has come; Arva leaves us; be happy till the return of the day

—pouzé men hantiné ezi vraini né touzé med vi ni ché chiré sainé—ké

—Pouzé, ami fidèle, mon désir est même pour toi et ton fils Sainé.—Que

—Pouzé, faithful friend, my wish is even for thee, and thy son Sainé.—May

zalisé téassé mianiné ni di daziné—eupié—pouzé

l'élément entier t'envéloppe et te garde!—Eupié!—Pouzé!

the entire element envelop thee and guard thee!—Eupié!—Pouzé!

15. modé tatinée cé ké mache radziré zé tarvini va nini nini triménêni il adzi

Mère chérie, je ne puis prononcer le langage ou nous nous comprenions si bien!

My dearest, I cannot pronounce the language in which we understood each other so well!

cé zé selimiré vétiche i modé inée kévi bérinir m hed kévi machiri cé di triné

Je le comprends cependant; ô mère adorée, quand reviendra-t-il? Quand pourrai-je te parler

I understand it, however; oh! adored mother, when will it return? When shall I be able to speak to thee

ti éstotiné ni bazée animina i modé cé méi adzi ilinée i modé inée

de ma demière et courte existence? Ô mere, je t' ai bien reconnue, ô mère adorée

of my last and short existence? Oh! mother I have well recognized thee, adored mother

cé ké lé nazère ani—mirâ mode itatinée mirâ mirâ mirâ

je ne me trompe pas!—Adieu mère chérie, adieu, adieu, adieu!

I am not mistaken!—Farewell, dearest mother, farewell, farewell, farewell!

16. astané ésenâle pouzé mêné simandini mirâ

Astane. Ésenale. Pouzé. Amie Simandini, adieu!

Astané. Ésenale. Pouzé. Friend Simandini, farewell!

17. taniré mis méch med mirivé éziné brima{; ti tès tensée—

Prends un crayon pour tracer mes paroles de cet instant.

Take a pencil to trace my words of this moment.

azini dé améir mazi si somé iche nazina tranei—Simandini cé kié mache di pédriné tès luné

Alors tu viendras avec moi admirer notre nouveau passage. Simandini, je ne puis te quitter ce jour.

Then thou wilt come with me to admire our new passage. Simandini, I cannot leave thee this day.

ké cé évé diviné—patrinèz kié nipuné ani

Que je suis heureux!—Alors ne crains pas!

How happy I am!—Then fear not!

Victory Henry

Le langage martien, étude analytique de la gènese d'une langue dans un cas de glossolalie somnambulique, 1901.

Martian Etymologies We have seen how the translation of Martian sentences into French is supposed to be the work of a spirit reincarnated on Mars, then disincarnated, who was still alive on our planet recently. Here, the name given him was "Alexis Mirbel." "Mirbel" is a pseudonym, but I have made sure, in private correspondence with M. Flournoy, that "Alexis" is not. This raises the following question: is there a connection between the two names, "Alexis" and "Ésenale" given to the same individual in two different worlds?

Admittedly, "Alexis" is not very rare; that said, it's not common, either, and no other name resembles it as far as the ending is concerned. It's not surprising, then, that this slightly unusual-sounding name set Mlle Smith's subconscious mind to work. We should note, from the outset, that she had all the time she needed to do so: in November 1894 we learned of the existence of Alexis on Mars, but his Martian name Ésenale was not revealed until October 1896. It took two years—*grande mortalis aevi spatium*—for something to be elaborated that, however complicated, would have taken less than a minute in a dream!

The sound of the two last syllables of *Alexis* calls to mind the Hungarian *csacsi*, especially if pronounced in the French manner. *Csacsi* means "donkey"—not in generic terms, we should note, but as a kind of affectionate diminutive, the sort of thing taught to children. The word may have sprung from [the father's] lips the first time he pointed a donkey out to little Hélène. . . . If we translate it into German, we get *Esel*, that is, practically the same as the first two syllables of the name "Ésenale." As for the ending, it's identical to the first syllable of the name "Alexis." (The final syllable, *-e*, is silent, of course.) The whole operation can be expressed in a formula of mathematical precision, namely: *al* + *csacsi* = *esel* + *al*. The two names are identical.

Or almost. The form should be **Eselale*. I don't think anyone will attach much importance to this minor discrepancy, however. It might just be the dissimilation of one of the two *l's*; the formulation obtained by translating the word back into French (the metathesis of *Esel* yields *Ésenale*); or the effect of words being run together, as in the Hungarian *ézen âllat*, "this animal." But even if we couldn't explain it at all, there's no reason to dwell on such a minimal discrepancy, given the perfect agreement in all other respects.

The ground having been cleared, all that remains is to follow alphabetical order, classifying each Martian word according to the lexical term from which it most likely derived. I stress that I'm quite aware that many of the connections proposed here are hypothetical. To be on the safe side, they will be qualified as "doubtful" or "very doubtful" on occasion. Some are mentioned just to set my mind at ease, to indicate a path for other scholars to follow in search of better.

Abadâ, "peu" [little/few], once, in the expression *mis abadâ*, "a little"; when pronounced in childlike fashion, it calls to mind French *abondant*, from which it may indeed derive via semantic contrast. Doubtful.

Acâmi, "astronome" [astronomer], once; the idea of "astronomer" suggests "scholar" and therefore "academy": note the medial long vowel, which seems to compensate for the loss of the penultimate syllable.

Alizé, "élément" [element], twice: concerns a rarefied element like the *fluidum* of spiritualists; this idea suggests that of "wind" and therefore French *alizé* [trade wind]—a word sufficiently uncommon and erudite to remain intact.

Animinâ, "existence" [existence] twice: this is the French *animé* (animated) with an arbitrary suffix added.

Anizié, "envoie" [sends], once: could be the metathesis, with an unvoiced consonant becoming voiced, of French *assigner* [to assign]; the latter may have been suggested by *consigner* [to consign], which, in commercial parlance, commonly means "to send." Mlle Smith works in sales and hears this word dozens of times a day. Doubtful nevertheless. [. . .]

Antéch, "hier" [yesterday], twice: this is the French word *antique*, or, more precisely, the first two syllables of the French *antérieur* [previous], with an adverbial suffix. [. . .]

Dorimé, "*sain*" [healthy], once: possibly a metathesis of the French *modéré*, which is linked in meaning to the expression *bien portant* (in good health).

Duméïné, "ancienne" [former {fem. sing.}]: Alexis addresses his earthly mother as *modé*, "mother"; then he corrects himself and says *duméïné modé*—she is no longer his mother, since he has been reincarnated on Mars and now has another one. This correction might have evoked *du moins* [at least], which would follow almost automatically in French; with a Martian suffix, the phrase has taken on the function of the adjective meaning "former."

Durée, "terre" [earth], occurs twice. A metathesis of German *Erde* [earth] fails to explain the term. Much more probable is the influence of a French locution such as *la dure terre* [the hard earth] or *coucher la dure terre* [sleep on the hard ground], especially since the first time the word is spoken, it is by an inhabitant of Mars, with extreme scorn for our unlucky planet.

Ébrinié, "[il] pense" [{he} thinks], once. Inasmuch as the thought here is extremely affectionate, it calls to mind French *épris* [enamoured], which would explain the first syllable.

Épizi, "rose," adjective [rose, pink], once: suggested by the association of the words *rose* [rose] and *épine* [thorn] in many a common phrase; then apocope and arbitrary suffixation.

Éspénié, proper name referring to the Martian paradise, twice: suggested by magical depictions of Spain [*l'Espagne*] in novels and romances.

Éssat, "vivant" [living], once, and *ëssate,* "vivre" [to live], twice: visibly contains the root of the verb *être* [to be]; as this root appears clearly in French only in the learned term *essence,* it is perhaps better to look to Italian *essere,* which it is possible to know without speaking the language. [. . .]

Finaïmé, "senteurs" [scents], once: suggested by the French "[odeur] fine" [delicate fragrance], with an assonated final suffix.

Forimé, "marques [d'écriture]" [marks {of writing}], once: *forme,* in French, is quite close; however, the commercial term *firme,* in the sense of "trademark," fits better, and Mlle Smith, a commercial employee, will be quite familiar with it; contamination between words is possible. [. . .]

Kavivé, "étrangers" [strangers], once: given that *kâ* means *qui* [who], *ka-vivé* could be broken down as *qui vive!* [who goes there!], an exclamation uttered when hearing or seeing something uncommon.

Kêmâ, "mâle" [male], once: a syllabic metathesis of French *mâle,* in which the letter *l* has been replaced by its immediate neighbour in the alphabet. Very doubtful.

Kin't'che, "quatre" [four], occurs once, at the very first appearance of Martian, when the language still lacks definition: arbitrary and garbled alteration of French *quatre.*

Léziré, "souffrance" [suffering], once: a clear derivative of French *léser* [to injure] or *lésion* [damage].

Luné, *"jour"* [day], six times. Here the choices are many: either French *lune* [moon], nighttime star, by semantic contrast; or French *lundi*, Italian *lunedi* [Monday], which begins the days of the week; or, more simply, the root *lu-*, taken from *luire* [to shine], *lumière* [light], etc., to which a Martian suffix has been added.

Mabûré, "grossier" [coarse], once. The idea suggests *bure* [homespun], or even *vêtement en bure* [homemade garment], a juxtaposition that also could be spelled *ambure*, of which *mâburé* is the exact metathesis.

Mazêté, "peine" [sorrow], twice: the word suggests the idea of a *masse* [mass] that is difficult to move; arbitrary suffixation.

Médache, "madame," once: jargon from the beginnings of Martian, where sibilants play a preponderant role.

Médinié, "entourent" [(they] surround], once: the first two syllables come from *méditerranée* [Mediterranean], which all geography books for children define as "sea *surrounded* on all sides by land."

Mervé, "superbes" [superb, plural], once: French *merveille* [marvel], or the first two syllables of *merveilleux* [marvelous].

Métaganiche, "mademoiselle," once, on the same day as *médâche*.

Mété, "tendre" [tender], once, in the alliterative juxtaposition *mété modé*, "tender mother." The idea of mother has suggested "maternal," which is shortened and jargonized. [. . .]

Midée, *"laide"* [ugly, fem.], once: likely a contamination of the words *misère* [destitution. woe] and *hideux* [hideous]. [. . .]

Vizêné, "distinguer" [to distinguish], once: Martian derivative of French *vision*, which, as a scholarly word, has a more technical meaning for Mlle Smith than *voir* (to see] in the ordinary sense; perhaps also related *viser* [to aim]. [. . .]

Zati, "souvenir" [memory], once: reminiscent of the last two syllables of *rnyosotis* (*Vergissmeinnicht*), the forget-me-not.

Ziné, "bleu" [blue], once: perhaps adapted and derived from *Chine* [China], because of the fine blue color of certain Chinese vases.

NOTES

FOREWORD

1. Mikhail Bakhtin, *Le Marxisme et la philosophie du langage* (1929) (Paris: Minuit, 1977). Translated into English by Ladislav Matejka and I. R. Titunik as *Marxism and the Philosophy of Language* (Cambridge, MA: Harvard University Press, 1986), with V. N. Vološinov as author (whom some have argued was a pen name of Bakhtin).

2. Françoise Gadet et al., *Les maîtres de la langue* (Paris: Maspero, 1979), contains brief excerpts.

3. First published by Gallimard (Paris), in 1938. André Blavier took up and expanded Queneau's project in *Fous littéraires* (Paris: Veyrier, 1982), revised with further additions by Éditions des Cendres (Paris, 2000). Queneau's work has since been published as *Aux confins des ténèbres: Les fous littéraires français aux xixe siècle* (Paris: Éditions Gallimard, 2002).

4. Self-published by the author around 1900, Brisset's works were rediscovered by André Breton and included in his *Encyclopédie de l'humour noir* (1930). They are now available in a single volume from Presses du Réel (Dijon, 2004). Michel Foucault wrote the preface for the 1970 edition of *La grammaire logique* published by Tchou.

5. Théodore Flournoy, *From India to the Planet Mars: A Case of Multiple Personality with Imaginary Languages*, ed. Sonu Shamdasani (Princeton, NJ: Princeton University Press, 1994).

6. Instead of slowing down the proceedings with lengthy quotations, I have placed reference texts at the end of the volume, where the reader may consult them at leisure; many of them, especially those from before 1900, are almost impossible to find outside of research libraries.

7. The fact that the Société linguistique de Paris, upon its foundation in 1866, excluded both the question of language's origins and utopian projects for a universal tongue shows the extent to which these two aspects of the linguistic imaginary are fused. Another telling example is the bibliography the editor of Court de Gébelin provides for the 1816 edition of *Histoire naturelle de la parole* (which first appeared in 1772): the same heading groups together "general grammar," "universal language," and "original language."

8. "Hence the profoundly paradoxical nature of language, at once immanent in the individual and transcendent for society" (Émile Benveniste, *Problèmes de linguistique générale II* [Paris: Gallimard, 1974], 85).

9. This term—which is hardly satisfying—refers to languages that seem to have issued "naturally" from the various cultures of humankind.

10. Thanks to the rigor of comparative philology and linguistics, "Primitive Indo-European" seems to be a valid (if contested) construction.

11. One should distinguish between pure science fiction, fantasy, and didactic-philosophical fiction. Science fiction (even before it was given this name) extrapolates from scientific data: everything must make sense, be justified, and have the air of probability. In contrast, fantasy does not care about verisimilitude: it portrays marvels, the irrational in its pure state. Finally, in the didactic-philosophical genre, authorial intention assumes the guise of a fiction that is, in fact, a matter of metaphor or allegory. Needless to say, the three forms can be mixed, and it isn't always easy to classify individual works. Those offering the most remarkable elaborations of invented languages often reveal a deep knowledge of linguistics; in some cases, they have even been written by a grammarian, linguist, or philosopher of language.

CHAPTER 1

1. Unavailable in English, but translated into French (Éditions OPTA).

2. Babylonian does not allow series of consonants; it is a matter of some importance that this invented language is distinguished by open syllables; see chapter 8, p. 121, on linguistic universals.

3. Cf. chapter 9, p. 133.

4. What is now known as speculative fiction, including science fiction, is rooted in utopian works and accounts of imaginary travel. The primary point of reference is *Utopia* by Thomas More, who coined the word in the book of the same name (1516). However, the tradition can be traced back to ancient authors including Plato and Lucian. In my estimation, Jules Verne should be credited with effecting the shift from one genre to the other, and it's no coincidence that his works were contemporaneous with the epistemological rupture of positivism, which laid a new foundation for science (and, of course, for the science of language). The phrase "science fiction" is obviously a contradiction in terms. Science and history, on one side, and fiction, myth, and utopia on the other, are antinomic (in the same way that in the nineteenth century the utopian socialism of Charles Fourier was opposed to the scientific socialism of Karl Marx).

5. According to Herodotus, the Phoenicians already circumnavigated Africa seven hundred years before Ptolemy.

6. On the history of the Austral continent, see L. Sprague de Camp, *Lost Continents: The Atlantis Theme in History, Science, and Literature* (New York: Gnome Press, 1954).

7. This is the Nostratic hypothesis of so-called Proto-World; see box, p. 104.

8. John Webb, *An Historical Essay Endeavouring the Probability that the Language of the Empire of China is the Primitive Language* (London: Nath. Brook, 1669).

9. Simon Berington, *Dissertation on the Mosaical Creation, Deluge, Building of Babel and Confusion of Tongues* (London: C. Davis, 1750).

10. Georges de Dubor, *Les langues et l'espèce humaine* (Louvain: Peeters, 1884).

11. This, incidentally, is the text of the last of Brahms's *Vier ernste Gesänge* (Op. 121). The two biblical chapters are reproduced in the appendix, p. 267.

CHAPTER 2

1. Michel Pierssens, *La Tour de Babil: La fiction du signe* (Paris: Éditions de Minuit, 1976); Umberto Eco, *The Search for the Perfect Language,* trans. James Fentress (Oxford: Blackwell, 1997).

2. Marcel Monnerot-Dumaine, *Précis d'interlinguistique générale et spéciale* (Paris: Maloine, 1960).

3. Few qualified linguists have taken an interest in the question; exceptions in the twentieth century include Edward Sapir, Otto Jespersen, and André Martinet.

4. "Interlinguistics" is the science of planned auxiliary languages. The other "bible" is the monumental *Histoire de la langue universelle* by Louis Couturat and Léopold Léau (Paris: Hachette, 1903).

5. Marr, who spent a large part of his life conducting fieldwork in the Caucasus and elsewhere, represents a notable exception; see chapter 8.

6. See appendix, p. 201 and p. 210, for the Cratylist writings of Court de Gébelin and Nodier.

7. Charles Callet, *Le mystère du langage* (Paris: Éditions de la Revue mondiale, 1925); cf. the extract on p. 220.

8. Charles Nodier, *Dictionnaire raisonné des onomatopées françaises* (Paris: Demonville, 1808).

9. That said, the term had not been invented yet. Interestingly, the author mentions "the conformity scholars have found between the language of the Persians and that of the Teutons." When these words were written, at the beginning of the eighteenth century, comparative grammar did not exist; the author simply believes that the Teutons, Greeks, and Romans borrowed from primitive Celtic (Paul-Yves

Pezron, *De l'antiquité de la nation et de la langue des Celtes, autrement appelés Gaulois* [Paris: Jean Boudot, 1703]).

10. Louis Poinsinet de Sivry, *Origine des premières sociétés, des peuples, des sciences, des arts et des idiomes anciens et modernes* (Amsterdam/Paris: Lacombe, 1769).

11. See Eco, *The Search for the Perfect Language*, chapter 4.

12. Both cited by Frédéric Baudry, *De la science du langage et de son état actuel* (Paris: Auguste Durand, 1864).

13. This thesis was advanced by Dr. John Rae; quoted in Max Müller, *Lectures on the Science of Language*, vol. 2 (London: Longman, Green, Longman, Roberts & Green, 1864), 10.

14. Onffroy de Thoron, *La langue primitive depuis Adam jusqu'à Babel, son passage en Amérique où elle est encore vivante* (Paris: Leroux, 1886).

CHAPTER 3

1. The study at hand takes Western culture as its framework; in early societies, it seems, glossolalia is a traditional component of shamanism and witchcraft, irrespective of sex.

2. Charles Nodier, *Bibliographie des fous: De quelque slivres excentriques* (Paris: Techener, 1835).

3. In a philological capacity, Leibniz is more the forerunner of Nikolai Marr than of Franz Bopp; however, his ideas agree with those of the times (and Marr was born a century too late).

4. Callet, *Le mystère du langage*; cf. appendix, p. 220.

5. Jaroslav Stuchlik, "Essai sur la psychologie de l'invention des langues artificielles," *Annales medico-pschologiques* 2 (1960).

6. Monnerot-Dumaine, *Précis d'interlinguistique.*

7. Cf. Marina Yaguello, *Language through the Looking Glass: Exploring Language and Linguistics*, adapted by Trevor Harris and the author (Oxford: Oxford University Press, 1998), chapter 11.

8. These formal aspects will be examined in detail in chapter 9.

9. Cf. Émile Lombard, *De la glossolalie chez les premiers chrétiens et des phénomènes similaires* (Lausanne: Imprimeries réunies, 1910).

10. The love of language (*langage*) does not necessarily overlap with the love of languages (*langues*): it is possible to love human tongues in all their diversity without seeking their underlying unity.

11. Jacques Damourette and Édouard Pichon, *Des mots à la pensée* (Paris: Éditions d'Artrey, 1911–1940).

12. Nuns are the exception that confirm the rule.

13. Literally, "He who loves well, punishes well."

CHAPTER 4

1. Etymologically, "utopia" does not have a "positive" sense; it connotes both the idea of a better world and the opposite: a fantasy that cannot be realized.

2. Eco, *The Search for the Perfect Language.*

3. Susan Bruce, ed., *Three Early Modern Utopias: Utopia, New Atlantis, The Isle of Pines* (Oxford: Oxford University Press, 1999), 74.

4. Frances Godwin, *The Man in the Moone* (London: John Norton, 1638).

5. Cf. Cyrano de Bergerac, *The Comical History of the States and Empires of the Worlds of the Moon and Sun,* trans. A. Lovell (London: Henry Rhodes, 1687). The journeys to the Moon and Sun were written, respectively, in 1649 and 1652 (and published posthumously in 1656 and 1662).

6. Thus, musicality is associated not just with universality, but also with naturalness. In the following century, Rousseau made it a trait of primitive language, and in the 1800s, François Sudre created *Solrésol,* a universal musical language.

7. The theory of stages (cf. chapter 5) will declare Chinese the prototype of primitive language, taking up, in "scientific" fashion, the hypothesis formulated by John Webb in 1669 (see chapter 5).

8. According to Leibniz, the Dutch mathematician Jacob Golius (1596–1667) deemed Chinese an artificial language, "invented all at once by some ingenious man to bring about verbal communication between the many different peoples inhabiting the great land we call China" (Leibniz, *New Essays on Human Understanding*, ed. Peter Remnant and Jonathan Bennett (Cambridge: Cambridge University Press, 1996), book 4, chapter 1, 275.

9. John Wilkins, *Mercury or the Secret and Swift Messenger* (London: J. Maynard, 1641), 145. In this same work Wilkins also suggests that it might be possible to base a universal character on Hebrew roots, which at that time were considered to be more consistent and fewer in number compared to other languages.

10. In a 1629 letter to Father Marin Mersenne (see appendix, p. 187), Descartes acknowledged the theoretical possibility of creating a truly philosophical language, but voiced skepticism about it ever gaining currency. His correspondent's *Harmonie universelle* (1636) would, in turn, seek a language with a natural foundation admitting direct communication—that is, one would understand it without having learned it first. All the same, Mersenne recognized that all languages rest on arbitrary foundations and that his project was utopian. One possible basis for such a design would be onomatopoeia.

11. Cyrano de Bergerac, *The Comical History of the States and Empires of the Worlds of the Moon and Sun*, 60–61.

12. Gottfried Wilhelm Leibniz, "Bref essai sur l'origine des peoples (1710)," in *Genèse de la pensée linguistique*, ed. André Jacob (Paris: Armand Colin, 1973).

13. Philosophy represents just one aspect—the most important one, to be sure—of the problem of universal language in the seventeenth century. There was also need for a vehicular interlanguage to replace Latin and serve practical ends. In fact, French came to play this role, which accounts for why the heyday of interlanguages did not occur until the nineteenth and twentieth centuries. Finally, religious motivations were significant for Athanasius Kircher and Comenius, among others. Persecuted for his Protestantism, Comenius sought a

means for uniting people set against each other by religious schism; for him, a universal language would bridge confessional divides and reestablish religious harmony (*Via Lucis*, 1668).

14. Leibniz, *New Essays on Human Understanding*, book 4, chapter 6, 399–400.

15. Cf. James Knowlson, *Universal Language Schemes in England and France* (Toronto: University of Toronto Press, 1975).

16. George Dalgarno, *Ars signorum* (London: J. Hayes, 1661); John Wilkins, *An Essay towards a Real Character and a Philosophical Language* (London: Gellibrand and Martin, 1668).

17. Gottfried Wilhelm Leibniz, *Dissertatio de arte combinatoria* (Leipzig: Johann Simon Fick and Johan Polycarp Seubold, 1666).

18. It is hardly surprising, then, that Louis Couturat, an eminent interlinguist and initiator of several projects for a universal language, also wrote a study on his forebear: *La logique de Leibniz d'après des documents inédits* (Paris: Félix Alcan, 1901).

19. Letter to Galloys (1677), quoted in Couturat, *La logique de Leibniz*. Until the end of his life, Leibniz retained interest in this problem and the related matter of finding the origin of language(s). Unfortunately, most of his relevant writings, which are in Latin, still have not been translated.

20. "The love of God" or "John loves Mary more than Peter" may both be interpreted in two ways. Leibniz foresees different structures for his scheme of improved Latin. In turn, possession—"I own this house"; "this house belongs to me"—will be rendered by a single expression.

21. Gunvor Sahlin, *César Chesneau du Marsais et son rôle dans l'évolution de la grammaire Générale* (Paris: Les Presses Universitaires de France, 1928), 2–3.

22. The anagram of Vairasse, of course.

23. We'll encounter the same complexity two centuries later with Volapük.

24. Denis Vairasse, *The History of the Sevarambians: A Utopian Novel* (Albany: State University of New York Press, 2006), 364.

25. Émile Pons, "Les langues imaginaires dans le voyage utopique: les grammairiens, Vairasse et Foigny," *Revue de littérature comparée* 12 (1932).

26. See appendix.

27. The reader will recall that Leibniz employed a combinatory system of numbers admitting infinite variation, which *then* were transcribed into pronounceable letters.

28. The principal defect of this invented language—which makes it inferior to any natural language—is that it does not avail itself of the resources provided by double articulation (which goes along with the arbitrariness of the sign—a notion that does not occur in speculations of the day). By making each letter (or spoken equivalent) a *significant* unit, rather than merely a *distinctive* one, Foigny loses the advantages of the economy at work in actual language. It is precisely because phonemes lack an inherent sense that, although limited in number, they allow for an unlimited array of meaningful combinations.

CHAPTER 5

1. Chevalier de Béthune, *Relation du monde de Mercure* (1750), in *Voyages imaginaires*, vol. 16, ed. C. Garnier (Paris: Garnier, 1787).

2. Sign language represents one of the most relevant implementations of the idea of a universal language in terms of cognition and communication without borders (although there are sign languages specific to countries, they are mutually intelligible for the most part), and as an illustration of theories of the gestural origins of language. It warrants mention that its inventor had no predecessor.

3. Étienne Bonnot de Condillac, *Cours d'étude pour l'instruction du prince de Parme*, vol. 1, *Grammaire* (Parma: Imprimerie Royale, 1775).

4. Charles de Brosses, *Traité de la formation mécanique des langues*, vol. 1 (Paris: Saillant, 1765), xii.

5. Cf. Roman Jakobson, "Why Mama and Papa," *Selected Writings*, vol. 1, *Phonological Studies* (The Hague: Mouton, 1962).

6. Anne-Marie Mercier-Faivre, *Un supplément à "L'Encyclopédie." Le "Monde primitif" d'Antoine Court de Gébelin* (Paris: Honoré Champion, 1999), 78.

7. Antoine Court de Gébelin, *Le monde primitif analysé et comparé avec le monde modern* (Paris: Durand, 1775).

8. Antoine Louis Claude Destutt de Tracy, *Éléments d'idéologie* (Paris: Courcier, 1803), 327.

9. Destutt de Tracy, *Éléments d'idéologie*, 331.

10. Destutt de Tracy, 338.

11. James Harris, *Hermes: Or, a Philosophical Inquiry Concerning Language and Universal Grammar* (London: H. Woodfall, 1751), 337.

12. Harris, *Hermes*, 340.

13. Harris, 335–336; emphasis added.

14. William Jones, *Discourses Delivered Before the Asiatic Society: And Miscellaneous Papers on the Religion, Poetry, Literature, Etc. of the Nations of India* (London: Charles S. Arnold, 1824), 28–29.

15. Thus, the comparatist Max Müller failed to obtain the chair of Sanskrit at Oxford in 1860.

16. Cf. Jakob Karl Ludwig Grimm, *On the Origin of Language*, trans. Raymond A. Wiley (Leiden: Brill, 1984).

17. For example, the so-called Grimm and Verner laws, which consider (among other things) the development of fricatives from aspirated occlusives. Sanskrit, Greek, Latin, and the Romance languages have an occlusive at the beginning of the different forms of the word *père, pater,* etc., whereas Germanic languages have a fricative: *father, Vater,* etc. (Grimm's law). The difference between English */th/*, which is fricative, and the occlusive in intervocalic position for its Germanic counterparts illustrates Verner's law: *father/Vater, mother/Mutter,* etc.

18. Prominent members at the time included Gaston Paris, [illegible] Bréal, and Frédéric Baudry.

19. The classification is Max Müller's.

20. Cf. Auguste Comte's theory of the three states: the theological (dogmatic) state, the metaphysical (critical) state, and the positive (scientific) state.

21. Claude Lévi-Strauss, *Race and History* (Paris: UNESCO, 1958), 13.

22. Grimm, *On the Origin of Language.*

23. In an 1869 paper for the *Société d'ethnographie.*

24. Louis Benloew, *De quelques caractères du langage primitif* (Paris: A Franck, 1863).

25. Baudry, *De la science du langage.*

26. Alfredo Trombetti, *L'unità d'origine del linguaggio* (Bologna: Beltrami, 1905).

27. Charles Lemaire, "De la parole," in *La tribune des linguistes: Philosophie des langues, études philologiques, questions grammaticales, réforme orthographique, alphabet universel, langue universelle, Volume 1* (Paris: Aux bureaux de la tribune des linguistes, 1858), 47.

28. Léon de Rosny, *De l'origine du langage* (Paris: Maisonneuve, 1869), 25.

29. Nazi racism found a natural extension in efforts to "purify" the German tongue.

30. Curiously, both predictions may be said to have come true: consider the remarkable vitality of English and the various vehicular forms of the same language spoken the world over.

31. Baudry, *De la science du langage.*

32. Baudry, *De la science du langage.*

33. Louis Couturat, "Des rapports de la logique et de la linguistique dans le problème de la langue universelle," *Revue de métaphysique et de morale* (July 1911).

...*ıts d'idéologie*, vol. 2, 394–395.

...*ıne langue universelle* (Paris, 1795).

...world a single means of communication is primarily a European idea. However, efforts have been made in Asia and Africa—for instance, Pham Xuan Thai's *Frater (Lingua Sistemfrater)* (Saigon: Zu-Hai, 1957); Fuishiki Okamoto's pasigraphic auxiliary language *Babm* (Tokyo, 1962); and K. A. Kumi Attobrah's *Afrihili Oluga* (Accra: Afrihili Centre, 1973).

4. Monnerot-Dumaine, *Précis d'interlinguistique*, 85.

5. Emphasis added.

6. The latter did not stay for long, however.

7. Forms that give birth to families of words in groups of related languages.

8. Cf. Harold E. Palmer, *The Principles of Language Study* (New York: World Book Company, 1921).

CHAPTER 7

1. Edgar Rice Burroughs, *A Princess of Mars* (New York: Grosset & Dunlap, 1917), 63.

2. In fact, many scholars have idealized this ancient language and wished to purge English of the Gallicisms and Latinisms that give it its hybrid nature. In the nineteenth century, the poet William Barnes (1801–1886) set about reconstructing the English language as a purely Germanic tongue—that is, as it would have been if William the Conqueror had not won the Battle of Hastings in 1066.

3. The past meets up with the future in science fiction as an element of disorientation; consider the "retro" atmosphere of *Blade Runner*, the "neo-ancient" costuming in *Star Wars*, the abundance of names with a Greco-Latin ring in many novels, the solemn and archaizing

bearing of leaders, the post-apocalyptic "return to nature" in the movie *Mad Max*, and so on.

4. Cf. Anthony Burgess, "Creating a Language for Primitive Man," *New York Times Magazine*, November 15, 1981, 102–109.

5. Benjamin Lee Whorf, *Language, Thought and Reality: Selected Writings* (Cambridge, MA: MIT Press, 1956), 252.

6. Edward Sapir, *Collected Works: I, General Linguistics* (Berlin: Walter de Gruyter, 2008), 498.

7. Sapir and Whorf (like Franz Boas) are to be credited for their noble intentions with regard to native populations, but that's another matter.

8. See appendix, p. 255.

9. Notably because Newspeak regularizes the process of lexical derivation: thus, the adjective "bad" is replaced by "ungood," which implies a value judgment that is hardly innocent.

10. We will return to this point in chapter 10.

11. Jack Vance, *The Languages of Pao* (St Albans: Mayflower, 1974), 47–48.

12. Vance, *The Languages of Pao*, 48.

13. Vance, 61.

14. Vance, 58.

15. Samuel R. Delany, *Babel-17* (New York: Ace, 1978), 152. Incidentally, to prevent others from reading her thoughts (a fairly common practice in this world), the heroine makes an effort to think only in Basque.

16. Returning to the conceptions of the *Grammaire générale et raisonnée de Port-Royal*, Noam Chomsky posits the distinction between deep structures and superficial ones; the latter derive from the former. To remove the ambiguity of a sentence (a "surface" phenomenon), one traces its generative history—that is, applies the rules of transformation in reverse—to arrive at the deep structure concerned.

17. Isn't the fact that generative and transformational grammar is an American invention—and that, consequently, English has received the most thorough theoretical treatment—another facet of "Anglo-Saxon" imperialism? Doesn't generative grammar promote English to the status of the universal language, both in the abstract sense (as an epistemological model) and in the concrete sense (as a vehicular language)? By the same token, *Grammaire générale et raisonnée de Port-Royal,* in spite of its "general" aims, served to consecrate the cultural hegemony of France and the role of French as a vehicular language. Finally, nineteenth-century comparative grammar was essentially a German undertaking—so much so that "Indo-Germanic" was long the term for "Indo-European," as if Germany were the center of Europe (if not the world).

18. Advances in computer science and automatic language processing have opened the prospect of replacing human translators with machines—a development presupposing the formal description of syntax and semantics.

19. Leaving aside ethical issues, it goes without saying that the demands of fiction prompt the author to treat the theoretical issues in a somewhat cavalier manner; nor could the experiment be conducted as described.

20. Specifically, the nested four-part poem of *Nouvelles Impressions d'Afrique,* in which branches spring from words and create a vast spider's web, forming four sentences that never end until the end of their respective section.

21. Ian Watson, *The Embedding* (New York: Scribner, 1973), 130.

22. Cf. Claude Hagège, *La grammaire générative: Réflexions critiques* (Paris: PUF, 1976).

23. That is, not linguistic *properties* (e.g., linearity, double articulation, redundancy), which are universal by definition.

24. In 1988, she also published *A First Dictionary and Grammar of Láadan* to disseminate the language, thereby passing beyond a purely fictional framework.

CHAPTER 8

1. As evidenced by Mikhail Bakhtin and V. N. Vološinov's critical analysis of his 1929 *Marxism and the Philosophy of Language.*

2. Nikolai Marr, *Izbrannye raboty I* (Leningrad: GAIMK, 1933), 6.

3. Cf. Sigmund Freud, "Psychoanalytic Notes Upon an Account of a Case of Paranoia (Dementia Paranoides) (1911)," in *Three Case Histories* (New York: Touchstone, 1963), 83–160.

4. Georgian, of course, is a language of venerable literary culture, but at the time its stature had been reduced; as a child, Marr spoke the Gourian dialect.

5. Marr, *Izbrannye raboty I*, 222.

6. Marr, 215.

7. Marr, 216.

8. Marr, 68.

9. Cf. Charles de Brosses, Antoine Court de Gébelin.

10. Marr, *Izbrannye raboty I*, 212–213; the modern theory of phonological universals affirms the precise opposite: a language only has affricates if it has occlusives first.

11. Marr, 217.

12. Marr, *Izbrannye raboty I*, 213. In his 1910 article, "The Antithetical Meaning of Primal Words," Freud draws on a study by Karl Abel (1884) and claims to have proven a parallel between dreams and the first words of human language. So Marr was not alone in thinking that the latter was able to signify contradictory meanings at the same time. The idea that "primitive" means "infantile" was quite widespread, hence Freud's equation of individualized language in the unconscious (which is regressive, childlike, and archaic) and collective language at its first beginnings. Benveniste had no difficulty demolishing this argument ("Remarks on the Function of Language in Freudian Theory," *Problems in General Linguistics* [Coral Gables: University of

Miami Press, 1971], 65–78) by showing that Abel's thesis rested on erroneous philological speculations that brought together words that seemed close for purely phonetic reasons. Imagine that Italian *caldo* ("hot") and German *kalt* ("cold") came from the same source!

13. Marr, *Izbrannye raboty I,* 11.

14. Gottfried Wilhelm Leibniz, "Bref essai sur l'origine des peoples (1710)," in *Genèse de la pensée linguistique,* ed. André Jacob (Paris: Armand Colin, 1973).

15. Marr, *Izbrannye raboty I,* 213–214.

16. Leibniz, "Bref Essai," 49; emphasis added.

17. Marr, *Izbrannye raboty I,* 211.

18. Marr, 217–218.

19. Note, in this context, the vitality of hybrid languages such as English and Swahili.

20. Marr, *Izbrannye raboty I,* 216.

21. Lawrence L. Thomas, *The Linguistic Theories of Nicolas Marr* (Berkeley: University of California Press, 1957).

22. The speech in which Stalin put an end to the Marrist controversy appeared in *L'Humanité* and is now available in two French translations; cf. Louis-Jean Calvet, *Marxisme et linguistique* (Paris: Payot, 1977), and Françoise Gadet et al., *Les maîtres de la langue* (Paris: Maspero, 1979).

23. Cf., Gadet, *Les maîtres de la langue,* and the special issue of *Langages* (1977) on Soviet linguistics.

24. Cf. the materials in Jacques Cosnier et al., *Les voies du langage* (Paris: Dunod, 1982). *Homo loquens* probably emerged 40,000 years ago. *Australopithecus,* on the other hand, goes back four million years. It seems that the capacity for symbolization, or semiotic activity, is an innate feature of human beings. A specialized auditory apparatus for verbal communication is likely a fairly recent development, as experiments on the acquisition of sign language by primates have

sought to demonstrate. That said, deaf children develop sign language spontaneously, without prior training. Likewise, the various languages used by deaf-mutes are far from being "transcriptions" of spoken language; they also develop autonomously, in ways that call to mind the "universals of simplification" observed in pidgins, with distinctive modalities adjusted to space that contrast with the linear unfolding of speech.

CHAPTER 9

1. *Studies on Hysteria*, co-written with Josef Breuer, appeared in 1894; *The Interpretation of Dreams* was not published until 1900.

2. Camille Flammarion, *Dreams of an Astronomer*, trans. E. E. Fournier D'Albe (New York: D. Appleton and Company, 1923), 111–112; translation slightly modified.

3. See Mireille Cifali, "Théodore Flournoy: La découverte de l'inconscient," *Le Bloc—Notes de la psychanalyse* 3 (1983): 111–131, and "Une glossolale et ses savants: Elise Muller, alias Hélène Smith," in Sylvain Auroux et al., *La linguistique fantastique* (Paris: Denoël, 1985), 236–244.

4. Not content to "stage" her stories by playing various characters, she also made beautiful naive drawings.

5. Cf. appendix; yet again, traces of the project for an ideal philosophical language are in evidence.

6. Cf. Justinus Kerner, *Die Seherin von Prevorst* (Stuttgart: Cotta, 1832); commentated by Lombard, *De la glossolalie*.

7. Note the similiarity between this pseudonym and the one Flournoy gave his medium.

8. While her lexicon is smaller and less interesting, "Mrs. Smead" developed a more remarkable syntax in trying to mark distance from English.

9. This rupture occurred specifically in response to the book, which stressed the diverging views of author and medium. See Théodore

Flournoy, "Nouvelles observations sur un cas de somnambulisme avec glossolalie," *Archives de psychologie de la Suisse romande* (1902): 100–255.

10. Cf. Felicitas Goodman, *Speaking in Tongues* (Chicago: University of Chicago Press, 1972).

11. See, especially, William John Samarin, "The Linguisticality of Glossolalia," *Hartford Quarterly* 8 (1968): 49–75, "Forms and Functions of Nonsense Language," *Linguistics* 50 (1969): 70–74; "Evolution in Glossolalic Private Language," *Anthropological Linguistics* 13, no. 2 (1971): 55–67; and *Tongues of Men and Angels: The Religious Language of Pentecostalism* (New York: Macmillan, 1972).

12. Although Flournoy's book largely conceals this fact, the records of the meetings make it quite clear (Mireille Cifali and Olivier Flournoy archives).

13. This case, observed by one Nicolo Cervello, a doctor, was not reported in French until *fifty years later* (1901) by another physician (L. Hahn).

14. Cf. César de Vesme, "Xénoglossie," *Annales de sciences psychiques* 15 (1905): 317ff., and "La xénoglossie de Laura Edmunds," *Annales de sciences psychiques* 17 (1907): 408–410 and 601–603.

15. Reported by John Sherrill, *They Speak with Other Tongues* (New York: McGraw-Hill, 1964).

16. Ennemond Boniface, *Thérèse Neumann, la crucifiée, devant l'histoire et la science* (Paris: Lethielleux, 1979).

17. Johann Wolfgang von Goethe, "Was heißt mit Zungen reden," quoted in Lombard, *De la glossolalie.*

18. Gustav Billroth, quoted in Lombard, *De la glossolalie.*

19. He found definitive proof only after publishing *From India to the Planet Mars* (1900).

20. A fact I've confirmed with my students—without reaching a state of trance or altered consciousness.

21. For example, in Czech, the tonic accent signals the end of a word, in French the end of a syntactic group.

22. Cf. appendix, p. 272.

23. Benveniste, "L'homme dans la langue," in *Problèmes de linguistique générale II*.

24. Flournoy, *From India to the Planet Mars*, 258–260: "Martian may be attributed to a survival or a reawakening under the lash of mediumistic hypnoses of that general function common to all human beings, which is at the root of language and manifests itself with the more [*sic*] spontaneity and vigor as we mount higher towards the birth of peoples and individuals.

"Ontogenesis, say the biologists, reproduces in abridged form and *grosso-modo* phylogenesis; each being passes through stages analogous to those through which the race itself passes; and it is known that the first ages of ontogenic evolution—the embryonic period, infancy, early youth—are more favorable than later periods and adult age to the ephemeral reappearances of ancestral tendencies, which would hardly leave any trace upon a being who had already acquired his organic development. The 'poet who died young' in each one of us is only the most common example of those atavic [sic] returns of tendencies and of emotions which accompanied the beginnings of humanity, and remain the appanage of infant peoples, and which cause a fount of variable energy in each individual in the spring-time of his life, to congeal or disappear sooner or later with the majority: all children are poets, and that in the original, the most extended, acceptation of the term. They create, they imagine, they construct—and language is not the least of their creations.

"I conclude from the foregoing that the very fact of the reappearance of that activity in the Martian states of Hélène is a new indication of the infantile, primitive nature left behind in some way and long since passed by her ordinary personality, of the subliminal strata which mediumistic autohypnotization with her puts in ebullition and causes to mount to the surface. There is also a perfect accord between the puerile character of the Martian romance, the poetic and archaic charms of its style, and the audacious and naïve fabrication of its unknown language."

25. Martin Joos and H. A. Gleason; cf. William John Samarin, "Salient and Substantive Pidginization," in *Pidginization and Creolization of Languages*, ed. Dell Hymes (Cambridge: Cambridge University Press, 1971).

26. Flournoy, *From India to the Planet Mars*, 249.

27. Flournoy, 250.

28. Many artificial languages devised by amateurs display weakness in this regard.

29. Japanese and Malagasy, for instance.

30. Here's a sample of the fictional language on "Nazar": *Spik antik flok skak mak tabu milahatt* ("The prince of trees orders that the being fallen from the sky be employed among his ordinary runners"); from Ludwig Holberg, *Nicolai Klimii Iter subterraneum novam telluris theoriam ac historiam quintae monarchiae adhuc nobis incognitae exhibens* (1741).

31. Martian corpus 33 in Flournoy, *From India to the Planet Mars*.

32. Samarin, *Tongues of Men and Angels*, and Goodman, *Speaking in Tongues*, collect important materials.

33. Dentals have a higher pitch than other consonants, as do the front closed vowels (*i, é*), which also predominate in Martian. Flournoy, who took an interest in "hearing colors," develops this point in his book.

34. Cf. Roman Jakobson, "Retrospect," *Selected Writings IV: Slavic Epic Studies* (The Hague: Mouton, 1966), 639.

35. Jakobson, "Retrospect," 640; emphasis in original.

36. In keeping with the linguistic substrate of local tongues.

37. Jakobson, "Retrospect," 641.

38. Émile Benveniste, "The Semiology of Language," in *Semiotics: An Introductory Anthology*, ed. Robert E. Innis (Bloomington: Indiana University Press, 1985), 226–246, at 241.

39. Benveniste, "The Semiology of Language," 242; emphasis added.

40. Vladimir Jankélévitch, *Music and the Ineffable,* trans. Carolyn Abbate (Princeton: Princeton University Press, 2003), 11.

41. Jankélévitch, *Music and the Ineffable,* 9.

42. Benveniste, "Subjectivity in Language," in *Problems in General Linguistics,* 230.

43. Quoted by Catherine Clément, *Opera: the Undoing of Women,* trans. Betsy Wing (Minneapolis: University of Minnesota Press, 1988), 176.

44. The vocalizations can be likened to the "hollers" of African Americans in the southern United States—which confirms the link between women and oppressed or disadvantaged minorities. Moreover, the predominance of the vowel *a,* which is the easiest sound to sing, has been universally noted in glossolalia.

45. This is a primary theme in Clément's book.

46. Quoted in Morton T. Kelsey, *Tongue Speaking: An Experiment in Spiritual Experience* (New York: Doubleday & Company, 1964).

47. Kelsey, *Tongue Speaking,* 199.

48. Winthrop Sargeant, *Geniuses, Goddesses, and People* (New York: E. P. Dutton, 1949).

49. Composers who have demonstrated interest in this link between glossolalia and music include Edgar Varèse and François-Bernard Mâche.

CHAPTER 10

1. "Ethnic languages" has been proposed as an alternative.

2. Benveniste, *Problèmes de linguistique générale II,* 25.

3. Benveniste, 94.

4. Preface to Henry Jacob, *A Planned Auxiliary Language* (London: Dobson, 1947).

5. Roman Jakobson, "On Linguistic Aspects of Translation," in *Selected Writings: Word and Language, Volume 2* (The Hague: Mouton, 1971), 260–266, at 263.

6. Benveniste, *Problèmes de linguistique générale II*, 229; emphasis added.

7. Benveniste, 228.

8. Benveniste, 64.

9. Benveniste, 224; emphasis added.

10. "We have seen that the semiotic unit is the sign. What will the semantic unit be? Quite simply, the word. After so many debates about, and definitions of, the nature of the word (a whole book has been filled with them), the word is restored to its natural function: the minimal unit of the message and the necessary unit for coding thought" (Benveniste, 225).

11. In caricatured fashion—and in the twentieth century, no less—the inventor of *Basic English* (which reduces the language to a mere 850 words), did not fail to include the word "kettle"; obviously, in all parts of the world, teatime is still five o'clock!

CHAPTER 11

1. Benveniste, *Problèmes de linguistique générale II*, 31; emphasis added.

2. Note that there are many points in common between policies of concerted language planning and creating a universal language, at least as far as practical and nonphilosophical purposes are concerned, i.e., actual speech.

3. Monnerot-Dumaine, *Précis d'interlinguistique*, 24.

4. Allomorphs are different forms, governed by context and mutually exclusive, of the same morpheme. Amalgamated morphemes fuse several grammatical morphemes, making segmentation impossible.

5. Cf. the languages created by Tyssot de Patot, Vairasse, etc., in the appendix.

6. As Claude Hagège has shown (*La grammaire générative*), the formal evolution of language often is cyclical or sinusoidal.

7. Cf. Arnold Van Gennep, "Essai d'une théorie des langues spéciales," *Revue des études ethnographiques et sociologiques* 1 (1908).

8. A contested notion, in point of fact.

9. This project—inspired by *Volapük, Esperanto, Kosmos, Spelin, Myrana, Mundolingual, Universala,* and *Novilatin*—didn't keep one of its creators, Edgar de Wahl, from devising *Occidental* later on.

10. Cf. Monnerot-Dumaine, *Précis d'interlinguistique*, 67.

BIBLIOGRAPHY

1 PRIMARY SOURCES

1.1 Projects for Creating or Describing Constructed Languages

Anon. *Essai sur la creation d'une langue nouvelle.* Saint-Dizier, 1864.

Comenius, Johann Amos (Jan Amos Komenský). *Via Lucis.* Amsterdam: Christopher Conrad, 1668. [*The Way of Light.* Trans. E. T. Campagnac. London: Hodder & Stoughton, 1938.]

Dalgarno, George. *Ars signorum, vulgo character universalis et lingua philosophica.* London: J Hayes, 1661.

Delormel, Jean. *Projet d'une langue universelle.* Paris, 1795.

Épée, Charles-Michel de l'. *Institution des sourds et muets, par la voie méthodiques; ouvrage qui contient le projet d'une langue universelle, par l'entremise des signes naturels assujettis à une méthode.* Paris: Nyon l'ainé, 1776.

Gajewski, Boleslas. *Grammaire du solrésol.* Paris: R. Moutier, 1902.

Harris, James. *Hermes: Or, a Philosophical Inquiry into Universal Grammar.* London: H. Woodfall, 1751.

Jacob, Henry. *A Planned Auxiliary Language.* London: Dobson, 1947.

Jespersen, Otto. *An International Language.* London: Allen and Unwin, 1928.

Kircher, Athanasius. *Ars Magna sciendi sive combinatoria.* Amsterdam: J. Janssonium & Waesberge, 1669.

Leibniz, Gottfried Wilhelm. *Dissertatio de arte combinatoria.* Leipzig, Johann Simon Fick and Johan Polycarp Seubold, 1666.

Letellier, Charles Louis Augustin. *Cours complet de langue universelle.* Paris: B. Duprat, 1861.

Letellier, Charles Louis Augustin. *Manuel de logologie.* Caen, 1891.

Lodwick, Francis. *The Groundwork or Foundation Laid for the Framing of a New Perfect Language and an Universal or Common Writing.* London, 1652. [Facsimile in Vivian Salmon, *The Works of Francis Lodwick.* London: Longman, 1972.]

Maimieux, Joseph de. *Pasigraphie.* Paris, 1797.

Pei, Mario. *One Language for the World.* New York: The Devin-Adair Company, 1958.

Platière, Roland de la. "Vocation de l'anglais à devenir la langue universelle." *Dix-huitième Siècle* 30 (1998): 317–330.

Saussure, René de. *La structure logique des mots dans les langues naturelles considérée au point de vue de son application aux langues artificielles.* Bern: Büchler, 1918.

Stoyan, Petro. *Vindiana, notre patrie historique retrouvée.* Arras: Stuit, 1946.

Sudre, François. *Langue musicale universelle, inventée par François Sudre, également inventeur de la Télephonie. Double dictionnaire.* Paris: G. Flaxland, 1866.

Wilkins, John. *The Discovery of a New World or a Discourse Tending to Prove that it is Probable that There May Be a Habitable World on the Moon.* London: J. Maynard, 1640.

Wilkins, John. *Mercury or the Secret and Swift Messenger.* London: J. Maynard, 1641.

Wilkins, John. *An Essay towards a Real Character and a Philosophical Language.* London: Gellibrand and Martin, 1668.

Wolfson, Louis. *Le Schizo et les langues.* Paris: Gallimard, 1970.

1.2 Theories on the Origin of Language

Baudry, Frédéric. *De la science du langage et de son état actuel*. Paris: Auguste Durand, 1864.

Benloew, Louis. *De quelques caractères du langage primitif.* Paris: A. Franck, 1863.

Berington, Simon. *Dissertation on the Mosaical Creation, Deluge, Building of Babel and Confusion of Tongues*. London: C. Davis, 1750.

Bouzeran, Joseph. *Essai d'unité linguistique raisonnée*, Paris: Hachette, 1847.

Brisset, Jean-Pierre. *La grammaire logique*. Paris: Leroux, 1883.

Brisset, Jean-Pierre. *Les origines humaines*. Angers, 1913.

Brisset, Jean-Pierre. *Le mystère de Dieu est accompli*. Angers, 1891.

Brosses, Charles de. *Traité de la formation mécanique des langues*. Paris: Saillant, 1765.

Callet, Charles. *Le mystère du langage*. Paris: Éditions de la Revue mondiale, 1925.

Condillac, Étienne Bonnot de. *Essai sur l'origine des connaissances humaines*. Amsterdam: P. Mortier, 1746.

Condillac, Étienne Bonnot de. *Cours d'étude pour l'instruction du prince de Parme*, vol. 1, *Grammaire*. Parma: Imprimerie Royale, 1775.

Condorcet, Jean-Antoine-Nicolas de Caritat, marquis de. *Esquisse d'un tableau historique des progrès de l'esprit humain*. Paris: Agasse, 1793.

Court de Gébelin, Antoine. *Histoire naturelle de la parole*. Paris: Boudet, 1772.

Court de Gébelin, Antoine. *Le monde primitif analysé et comparé avec le monde moderne*. Paris: Durand, 1775.

Destutt de Tracy, Antoine-Louis-Claude. *Éléments d'idéologie*. Paris: Courcier, 1803.

Drojat, François. *La maîtresse-cléf de la tour de Babel*. Paris: B. Duprat, 1857.

Dubor, Georges de. *Les langues et l'espèce humaine*. Louvain: Peeters, 1884.

Grimm, Jacob von. *Über den Ursprung der Sprache*. Berlin: Dümmler, 1851.

Guichard, Étienne. *L'harmonie étymologique des langues . . . où se démontre que toutes les langues sont descendues de l'hébraïque*. Paris: Chez Victor Le Roy, 1606.

Hennequin, Amand. *Essai sur l'analogie des langues*. Besançon: Douai, 1838.

Herder, Johann Gottfried. *Abhandlung über den Ursprung der Sprache*. Berlin: C. F. Voss, 1772.

Humboldt, Wilhelm von. *Über das Entstehen der grammatischen Formen und ihren Einfluss auf die Ideenentwicklung*. Berlin: Königliche Akademie der Wissenschaften, 1822.

Holberg, Ludvig. *Nicolai Klimii iter Subterraneum. A Journey to the World Underground. By Nicholas Klimius, Translated from the Original*. London: T. Astley, 1741.

Leibniz, Gottfried Wilhelm. *New Essays on Human Understanding*, ed. Peter Remnant and Jonathan Bennett. Cambridge: Cambridge University Press, 1996.

Leibniz, Gottfried Wilhelm. *Brevis designatio meditationum de originibus gentium ductis potissimum ex indicio linguarum*. In *Opera omnia*, ed. L. Dutens, vol. IV, no. 2, 186–198. Geneva, 1768.

Le Quen d'Entremeuse. *Sirius: Aperçus nouveaux sur l'origine de l'idolâtrie*. Paris: V. Didron, 1852.

Marcillac, Jacques. *Les vraies origines de la langue française, ses rapports avec l'anthropologie et la physique du globe*. Paris: Reinwald, 1900.

Marr, Nikolai Yakovlevich. *Izbrannye raboty*. Leningrad: GAIMK, 1933.

Marr, Nikolai Yakovlevich. *Voprosy jazyka v'osvescenije jafeticeskoj teorii*. Leningrad: GAIMK, 1933.

Maupertuis, Pierre Louis Moreau de. *Réflexions philosophiques sur l'origine des languages et la signification des mots*. Dresden: Georg Conrad Walther, 1752.

Müller, Max. *Lectures on the Science of Language*. London: Longman, Green, Longman, Roberts & Green, 1864.

Nodier, Charles. *Dictionnaire raisonné des onomatopées françaises*. Paris: Demonville, 1808.

Nodier, Charles. *Archéologue ou système universelle et raisonné des langues*. Paris: Didot, 1810.

Nodier, Charles. *Notions élémentaires de linguistique, ou histoire abrégeee de la parole et de l'écriture*. Paris: P. Baudouin, 1834.

Nodier, Charles. *Bibliographie des fous: De quelque slivres excentriques*. Paris: Techener, 1835.

O'Donnelly, Terence Joseph. *Extrait de la traduction authentique des hiéroglyphes de l'Obélisque de Louqsor à Paris*. Paris: Schlesinger, 1851.

Paget, Richard. *Human Speech: Some Observations, Experiments, and Conclusions as to the Nature, Origin, Purpose and Possible Improvement of Human Speech*. London: Routledge, 1930.

Pezron, Paul-Yves. *De l'antiquité de la nation et de la langue des Celtes, autrement appelés Gaulois*. Paris: Jean Boudot, 1703.

Poinsenet de Sivry, Louis. *Origine des premières sociétés, des peuples, des sciences, des arts et des idiomes anciens et modernes*. Amsterdam: Lacombe, 1769.

Rambosson, Jean. *Langue universelle: langage mimique mime et écrit*. Paris: Garnier, 1853.

Rambosson, Jean. *Origine de la parole et du langage parlé*. Paris: A. Picard, 1881.

Renan, Ernest. *De l'origine du langage*. Paris: Michel Lévy, 1858.

Rosny, Léon de. *De l'origine du langage*. Paris: Maisonneuve, 1869.

Rousseau, Jean-Jacques. *Essay on the Origin of Languages*. Trans. John T. Scott. Hanover, NH: University Press of New England, 1998.

Saint-Mars, Desdonitz de. *Essai d'un dictionnaire d'étymologies gauloises*. Rouen: Mari, 1785.

Thessalus, Félix. *Traité de l'origine du langage ou formation et déformation des mots*. Brussels: Gay et Doucé, 1882.

Thiébault, Dieudonné. *Observations générales sur la grammaire et les langues*. Paris: n.p., 1776.

Thoron, Enrique Onffroy de. *La langue primitive depuis Adam jusqu'à Babel, son passage en Amérique où elle est encore vivante*. Paris: E. Leroux, 1886.

Timmermans, Adrien. *Traité de l'onomatopée ou clef des racines irréductibles*. Paris: É. Bouillon, 1890.

Trombetti, Alfredo. *L'unita d'origine del linguaggio*. Bologna: Beltrami, 1905.

Vertus, Rémy-Amand de. *La langue primitive basée sur l'idéographie lunaire*. Paris: Maisonneuve, 1868.

Webb, John. *An Historical Essay Endeavouring the Probability that the Language of the Empire of China is the Primitive Language*. London: Nathan Brook, 1669.

1.3 Works of Fiction That Include the Invention of a Language

Anon. *Human Vicissitudes or Travels into Unexplored Regions*. London: G. G. and J. Robinson, 1798.

Béthune, Chevalier de. *Relation du monde de Mercure* (1750). In *Voyages imaginaires*, ed. C. Garnier, vol. 16. Paris: Garnier, 1787.

Bogdanov, Alexander. *Red Star: The First Bolshevik Utopia*. Trans. Charles Rougle. Bloomington: Indiana University Press, 1984.

Bulwer-Lytton, E. G. *The Coming Race*. London: William Blackwood, 1871.

Burroughs, Edgar Rice. *A Princess of Mars*. New York: Grosset & Dunlap, 1917.

Colin, Vladimir. *Babel*. Bucharest: Albatros, 1978.

Cyrano de Bergerac, Savinien. *The Comical History of the States and Empires of the Worlds of the Moon and Sun*. Trans. A. Lovell. London: Henry Rhodes, 1687.

Defoe, Daniel. *The Consolidator, or Memoirs of Sundry Transactions from the World in the Moon*. London: Benjamin Bragg, 1705.

Delany, Samuel. *Babel-17*. New York: Ace, 1966.

Desfontaines, Pierre-François Guyot. *Le nouveau Gulliver* (1730). In *Voyages imaginaires*, vol. 15, ed. C. Garnier. Paris: Garnier, 1787.

Elgin, Suzette Haden. *Native Tongue*. London: The Women's Press, 1984.

Elgin, Suzette Haden. *A First Dictionary and Grammar of Láadan*. Madison, WI: Society for the Furtherance and Study of Fantasy and Science Fiction, 1988.

Foigny, Gabriel de. *Les aventures de Jacques Sadeur dans la découverte et le voyage de la Terre Austral* (1676). In *Voyages imaginaires*, vol. 24, ed. C. Garnier. Paris: Garnier, 1787.

Godwin, Francis. *The Man in the Moone or a Discourse of a Voyage Thither by Domingo Gonsales, the Speedy Messenger*. London: John Norton, 1638.

Karinthy, Ferenc. *Epepe*. Budapest, 1970.

Lewis, C. S. *Out of the Silent Planet*. New York: MacMillan, 1938.

More, Thomas. *Utopia, the Best of Republics Sited in the New Island of Utopia*. London, 1516.

Mouhy, Charles de Fieux de. *Lamékis, ou les voyages extraordinaires d'un Égyptien dans la terre intérieure* (1735). In *Voyages imaginaires*, vol. 20, ed. C. Garnier. Paris: Garnier, 1787.

Orwell, George. *1984*. London: Penguin, 1948.

Psalmanaazaar, George. *An Historical and Geographical Description of Formosa*. London: Daniel Brown, 1704.

Tolkein, J. R. R. *The Hobbit*. London: Allen and Unwin, 1937.

Tolkein, J. R. R. *The Lord of the Rings*. London: Allen and Unwin, 1954–1955.

Vairasse, Denis. *The History of the Sevarambians: A Utopian Novel*. Albany: State University of New York Press, 2006.

Vance, Jack. *The Languages of Pao*. St Albans: Mayflower, 1974.

Watson, Ian. *The Embedding*. New York: Scribner, 1973.

2 CRITICAL AND ANALYTIC WORKS AND COMMENTARIES

2.1 Studies on Universal Languages and on Linguistic Theories

Albani, Paolo and Berlinghiero Buonarroti. *Dictionnaire des langues imaginaires*. Paris: Les Belles Lettres, 1994.

Auroux, Sylvain et al. *La linguistique fantastique*. Paris: Denoël, 1985.

Auroux, Sylvain *Histoire des idées linguistiques*. Brussels: Pierre Mardaga, 1989.

Calvet, Louis-Jean, ed. *Marxisme et linguistique*. Paris: Payot, 1977.

Cavalli-Sforza, Luigi Luca. "Genes, Peoples and Languages." *Scientific American*, no. 265 (1991): 104–110.

Clark, Walter John. *International Language, Past, Present and Future, with Specimens of Esperanto and Grammar*. London: J. M. Dent & Company, 1907.

Couturat, Louis. *La logique de Leibniz d'apres des documents inedits*. Paris: Alcan, 1901.

Couturat, Louis. "Des rapports de la logique et de la linguistique dans le problème de la langue universelle." *Revue de métaphysique et de morale* (July 1911).

Couturat, Louis, and Léopold Léau. *Histoire de la langue universelle*. Paris: Hachette, 1903.

Couturat, Louis, and Léopold Léau. *Les nouvelles langues internationales*. Paris: Paul Brodard, 1907.

De Mott, Benjamin. "Comenius and the Real Character in England." *Publications of the Modern Language Association of America*, no. 70 (1955): 1068–1081.

Eco, Umberto. *The Search for the Perfect Language*. Trans. James Fentress. Oxford: Blackwell, 1995.

Gadet, Françoise et al. *Les maîtres de la langue*. Paris: Maspero, 1979.

Genette, Gérard. *Mimologiques*. Paris: Éditions du Seuil, 1976.

Hagège, Claude. "Babel: Du temps mythique au temps du langage." *Revue philosophique* 4 (1978): 465–479.

Harnois, Guy. *Les théories du langage en France de 1660 à 1821*. Paris: Les Belles Lettres, 1929.

Higley, S. L. "Audience, Uglossia, and CONLANG: Inventing Languages on the Internet." *M/C: A Journal of Media and Culture* 3, no. 1 (2000).

Jacob, André, ed. *Genèse de la pensée linguistique*. Paris: Armand Colin, 1973.

Joseph, Brian D., and Joseph C. Salmons. *Nostratic: Sifting the Evidence*. Amsterdam: John Benjamins, 1997.

Knowlson, James. *Universal Language Schemes in England and France, 1600–1800*. Toronto: University of Toronto Press, 1975.

"Le mythe de la langue universelle." *Critique*, no. 387–388 (Aug.–Sept. 1979).

Lehmann, Winfried P, and Ladislav Zgusta. "Schleicher's Tale after a Century." In *Festschrift for Oswald Szemerényi on the Occasion of His 65th Birthday*, ed. B. Brogyanyi, 455–466. Amsterdam: John Benjamins, 1979.

Mahieu, Stéphane. *Le phalanstère des langages excentriques*. Paris: Gingko, 2005.

Martinet, André. *Des steppes aux oceans: L'indo-européen et les Indo-Européens*. Paris: Payot, 1986.

McCracken, George E. "Athanasius Kircher's Universal Polygraphy." *Isis* 39 (1948): 215–228.

Mercier-Faivre, Anne-Marie. *Un supplément à "L'Encyclopédie." Le "Monde primitif" d'Antoine Court de Gébelin.* Paris: Honoré Champion, 1999.

Mikhankova, V. A. *N. Y. Marr, ocherk yego zhyzni i nauchnoy deyatel'nosti.* Moscow: Izd-vo Akademii nauk SSSR, 1949.

Mitrović, Paul. "Deux sabirs balkaniques." *La Linguistique* 8, no. 1 (1972): 134–141.

Monnerot-Dumaine, Maurice. *Précis d'interlinguistique générale et speciale.* Paris: Maloine, 1960.

Ogden, Charles K. *Debabelization: With a Survey of Contemporary Opinion on the Problem of a Universal Language.* London: Routledge, 1931.

Ogden, Charles K. *Counter-Offensive: An Exposure of Certain Misrepresentations of Basic English.* London: Routledge, 1935.

Olender, Maurice. *Les langues du paradis: Aryens et Sémites, un couoke providential.* Paris: Éditions du Seuil, 1989.

Olender, Maurice. "Les langues mégalomanes." *Le Genre humain,* no. 21. Paris: Éditions du Seuil, 1990.

Pierssens, Michel. *La Tour de Babil: La fiction du signe.* Paris: Éditions de Minuit, 1976.

Ruhlen, Merritt. *A Guide to the World's Languages,* vol. 1, *Classification.* Stanford: Stanford University Press, 1987.

Salmon, Vivian. *The Works of Francis Lodwick: A Study of His Writings in the Intellectual Context of the Seventeenth Century.* London: Longman, 1972.

Sapir, Edward. "Wanted: A World Language." *American Mercury* (February 1931): 202–209.

Thomas, Lawrence Leslie. *The Linguistic Theories of N. Ja Marr.* Berkeley: University of California Press, 1957.

Van Gennep, Arnold. "Essai d'une théorie des langues speciales." *Revue des études ethnographiques et sociologiques* 1 (1908): 327ff.

Vaquera, Maria Luisa Calero. *Projectos de lengua universal, la contribucion Española*. Córdoba: Universidad de Cordoba/Caja Sur, 1999.

2.2 Studies on Language in Fiction

Atkinson, Geoffroy. *The Extraordinary Voyage in French Literature before 1700*. New York: Columbia University Press, 1920.

Burgess, Anthony. "Creating a Language for Primitive Man." *New York Times Magazine*. November 15, 1981.

Carpenter, Humphrey. *Tolkein: A Biography*. New York: Ballantine Books, 1978.

Cornelius, Paul. *Languages in Seventeenth- and Early Eighteenth-Century Imaginary Voyages*. Geneva: Droz, 1965.

Goimard, Jacques. "Science-Fiction." In *Dictionnaire critique de la communication*, vol. 2, 1621–1624. Paris: PUF, 1993.

Gove, Philip Babcock. *The Imaginary Journey in Prose Fiction with an Annotated Check List of 215 Imaginary Voyages from 1700 to 1800*. New York: Columbia University Press, 1941.

Gros, Léon-Gabriel. "Langues imaginaires et langage secret chez Swift." *Cahiers du Sud* 46 (1957): 3–44.

Kloczko, Édouard. *Dictionnaire des langues elfiques*. Paris: Éditions Tamise, 1995.

Meyers, Walter Earl. *Aliens and Linguists*. Athens: University of Georgia Press, 1980.

Nicolson, Marjorie Hope. *Voyages to the Moon*. New York: Macmillan & Co., 1948.

Pons, Émile. "Les langues imaginaires dans le voyage utopique: un precurseur, Th. Morus." *Revue de littérature comparée* 10 (1930): 592–603.

Pons, Émile. "Les langues imaginaires dans le voyage utopique: les jargons de Panurge clans Rabelais." *Revue de littérature comparée* 11 (1931): 185–218.

Pons, Émile. "Les langues imaginaires clans le voyage utopique: les grammairiens, Vairasse et Foigny." *Revue de littérature comparée* 12 (1932): 500–532.

Seeber, Edward D. "Ideal Languages in the French and English Imaginary Voyage." *Publications of the Modern Language Association* 60 (1945): 586–597.

Sériot, P. "Le sexe des anges ou la tentation iconique." In *O Feminino nas Linguas, Culturas e Literaturas*, ed. M. E. Almeida and M. Maillard, 395–402. Madeira: Centro Metagram, universidade da Madeira, 2000.

Sfez, Lucien. "Utopie et imaginaire de la communication." *Quaderni* 28 (1996): 7–10.

2.3 Studies on Glossolalia, Spiritualism, Other Worlds

Alphandéry, Paul. "La glossolalie dans le prophétisme médiéval latin." *Revue de l'histoire des religions* 104 (1931): 417–436.

Bobon, Jean. "Les pseudo-glossolalies ludiques et magiques." *Journal belge de neurologie et de psychiatrie* 47 (April–June 1947): 327–395.

Bobon, Jean. *Introduction historique à l'étude des néologismes et des glossolalies en psychopathologie*. Paris: Masson, 1952.

Boniface, Ennemond. *Thérèse Neumann, la crucifiée, devant l'histoire et la science*. Paris: Lethellieux, 1979.

Bozzano, Ernesto. *La Médiumnité polyglotte*. Paris: Éditions Jean Meyer, 1934.

Cifali, Mireille. "Théodore Flournoy: La découverte de l'inconscient." *Le bloc—Notes de la psychanalyse* 3 (1983): 111–131.

Cifali, Mireille. "Une glossolale et ses savants: Elise Muller, alias Hélène Smith." In S. Auroux et al., *La linguistique fantastique*, 236–244. Paris: Denoël, 1985.

Claparède, E. "Théodore Flournoy, sa vie, son oeuvre." *Archives de psychologie de la Suisse romande* 18 (1921): 1–125.

Courtine, Jean-Jacques, ed. "Les glossolalies." In *Langages* 91. Paris: Larousse, 1988.

Cutten, George Barton. *Speaking with Tongues*. New Haven: Yale University Press, 1927.

Dubleumortier, Nathalie. *Glossolalie: Discours de la croyance dans un culte pentecôtiste*. Paris: L'Harmattan, 1997.

Flammarion, Camille. *La pluralité des mondes habités*. Paris: Mallet-Bachelier, 1862.

Flammarion, Camille. *Les mondes imaginaires et les mondes réels: Voyage pittoresque dans le ciel et revue critique des théories humaines, scientifiques et romanesques, anciennes et modernes sur les habitants des astres*. Paris: Flammarion, 1865.

Flammarion, Camille. *Rêves étoilés*. Paris: Flammarion, 1888.

Flammarion, Camille. *La planète Mars et ses conditions d'habitabilité*. Paris: Gauthier-Villars, 1892.

Flammarion, Camille. *Dreams of an Astronomer*, trans. E. E. Fournier D'Albe (New York: D. Appleton and Company, 1923).

Flournoy, Théodore. *Des Indes à la planète Mars, étude sur un cas de somnambulisme avec glossolalie*. Paris and Geneva, 1900. [Critical ed., 1983, by M. Yaguello and M. Cifali.]

Flournoy, Théodore . "Nouvelles observations sur un cas de somnambulisme avec glossolalie." *Archives de psychologie de la Suisse romande* 1 (1902): 100–255.

Flournoy, Olivier. *Théodore et Léopold: de Théodore Flournoy à la psychanalyse*. Neuchâtel: À la Baconnière, 1986.

Fontenelle, Bernard Le Bovier de. *Entretiens sur la pluralité des mondes*. Paris, 1686.

Franche, Paul. *Sainte Hildegarde*. Paris: Lecoffre, 1903.

Giacomelli, Roberto. *Dossier Hélène Smith*. Milan: CUEM, 1999.

Goodman, Felicitas. *Speaking in Tongues: A Cross-Cultural Study of Glossolalia*. Chicago: University of Chicago Press, 1972.

Henry, Victor. *Le Langage martien, étude analytique de la gènese d'une langue dans un cas de glossolalie somnambulique*. Paris: Maisonneuve, 1901.

Hine, Virginia. "Pentecostal Glossolalia: Toward a Functional Interpretation." *Journal for the Scientific Study of Religion* 8 (1969): 211–226.

Hyslop, V. "La médiumnité de Mme. Smead." *Annales des sciences psychiques* (1906): 461–500.

Jaquith, J. R. "Towards a Typology of Formal Communication Behaviour: Glossolalia." *Anthropological Linguistics* 9, no. 8 (1967).

Kelsey, Morton Trippe. *Tongue Speaking: An Experiment in Spiritual Experience*. New York: Doubleday & Company, 1964.

Kerner, Justinus. *Die Seherin von Prevorst*. Stuttgart: Cotta, 1832.

Lapsley, James N., and John H. Simpson. "Speaking in Tongues: Infantile Babble or Song of the Self." *Pastoral Psychology* 15, no. 146 (1964): 16–24.

Lombard, Émile. *De la glossolalie chez les premiers chrétiens et des phénomènes similaires*. Lausanne: Imprimeries réunies, 1910.

Maeder, Alphonse. "La langue d'un aliéné, analyse d'un cas de glossolalie." *Archives de psychologie* (Mar. 1910): 208–216.

May, L. Carlyle. "A Survey of Glossolalia and Related Phenomena in Non-Christian Religions." *American Anthropologist* 58 (1956): 75–96.

Richet, Charles. "Xénoglossie: L'écriture automatique en langues étrangères." *Proceedings of the Society for Psychical Research* 19, part 51 (December 1905): 162–194.

Samarin, William J. "The Linguisticality of Glossolalia." *Hartford Quarterly* 8 (1968): 49–75.

Samarin, William J. "Forms and Functions of Nonsense Languages." *Linguistics* 50 (1969): 70–74.

Samarin, William J. "Evolution in Glossolalic Private Language." *Anthropological Linguistics* 13, no. 2 (1971): 55–67.

Samarin, William J. *Tongues of Men and Angels: The Religious Language of Pentecostalism*. New York: Macmillan, 1972.

Sherill, John. *They Speak with Other Tongues*. New York: McGraw Hill, 1964.

Stuchlik, Jaroslav. "Essai sur la psychologie de l'invention des langues artificielles." *Annales médico-psychologiques* 2 (1960): 225–232.

Sullivan, F. A. "Ils parlent en langues." *Lumen Vitae* 21 (1976): 1ff.

Swedenborg, Emanuel. *The Earths in Our Solar System, Which Are Called Planets, and the Earths in the Starry Heaven, Their Inhabitants, and the Spirits and Angels There: From Things Heard and Seen*. London: Swedenborg Society, 1894.

Vesme, C. de. "Xénoglossie." *Annales des sciences psychiques* 15 (1905): 317–412.

Vesme, C. de. "La xénoglossie de Laura Edmunds." *Annales des sciences psychiques* 17 (1907): 408–410, 601–603.

2.4 General Works

Arnauld, Antoine, and Claude Lancelot. *Grammaire générale et raisonnée de Port-Royal*. Paris: Le Petit, 1660.

Bach, Emmon W, and Robert Thomas Harris., eds. *Universals in Linguistic Theory*. New York: Holt, Rinehart and Winston, 1968.

Bakhtin, Mikhail. *Marksizm ifilosofiya yazyka*. Leningrad, 1929. [Originally published under the name V. N. Vološinov, *Marxism and the Philosophy of Language*. Trans. L. Matejka and I. R. Titunik. New York: Seminar Press, 1973.]

Benveniste, Émile. *Problèmes de linguistique générale*, I and II. Paris: Gallimard, 1966 and 1974.

Chomsky, Noam. *Syntactic Structures*. The Hague: Mouton, 1957.

Chomsky, Noam. *Aspects of the Theory of Syntax*. Cambridge, MA: MIT Press, 1965.

Chomsky, Noam. *Cartesian Linguistics*. New York: Harper and Row, 1966.

Comrie, Bernard. *Language Universals and Linguistic Typology*. Oxford: Oxford University Press, 1981.

Comrie, Bernard. *The World's Major Languages*. Oxford: Oxford University Press, 1990.

Cosnier, Jacques et al. *Les voies du langage*. Paris: Dunod, 1982.

Croft, William. *Typology and Universals*. Cambridge: Cambridge University Press, 1990.

Damourette, Jacques, and Édouard Pichon. *Des mots à la pensée*. Paris: Editions d'Artrey, 1911–1940.

Freud, Sigmund. "The Antithetical Meaning of Primal Words." In *The Standard Edition of the Complete Psychological Works of Sigmund Freud*, vol. 11 (1910), Five Lectures on Psycho-Analysis, Leonardo da Vinci and Other Works, trans. and ed. James Strachey. London: Vintage Books, 2001, 160–161.

Gobineau, Arthur de. *Essai sur l'inégalité des races humaines*. Paris: Firmin Didot, 1853.

Greenberg, Joseph H. *Language Universals*. Cambridge: MIT Press, 1963.

Greenberg, Joseph H., Charles Albert Ferguson, and Edith Moravczik, eds. *Universals of Human Language*. Stanford: Stanford University Press, 1978.

Hagège, Claude. *La grammaire générative: Réflexions critiques*. Paris: PUF, 1976.

Hagège, Claude. *La structure des langues*. Paris: PUF, 1982.

Hagège, Claude. "Contribution des recherches typologiques à l'ét ude diachronique des langues." In *Table ronde, la diachronie hier et demain*. Lille: Publications de l'Universite de Lille, 1983.

Hagège, Claude. *The Language Builder*. Amsterdam: John Benjamins Publishing Company, 1993.

Hagège, Claude. *Halte à la mort des languages*. Paris: Odile Jacob, 2001.

Hombert, Jean-Marie, ed. *Aux origines des langues and du langage*. Paris: Fayard, 2005.

Hymes, Dell, ed. *Pidginization and Creolization of Languages*. Cambridge: Cambridge University Press, 1971.

Jakobson, Roman. "Why Mama and Papa." In *Selected Writings*, vol. 1, *Phonological Studies*, 635–644. The Hague: Mouton, 1962.

Jakobson, Roman. "Retrospect." In *Selected Writings*, vol. 4, *Phonological Studies*, 637–664. The Hague: Mouton, 1966.

Jakobson, Roman. *Essaies de linguistique générale*, vols. 1 and 2. Paris: Éditions de Minuit, 1963, 1973.

Jakobson, Roman. *Langage enfantin et aphasie*. Paris: Éditions de Minuit, 1969.

Lacan, Jacques. *De la psychose paranoïaque dans ses rapports avec la personnalité*. Paris: Éditions du Seuil, 1975.

Lakoff, George. *Women, Fire, and Dangerous Things*. Chicago: University of Chicago Press, 1987.

Langacker, Ronald W. *Concept, Image and Symbol: The Cognitive Basis of Grammar*. New York: Mouton/De Gruyter, 1990.

Lapouge, Gilles. *Le singe de la montre: Utopie et histoire*. Paris: Flammarion, 1982.

Levi-Strauss, Claude. *Race et histoire*. Paris: Albin Michel, 1952.

Nettle, Daniel, and Suzanne Romaine. *Vanishing Voices: The Extinction of the World's Languages*. Oxford: Oxford University Press, 2000.

Palmer, Harold E. *The Principles of Language Study*. New York: World Book Company, 1921.

Renfrew, Colin. *Archaeology and Language*. Cambridge: Cambridge University Press, 1987.

Roussel, Raymond. *Nouvelles impressions d'Afrique*. Paris: Lemerre, 1932.

Sapir, Edward. *Language: An Introduction to the Study of Speech.* New York: Harcourt, Brace & Co., 1921.

Sapir, Edward. *Collected Works: I, General Linguistics.* Berlin: Walter de Gruyter, 2008.

Schaff, Adam. *Langage et connaissance.* Paris: Anthropos, 1969.

Slobin, Dan Isaac, ed. *The Ontogenesis of Grammar.* New York: Academic Press, 1971.

Sprague de Camp, Lyon. *Lost Continents: The Atlantis Theme in History, Science, and Literature.* New York: Gnome Press, 1954.

Steiner, George. *After Babel.* Oxford: Oxford University Press, 1975.

Whorf, Benjamin Lee. *Language, Thought and Reality: Selected Writings.* Cambridge: MIT Press, 1956.

Yaguello, Marina. "L'invention des langues." In Hombert, *Aux origins des langues and du langage,* 362–389.

INTERNET RESOURCES

Information on published auxiliary international languages can be found on several sites. The Internet has given rise to an incredible amount of activity by Esperantists, along with other inventors of languages.

Internet Sites

www.esperanto.net: main website for information on Esperanto, presented in a variety of languages. An in-depth presentation on the Lingvo Internacia can be accessed through a choice of fifty-seven different languages.

Ikurso.net: for learning Esperanto.

esperanto.net/veb: *La Virtuala Esperanto-Biblioteko.* The main web resources on Esperanto gathered together in a virtual library.

dmoz.org/World/Esperanto/: A listing of the best sites in Esperanto.

eo.wikipedia.org: *Vikipedeo, la libera enciklopedio.* Wikipedia, an encyclopedia containing over 10,000 articles in Esperanto.

Francalingualal pagino pri Ido: Welcome page of the IDO.

The site TOLKLANG is devoted to Tolkein and his languages.

The site CONLANG is devoted to the invention of languages.

The site of Patrick Sériot, professor at the University of Lausanne (Slavic Studies), offers numerous studies on the status of languages in the USSR.